"Maria Golia's well-researched volume paints a portrait of a man who looked different, ate differently (being a vegetarian in Texas was no joke), and, of course, played differently . . . we learn a great deal about Coleman's musical beginnings, his subsequent motivations, and the broader landscape of which he was a part."—*Record Collector*

"Maria Golia eloquently describes the Ornette phenomenon in a book laden with musical and social insights."
—CHRIS SEARLE, *The Morning Star*

"A giant step in the right direction and the first significant book on Ornette Coleman since John Litweiler's *Ornette Coleman: The Harmolodic Life* was published in 1992 . . . Golia is very good at contextualising and explaining . . . and succeeds in exploring in a non-systemically musicological way the mysteries of harmolodics by shedding light on the more arcane side of Ornette's vast artistic curiosity. *Ornette Coleman: The Territory and the Adventure* also is excellent in enhancing our biographical knowledge of Ornette's early life in a very considered way."
—STEPHEN GRAHAM, Marlbank.net

"The history of jazz is often told as a geographical adventure in which a great art enlightens and assimilates a chain of territories in the course of world conquest. Maria Golia revitalizes that narrative in exploring the life and genius of Ornette Coleman. This is the most incisive portrait we have of him—a joyous addition to the literature of music."
—GARY GIDDINS, music critic, author and biographer

"It's always good to learn more about one of America's greatest musicians, and Golia's work has much that is new, especially (at last) a proper overview of Ornette's experience in his hometown of Fort Worth, both in his youth and the 1980s. *The Territory and the Adventure* is the best book on Ornette Coleman yet."—ETHAN IVERSON, musician and music critic

"Following Ornette's departure from the planet, his presence in the world only seems to increase and his music's influence will no doubt continue far into the future. The poetic conception of music, sound, and life in the broadest sense that Ornette embodied is addressed here through the terrific writing of Ms. Golia. This volume is an excellent addition to the ongoing study of one of the greatest improvising musicians of all time."
—PAT METHENY, musician, composer, educator

ORNETTE
THE TERRITORY
COLEMAN
AND THE ADVENTURE

MARIA GOLIA

REAKTION BOOKS LTD

To the memory of my brother
Francis J. Golia Jr.,
(August 10, 1945–February 2, 2019)
musician, educator, and composer,
"one for the books."

Published by
Reaktion Books Ltd
Unit 32, Waterside
44–48 Wharf Road
London NI 7UX, UK

www.reaktionbooks.co.uk

First published 2020, reprinted 2020

Printed and bound in Great Britain by
TJ International, Padstow, Cornwall

A catalogue record for this book is available from the British Library

ISBN 978 1 78914 223 5

CONTENTS

Music, states of happiness, mythology, faces worn by time, certain twilights and certain places, all want to tell us something . . . or are about to tell us something: that imminence of a revelation as yet unproduced is, perhaps, the aesthetic fact.

—JORGES LUIS BORGES,
"The Wall and the Books" (1959)

Sleeve of *The Art of the Improvisers* (Atlantic, 1970),
reproducing a painting by Ornette Coleman.

Introduction

The theme you play at the start of the number is the territory.
And what comes after, which may have very little to do with it,
is the adventure.
ORNETTE COLEMAN (March 9, 1930–June 11, 2015)

The individuals who may be said to define an era have distilled its characteristic forces and possibilities into a body of work that in turn informed their times. Born in segregated Fort Worth, Texas, during the Great Depression, African American composer and musician (sax, trumpet, violin) Ornette Coleman was zeitgeist incarnate. Steeped in the Texas blues tradition, he and jazz grew up together, as the brassy blare of big band swing gave way to bebop, a faster music for a faster, postwar world. If jazz were an aircraft, then New Orleans trumpeter Louis Armstrong winged it over the Atlantic, Kansas City saxophonist Charlie Parker shattered the sound barrier, and Ornette achieved escape velocity, forging a breakaway art appropriate to the Space Age, often referred to as "free jazz."

I met Ornette in his hometown at the Caravan of Dreams Performing Arts Center where I worked and where he played and recorded in the 1980s. He was unassuming and soft-spoken; he lisped and wore shirts that resembled painters' drop cloths, but he was tougher than he looked. Self-taught and proud, Ornette had a nonconformist approach to music that attracted ridicule and censure. Marginalized by his peers for abandoning jazz conventions and feared for the unmistakable authenticity of his sound, he posed a threat to the status quo and to the musicians who staked their careers on it. It would have been simpler to join the in-crowd but Ornette held his course and made the margins the place to be. "How do I turn emotion into knowledge? That's what I try to do with my horn," he said. Ornette used music to advance his self-understanding and in doing so, expanded the musical boundaries of the known.

Jazz is considered a "democratic" music for the equal weight it gives the individual and the collective, where the ensemble's role is not to subsume its members but to make room for their greater expression. Integral to the language of jazz is improvisation, the art of the immediate, an interactive process involving receptive listening and cogent response that Ornette wished to rescue from ephemerality by presenting it as a model for all genuine communication. His approach to music would reach beyond jazz to touch all manner of creative endeavor, and it is no coincidence that reviewers wrote some of their most inspired prose when describing Ornette's sound.

More a compendium than a comprehensive biography or technical analysis, this book helps contextualize Ornette's work, using archival and primary sources to describe some of the pivotal places, people, and struggles that shaped his music and his life. It begins in Fort Worth, a hardscrabble town where music was the only thing that brought black and white citizens together aside from the latter's need for cheap labor. Part One ("Coming Up") reconstructs the social conditions and sonic ambiance of Ornette's youth, an idiosyncratic collage of radio broadcasts from Harlem, western swing fiddlers, Tejano two-steps, high-school marching bands, and the rhythm and blues (R&B) that issued from storefront churches where congregations spoke in tongues.

"I created everything about me," Ornette once said, but he was heir to an exceptional legacy. Texas produced innovators at every stage of jazz evolution, from blues and ragtime to bebop and beyond. Music flourished in the dives and dance halls of Ornette's hometown, frequented by Texan contributors to jazz history who influenced, mentored, or collaborated with him. While Fort Worth and nearby Dallas were not jazz crucibles like New Orleans, New York, or Los Angeles, Texas was nonetheless a field of encounter and synthesis. Musicians who left home seeking a living roamed the vast Southwest in fluidly configured territory bands, folding the impressions they found on the road into their homegrown sound. Restlessness and mobility were built into Ornette's generation; inured to discrimination and hardship, and intent on overcoming them, musicians were explorers charting new ground and eager to share their discoveries.

Part Two ("Ignition") tracks Ornette's music-driven trajectory from Texas via New Orleans and Los Angeles to New York, where he found a home, and Europe, where he communed with the fervent free jazz diaspora he helped create. By the time he arrived in New York in 1959, jazz had become aware of itself and its strengths, with intellectual bebop and its technical prowess the accepted norm. Ornette and a handful of contemporaries found this self-consciousness restrictive and contrary to the purpose of deeper exploration. His album *Free Jazz* (1961) lent a name to what he and his companions were after, but Ornette disliked the connotation of randomness. His music required discipline and mastery alongside an alertness of body, intellect, emotion, and memory. If this was freedom, skillful vigilance was its price.

The same heightened awareness of possibilities and urge to rebel against constraints was manifest in painting, theater, literature, dance, film, and photography. The 1960s witnessed an exuberant cross-fertilization of the arts as practitioners of every discipline staked out new, overlapping territories, sharing inspiration and resources, with jazz embodying the values of experimentation and collaboration that characterized an increasingly international avant-garde. The same impulses driving artists guided movements that challenged authority, taking a stand against war, racism, and inequality, a wave of change that swept across the Atlantic. Ornette pursued his lines of inquiry immersed in a milieu he helped advance—of open doors, loft jams, chance meetings, group performances, conversations, and projects—a lifestyle that reaffirmed the interconnectedness of both the arts and human beings that he called "unison."

When Ornette returned to Fort Worth for his first performance there in nearly two decades, he was a 53-year-old world traveler and a living legend to a discrete global tribe of listeners. The hero's welcome he received was orchestrated by new friends, the founders of a night-club and theater venue called the Caravan of Dreams Performing Arts Center, an anomalous venture backed by a Texan tycoon. Richly endowed, multidimensionally conceived, accessible to a spectrum of performers and audience, and until now virtually absent from the (pre-Internet) record, the Caravan of Dreams was designed to cata-lyze the arts and urban renewal in downtown Fort Worth. Ornette was intrigued by the prospect and the people behind it, a group of individuals who executed projects at the intersection of the arts with emerging technologies and environmental science.

Part Three ("Atmospherics") documents Ornette's homecoming and the week-long inauguration extravaganza at the Caravan of Dreams, "a palace of the avant-garde," as it was fatefully billed, that was built around him. Each of the events purposefully celebrated a milestone of his career, including concerts of his symphony, *Skies of America*, and a composition honoring Buckminster Fuller, whom Ornette called "my best hero." The Caravan's nightclub opened with Ornette and his group, Prime Time; the upstairs theater with a reading by William Burroughs and Brion Gysin, whom Ornette met in the Moroccan village of Joujouka in 1972, an adventure that served to coalesce his thinking about music.

In his mannerisms, the way he spoke and dressed, Ornette was a character whose laconic asides and elliptical anecdotes provoked both laughter and reflection. He called his theory of music "harmo-lodics," saying it applied to all other art forms, including life. Part Four ("Transmissions") follows Ornette's trains of thought regarding musical methodologies and his attitudes towards language, paint-ing, women, celebrity, teaching, and death, tracking events in his later life, his influence and his legacy. As an actively touring octo-genarian, he was showered with awards, while artists and scholars of every persuasion acknowledged how his work advanced their own creative processes.

In the course of producing this book I lost count of the people who said Ornette had changed their lives, even though he once remarked that aside from music he was just an ordinary guy. But Ornette was all about music, and the attributes he ascribed to it defined his idea of what "ordinary" might mean. He saw music as a natural, healing power, a tool for the acquisition of knowledge, and a language that transcends culture and category, a message freighted with the experience of surviving the darkest hours of racial oppression in America. His life nonetheless traversed a luminous few decades; in the larger scheme of things, a click of the shutter, an opening that lasts an instant.

The snapshot offered here is of an ever-receding era, more receptive and inquisitive, less pressured and afraid, when a city's live music clubs were among its most sought-after destinations, where everyone looked forward to the unpredictable. Now that so much contact occurs at a sterile, screen-mediated distance, it's worth recalling the spontaneous complicity of jazz, the palpable exchange of energy that occurs within an ensemble and its audience. Ornette once remarked that the most important thing about music is that it be heard. Hopefully these pages will tempt readers to follow his advice, and listen.

Ornette and Denardo Coleman, Los Angeles, *c.* 1958.

Part One: Coming Up

Jazz is existence music. It puts you in the world.

WYNTON MARSALIS

However integral their narratives may have been to the nation's foundation, none of the United States produced as robust a narrative as Texas. The frontier settlers' Texas Revolution, a battle for independence from Mexico that resulted in the establishment of a Texan republic (1835–45), contributed to its freedom-loving élan. The vastness of the territory, considerably larger than Ukraine or mainland France, and the promise of wealth it so amply fulfilled ensured its iconic status. Encompassing prairies, grasslands, forests, coastal swamps, natural harbors, sandy beaches, piney woods, and vast tracts of desert and mountains, Texas held the allure of undiscovered possibilities. In this and other ways it was America in microcosm, at its best expansive, liberating, enterprising, a place where courage and individuality served the greater good; at its worst insular and paranoid, pioneers circling the wagons, waiting for the cavalry to shoot their way out. Many attributes comprising the American self-image are Texan by association if not origin: resilience, pride, individuality, common sense, and entitlement to as much of everything as possible. And in this land of plenty, no state gave more abundantly of its nation-building flesh and blood, red meat and crude oil.

All blessings came from the land, beginning with the cattle that arrived with the Spanish missionaries and conquistadores in Christopher Columbus's wake and were left to multiply, undisturbed, on the open range. By 1860 Texans were outnumbered six to one by quarter-ton longhorns, feral descendants of the calves and heifers that crossed the Atlantic. When the railroads brought the market within a thousand-mile reach, the rangy longhorn distinguished itself by its ability to thrive, camel-like, on the long march. The forced migration of over six million head in the late 1860–70s took place along the Chisholm Trail, running due north from the Texan heartland to a railhead in Abilene, Kansas. Among the towns offering respite en route, Fort Worth was the most anticipated, the "Paris of the Plains," famed for its saloons and brothels.

Peopled by the neotypes of American mythology—wranglers, sports and demimondes, card sharks, stage coach, train and bank robbers, Wyatt Earp and the Sundance Kid—Fort Worth's downtown district was called Hell's Half Acre, where outlaws did real and metaphysical battle with the defenders of order who kept one hand on the Bible, the other on the trigger of their guns. The unbridled testosterone that fueled the Acre's narrative was soon redirected towards commerce. The arrival of the Texas and Pacific Railway in 1876 transformed Fort Worth from a stopover to a destination; the establishment of the Swift & Co. meatpacking companies in 1902 caused its population to triple. Fort Worth became America's beef factory and its sprawling stockyards and slaughterhouses made the city's first large, legitimate fortune.

"Other states were carved or born / Texas grew from hide and horn," wrote poet Berta Hart Nance, and while it is true that Fort Worth merits the sobriquet "Cowtown," it was originally, as the name implies, a military outpost. Established in 1849 and tasked with protecting settlers, Fort Worth was disruptively situated beside the game-rich banks of the Trinity River, a well-known Native American hunting ground; its founding officers had farms, killed "injuns," and kept slaves. A courthouse had replaced the fort in the late 1870s and over the next half-century a low-slung skyline, dominated by the courthouse steeple, etched itself against the horizon. Seen from above, Fort Worth juts from the featureless plain like a skeletal reef on the

Longhorn steer in livestock pen at the Swift & Co. stockyards, Fort Worth, *c.* 1940s.

floor of a vanished sea. The torpor of its blazing summers helps account for the spare, languidly cadenced dialect, the parched brush sprouting along roads, the wide-brimmed ten-gallon hats favored by inhabitants, the sound of crickets at night, the buzz of flies in the daytime; Fort Worth was neither urban nor rural. Prone to savage tornadoes, floods, and freakish storms, its uneasy truce with nature was mirrored in the ambivalence of society. In Ornette Coleman's recollection:

> Sometimes the sun is shining and beautiful on one side of the street, and across the street, just maybe three feet [1 m] apart, there'd be big balls of hail and thunderstorms, and that reminded me of something that happened with people . . . they're the same way as the elements.[1]

At the time of Ornette's birth, Fort Worth was a mix of the small-town ordinary and the larger-than-life, a city of us and them, the powerful and those who served at their pleasure.

OWING TO ITS frontier history, Fort Worth considered itself culturally western as opposed to southern, a place where individual freedom was valued and the race issue handled more genteelly than in the Deep South. While no lynching of African Americans was recorded there, historic attitudes may be judged by the 1860 hanging of two white abolitionists (who advocated an end to slavery) at the hands of Fort Worth's "Vigilance Committee." Abraham Lincoln's 1863 Emancipation Proclamation was late in reaching Fort Worth, but on June 19, 1865, when General Gordon Granger delivered the news, "there was no jubilee of freedom" or "reports of a mass exodus of freedmen."[2] After the Civil War, the Texas legislature's "black codes" restricted movement, property ownership, and labor contracts not only to all visibly African Americans, but to so-called "octoroons," anyone with a single black grandparent, that is, an eighth of African heritage.

In 1868 a branch of the Ku Klux Klan opened in Fort Worth shortly after the one established in Dallas. With black lives held hostage to punitive laws, white populations openly enacted race hatred. Between 1900 and 1920 some one hundred African Americans were publicly tortured and murdered in Texas.[3] These crimes were sometimes perpetrated in broad daylight amid a cheering crowd, photographed, and made into souvenir postcards. "This is the Barbeque we had last night" reads the script on the back of a postcard sent from Robinson, Texas, in 1916, referring to the charred corpse of a man depicted on the front.[4]

Despite its wide-open spaces and the independence and individualism that Texans wished to embody, the "Lone Star State" was trapped in the same racist norms as the claustrophobic South. If Fort

Worth was less guilty of violence towards blacks than other cities, including neighboring Dallas, the possibility of such violence was ever present. Fort Worth prided itself on relatively calm race relations largely because its black population was small and powerless enough to pose minimal threat; white residents tended to ignore black communities altogether and African Americans entered their lives almost exclusively as employees. The tensions that arose from the contradiction between self-myth and reality defined this society and arguably fueled its vibrant and progressive music scene. In black communities, music offered a means of self-improvement and expression, and livelihoods were earned through teaching and performance.

In 1896 the u.s. Supreme Court ruled that segregation was not discrimination, so long as the racially separate facilities were "equal," a word whose meaning was broadly interpreted in the raft of laws issued throughout the early decades of the twentieth century. "Jim Crow," the name of a blackface minstrel performer, became the shorthand term for practices projecting the appearance of equality while maintaining a racist status quo. In 1930, when Ornette Coleman was born, Fort Worth, a city of 163,000 people (including approximately 22,000 African Americans and 4,000 Mexican Americans), was thoroughly segregated: schools, hospitals, restaurants, hotels, public transport, and neighborhoods. Blacks were obliged to travel in separate train cars and railroad stations were equipped with separate waiting rooms. African American citizens could visit the city's parks only on "Juneteenth" (June 19th), the anniversary of the Emancipation Proclamation's arrival in Texas. They were either altogether barred from sports or cultural events, or able to attend only when separate seating and restrooms were provided. The 1936 Texas Centennial Exposition (June 6–November 29), an extravaganza held in Dallas marking one hundred years of Texas independence, featured a "Hall of Negro Life," "the first recognition of black culture at a world's fair," which blacks were allowed to visit only on "Negro Day."[5]

Main Street, Fort Worth, Texas, in the late 1920s.

In Fort Worth, African Americans had to step off the sidewalk when white people passed and to address them as "Ma'am" or "Mr." if not "Sir." Profit occasionally trumped prejudice: Leonard Brothers, one of Fort Worth's several large department stores, courted a black clientele while maintaining the obligatory "colored" restrooms, drinking fountains, and seating in the store's cafeteria. Mexican Americans fared slightly better; while "unofficial" discrimination relegated them to an inferior social position, they could, for example, be buried in white cemeteries, whereas African Americans had their own separate but equal ones.[6] Nor did white Christians feel that Galatians 3:26 ("[We] are all the children of God by faith in Christ Jesus") applied to black Christians, who in any case had long established their own churches in order to worship as they pleased.

That segregation was an artificial means of negotiating deeply racist attitudes is clear in hindsight; the burden it represented to African Americans denied their dignity at every turn is less easily grasped. The word "denigration" (from the Latin "to blacken") has been simplistically associated with racial prejudice, but its significance lies in its connotation of darkness, the kind that envelops the soul of individuals whose self-esteem has been ceaselessly battered. Consider the pervasive shadow that racism cast on black communities, augmented by the hardships of the Great Depression, when an estimated 50 percent of African Americans were unemployed, and one may begin to approach the importance of the Church as refuge. Centers of moral and material support, education, and cultural affirmation, churches provided a platform for community organizations and formed the backbone of the nascent black middle class.[7]

In all the world throughout all time, there has never been a surer means of wringing exaltation from the heart of despair than hearing voices lifted in song. Fort Worth's oldest black churches were located within a block or two of Ornette's childhood homes and he recalled "all the time going from one church to the other, listening to gospel music."[8] These relatively modest buildings housed the largest meeting rooms available to the black community and appeared the more imposing for their contrast with the makeshift housing that surrounded them. Built with donations eked out of meager familial earnings, they radiated pride and accomplishment. Musician and composer John Wallace Carter (1929–1991), who attended high school with Ornette, recalled the services at Mount Gilead Baptist Church and their lasting effect on his music:

> As I search my experiences now, looking for areas to call upon for thematic material, for the excitement for an out chorus, for the gutty feeling for a blues, for the beauty of a ballad, I go back often to the scenes of my early childhood. I wish I could capture the raw power of my baptizing pastor, Rev. J. L. Lenley in the out chorus on his sermon of Jesus cheating the devil out of the grave after having been entombed—the angels removing the gravestone and Jesus

stepping forth in triumph. Reverend Lenley at this point always stepped off the pulpit with great drama, took the tails of his frock-tailed coat in front of him in his left hand and marched through the church, right hand fully extended, shouting at the top of his voice, "All power, good God, all power, won't you try him today church, all power." . . . The church would be in absolute chaos, the "amen" corner echoing, "Yas Suh, Yas suh," and the church nurses running around from one emotionally-wrought person to another. I would sit and smile . . . beautiful music.[9]

The preacher-to-congregation interaction characteristic of these sermons corresponds to the practice of "call and response" present in African and other musical traditions. Preachers like Lenley could orchestrate a rhythmic back-and-forth that built to a cathartic climax. Carter, who sang in the Mount Gilead choir, described the excitement of Sunday service as "akin to the feeling of being on the stand playing jazz . . . branches of the same tree."[10]

Despite the presence of these respected religious institutions, Ornette's neighborhood, Hillside (slightly east of downtown), was considered one of Fort Worth's least privileged. "The Southside was more wealthy territory," Ornette recalled, "Dewey Redman [schoolmate and later collaborator] had indoor plumbing down there. We had a honey pot."[11] Ornette's childhood homes, hard by the Santa Fe Railway tracks, were rented "shotgun shacks," so-called because it was a straight shot from the front door to the back. These wooden pier and beam (as opposed to foundation-supported) dwellings were typically around 12 feet (3.5 m) wide and twice as long, with a small front porch. Also called "railroad houses," they were situated on properties considered undesirable by whites because of their proximity to the tracks and the accompanying danger of derailment, the engine smoke, house-rattling noise, and, especially in Fort Worth's sweltering summers, the stench of cattle cars.

Yet in the popular imagination, trains evoked freedom and the romance of travel and adventure described in many a period song, including guitarist Henry "Ragtime Texas" Thomas's "Railroadin' Some" (recorded circa 1927). Thomas (1873–1930?) was seventeen when he escaped farm-bound drudgery in Big Sandy, Texas, to travel by hitching rides on freight trains (to "hobo"). In his song, he calls out the stops like some magical incantation:

> Change cars on the T.P.! [Texas & Pacific Railroad]—
> Leaving Fort Worth, Texas! Going through Dallas! Hello,
> Terrell! Grand Saline! Silver Lake! Mineola! Tyler! Longview!
> Jefferson! Marshall! Little Sandy! Big Sandy! And double back
> to Fort Worth![12]

The passage of trains, their insistent rhythms, the barrage of bells announcing their arrival, the forlorn whistle of departure, what author Albert Murray called "railroad onomatopoeia" and a "very

Letitia Eldredge, *Shotgun Houses*, 1961, ebony pencil on paper. Ornette told Eldredge that her drawing looked just like his childhood home in Hillside.

fundamental matter" relating to the blues, formed an aural backdrop for Ornette's youth and a vocabulary later referenced in his music.[13]

Men who worked for the railroads were held in high regard. Aside from educators, no profession was more admired in Fort Worth's black community than that of Pullman train porter. They traveled over 10,000 miles (16,000 km) a month, slept a few hours a night, and augmented their minimal wages with tips earned while serving a wealthier, more mobile white clientele. Meanwhile, in every city the porters gathered stories, experiences, the latest fashions, and records, and brought them all back to their hometowns. Porters were also admired for belonging to America's first African American labor union, the Brotherhood of Sleeping Car Porters (BSCP), established in 1925 following a civil rights struggle led by A. Philip Randolph, who visited Fort Worth's Southside to hold union meetings. The Southside was considered the "elite" black neighborhood: residents included teachers, small business owners, and railroad men. Marjorie Crenshaw (1927–2019), a Southside resident whose father was a braker on the Texas and Pacific Railway, noted, "My mother didn't work, sometimes she had people come and help her. This area was really exclusive, as we called that then," whereas Ornette's neighborhood "was anything but right."[14]

Ornette's father Randolph, son of Virginia-born William and Lucy Coleman, was listed as a seventeen-year-old farmer in the 1910 U.S. Federal Census, living in his father's home in Calvert, Texas (150 miles, or 240 km, south of Fort Worth). The births of America's rural poor, black and white, were not always officially registered prior to the First World War and some dates remain approximate. Randolph was born Christmas Day around 1893; it is uncertain when he married Rosa Jackson, who shared the same birthday and was very young when she had their first son, Allen Grover, in 1916. During the First World War, Randolph served as a cook in the army (1918–19), a duty considered menial and therefore reserved for African Americans. In 1920 a daughter, Truvenza, was born while the family resided in Rio

Vista (40 miles, or 64 km, south of Fort Worth), followed by another daughter, Vera, in 1922.[15] At the time of Ornette's birth (March 9, 1930), Randolph was employed as a mechanic and Rosa as a "hotel maid" in Fort Worth. But like many other African American families, the Colemans' was a musical one.

In Fort Worth's black communities, home life revolved around music. The tradition of weekly musical gatherings where friends and family played and sang together was passed from generation to generation. Brenda Sanders-Wise of Garden of Eden, a community founded just outside Fort Worth by Tennessee and Kentucky freedmen, recalled a scene replicated in many local homes:

> On Saturday mornings we'd do our chores then go next door to our grandparents' house . . . everybody would congregate, our grandmother would come down and play piano. We'd have talent shows in the morning and in the afternoon we'd go to church for choir rehearsal because we had to sing Sunday morning.[16]

That children were afforded music lessons despite the family's financial straits suggests the importance of cultural achievement to social status. From elementary school age, many children studied privately, paying 25 cents per lesson. According to Ornette's friend and collaborator, trumpeter Bobby Bradford (1934–), who grew up in Dallas:

> "Middle-class" meant people who have the same values as people who had money. Black middle-class people didn't have money but they embraced the values, which meant you had to go to school and you had to take music lessons, even if you didn't have any talent.[17]

A social hierarchy grounded in the church, where the titles of pastor, minister, deacon, and usher conferred degrees of status, extended to forms of music. Organist Jack Carter never played with Ornette because "he was on the jazz side and I was on the religious side."[18] Marjorie Crenshaw echoes the same sentiment: "my father played violin, upright bass . . . and he just loved music . . . but remember he was a church man." Crenshaw's father saw to it that his children heard musicians "who counted," notably Duke Ellington, but the music the family played at home was "classical."[19]

Music involving improvisation was considered inferior to scored compositions from hymnals or European canons, not to mention vulgar for the indecorous dancing it engendered. People who frequented blues or jazz clubs were referred to as "backsliders," for taking their religious commitments lightly. "If you can dress up for the devil on Saturday night," preachers admonished their congregations, "then you can dress up for Jesus on Sunday morning."[20] In describing the defining role of the church in African American lives, LeRoi Jones affirmed that "the 'backslider' (the sinning churchgoer) and 'the heathen' became, in the new theocracy, the lowest rungs of the social ladder." These late nineteenth-century norms remained firmly in place throughout Ornette's youth and early adulthood.[21]

Derogatory attitudes towards certain kinds of music were largely owed to the places where they were performed, where liquor was served and gambling common, but they also reflected opinions held by the white middle class since the dawn of the decadent Jazz Age. "Unspeakable Jazz Must Go!" was the title of a 1921 article in the *Ladies' Home Journal*, declaring it "worse than saloon and scarlet vice." Conservative backlash to the audacious new music was typically couched in racist terms, like the diatribe against jazz published that same year in the *New Republic*:

> impudence is its essence . . . After impudence comes the determination to surprise . . . Irony and wit is for grown-ups. Jazz dislikes them as much as it dislikes Nobility and Beauty. They are the products of a cultivated intellect . . . Niggers can

be admired artists without any gift more singular than high spirits: so why drag in the intellect?[22]

When the Benny Goodman Orchestra played Carnegie Hall in 1938, jazz achieved a degree of respectability, as did the African Americans performing in his predominantly white band. But the event's success reflected Goodman's popularity more than a shift in perceptions. The idea that jazz musicians possessed no less virtuosity than classical ones and consequently deserved an equal place in concert halls was radical when placed into action by 26-year-old aficionado and impresario Norman Granz.

In 1944 Granz produced the first of an extended series of jazz concerts, recordings, and nationwide tours featuring a stellar line-up of black musicians and vocalists entitled "Jazz at the Philharmonic" (JATP). For African Americans who believed that in a better world, their children would have become concert musicians playing in symphony halls, the JATP was a revelation. By moving jazz to cultural venues where listening was encouraged instead of dancing, the JATP, which toured Dallas and Fort Worth in the 1940s, presented jazz as "serious" music, instilling a powerful sense of pride in black audiences nationwide.[23]

It would have been hard to find an African American in Fort Worth in the 1930s–40s who did not enjoy listening to blues and/ or rhythm and blues and the big swing bands of the era, but while they admired the recording artists, they still wanted their children to become music educators, not performers, because it was a steadier, more reputable job. The only acceptable reason for young people to play in nightclubs or touring bands was that their families needed the money. The need to leverage musical talent to earn a living under objectionable conditions came with a certain stigma, one that Ornette felt throughout his early professional life. That some forms of music were regarded as more "serious" than others inspired him to create one that defied categorization.

Ornette's older sister, Truvenza Coleman, a blues singer and bandleader, said that their mother encouraged them to study music. Ornette's first instrument was the kazoo, which he played with friends, imitating the swing bands on the radio. Randolph Coleman sang both at church and in a quartet that sometimes rehearsed at their home. According to Truvenza, the popular (now legendary) guitarist and vocalist Aaron Thibeaux "T-Bone" Walker visited often and showed her to play the family's old upright piano. In Truvenza's recollection, their home was alive with people, music, and parties:

> We didn't have money to throw away, but I don't remember going without anything. I may have had to but I didn't realize it. We had so much love in our family, maybe we were poor and didn't know it. There's a song: "we ate every night and the roof stayed on tight."[24]

Ornette, who was perhaps too young to recall these happier times, remembers instead being "poorer than poor."[25] Judging by scores of interviews and his usually curt response to questions regarding his youth, Ornette's childhood memories were relatively scant and often tinged with bitterness.

Randolph Coleman died of a "stroke of paralysis" on February 21, 1938, when Ornette was just shy of his eighth birthday. In those Depression days, one way of ensuring a proper burial was to belong to the local black lodge of the Masons, where annual dues doubled as a kind of insurance policy covering funeral costs. But membership in the Masons constituted a step up the social ladder that the Colemans either could not afford or chose not to take.[26] Randolph's grave went unmarked for over a year until Rosa, then working as a laundress, petitioned the u.s. Military for a tombstone, part of a benefit package offered to First World War veterans. After their father's death, Ornette's brother Allen left home to seek work in Los Angeles, joining the exodus of some five million southern blacks to points north and west known as the Second Great Migration.

In 1941 Vera, fresh out of high school with all the promise her diploma represented, was killed in a car accident in Palo Pinto, 65 miles (105 km) west of Fort Worth. Truvenza signed the death certificate and brought her sister's body home for burial in the "colored cemetery." Less than two years later, Allen died at the age of 26.[27] Rosa lost her eldest son and presumably whatever income he was sending home. Ornette surely registered his mother's grief and the repeated shock of loss to his family. The ambiance in the Coleman household grew somber. Ornette recalled the long walk to elementary school, "over a lot of train tracks . . . and I'd get tired and some days I'd never make it. When my mother found out she near beat me to death."[28] He characterized Rosa as strict and religious. Church, for different reasons, was an important part of both of their lives.

Churches were often the first venues where young people heard music performed but also where they first performed it, in church-sponsored youth orchestras. According to Marjorie Crenshaw, who knew Ornette from childhood, he studied briefly under William Arthur Fowler (1872–1952), a private teacher and leader of the band that played at Mount Gilead and St. James Baptist Church events.[29] When he wasn't giving lessons or holding rehearsals in his Veal Street home, Fowler patrolled the Southside with a walking stick to discourage kids from skipping school. He groomed his sixty-piece band for nationwide competitions, soliciting William "Gooseneck" McDonald, Fort Worth's leading African American businessman, to supply instruments and uniforms. The repertoire of church youth bands was hymn-based and relatively staid. For musical variety, the Baptists and Methodists could not compete with "Holiness churches" (sometimes called "sanctified churches"), the Pentecostal and Evangelical branches of Protestantism, whose services featured bands with a rhythm section and often at least one horn.

Trumpeter and drummer Charles Moffett (1929–1997), who befriended Ornette in high school, attended a "sanctified church" as a child with his family, not just on Sunday but every day:

> We were going to church to have a good time . . . I remember a lady playing a tambourine, someone playing the trombone, there was a drummer and a piano player . . . everybody in church always clapped. You'd be groovin' all the time.[30]

Fort Worth's Baptists and Methodists found the abandon of so-called "Holy Rollers" unseemly, or at least better suited to a dance hall. That didn't stop neighborhood children from hanging around to hear the music and many a jazz great had a formative musical experience in such a church, whether attending services or playing for them.[31] According to church organist Jack Carter,

> I never played for the Pentecostal church because I didn't play that type of music . . . see I was a Baptist and we were completely different from their style of music. They played and danced and sang . . . and the music was like rhythm and blues . . . fast music and they clapped as they danced, they kept the rhythm. As a kid, my brother and I, we'd go up and watch them dance and it was an amusement thing for us and at that time we didn't realize they were worshiping God in their own way . . . [32]

Music teacher Marjorie Crenshaw drew the same distinction:

> See, the Holiness church always added, they added their chords and things, they were different. We played it like it was written in the Methodist church, but they had a creative mind . . . and they didn't have to use the book [written music], they had this ear—that's a blessing—but at that time if my

piano teacher had caught me trying to play something like that I'd get in trouble, none of them allowed us to do that.[33]

Both the Pentecostal and Evangelical church services retained aspects of traditional African worship, such as the use of drums and dancing, that were dismissed by other denominations as untoward. But the presence of music in all black churches reflected the African dictum that "the spirit will not descend without song," and was regarded as essential to overcome suffering and achieve the spiritual healing that was every worshiper's goal.[34] Ornette was witness and participant in these musical catharses:

> Well, I've heard lots of music and it just sounds like music, but [sometimes] the air smelled so differently and the activity of the people around [was affected] . . . [the music] changed them . . . In Texas when I used to have to play for a country evangelist, healing people, doing things . . . We'd get there and the piano would be [out of tune], but those same things would happen. So I had that experience myself, when I was playing for evangelists or in the church, that particular thing we're talking about—I think that's more in church music. What I mean by church music, [is] music that is totally created for an emotional experience.[35]

At an early age, Ornette observed that the value of music was perhaps less a matter of form than function. "I didn't need to worry about keys, chords, melody," he later remarked, "if I had that emotion that brought tears and laughter to people's hearts."[36] It seems likely that the concept of "unison" he developed in later life, which beyond its musical definition denoted a deeper attunement available to all human beings, originated in his early encounters with music in the church.

WHEN ORNETTE WAS growing up, music was shared largely via radio and jukeboxes. By the 1940s portable phonographs were widely available but remained a luxury item, and jukeboxes, a descendant of coin-operated player pianos, served as communal record players. Ornette's friend, saxophonist Dewey Redman (1931–2006), recalled a juke joint across the street from his childhood home on the Southside:

> it went on almost every day and every night. I would sit [outside] and listen just to the blues, or whatever was happening . . . and this was one of the biggest thrills in my life . . . I listened to it for hours.[37]

To restaurant and bar owners, jukeboxes were a means of cutting corners on live entertainment while still attracting clientele, according to Bobby Bradford:

> Almost any little beer joint would have a jukebox with like 40 songs on it . . . That was the source of black entertainment and it generated some serious money. Sometimes they called that jukebox a Seeburg. We'd say, "go put a nickel in the Seeburg" and that was a synonym for jukebox.[38]

Putting a nickel in the Seeburg represented a significant expenditure at a time when jobs were scarce and laborers might earn 25–75 cents per hour. Considering that the average tune lasted around three minutes, jukeboxes were making more money than a lot of people. With their futuristically illuminated chrome or brass-fitted housings, their success reflected the fascination that greeted both the music emerging from the Jazz Age and new technologies whose praises were sung in a 1932 article in *Popular Mechanics*:

> You live in an automatic age. By merely dropping a coin in the slot you can buy recreation, food . . . without contact

with a single clerk. The machines that make this possible are legion, developed to a high state of perfection in half a century of experiments. They are produced and serviced by a constantly growing industry employing several hundred thousand men. Dispensing with the services of salesmen, cashiers and attendants, these machines offer standard products at low prices . . ."[39]

On the Southside, jukeboxes were supplied by Bill Jackson, the father of percussionist Ronald Shannon Jackson (1940–2013), who later toured and recorded with Ornette. Bill Jackson must have been a savvy businessman, since the lucrative jukebox trade was typically handled by white men. His advantage was probably the ability to provide best-selling records to stock the jukeboxes from his store, House of Music on Evans Street. Jackson understood local tastes and specialized in "race music," the industry name coined in the early 1920s for records targeting black audiences, including gospel, blues, and swing.[40]

By the 1940s, when more families could afford radios, they had become as important to daily life as the Internet is today. "Without a radio I don't know what we would have done," said one Fort Worther, "it kept us up with the news and with music, and sometimes some of that music *was* the news."[41] Philco's battery-operated Farm Set must have been popular in neighborhoods like Ornette's that lacked electricity. Beginning in the 1930s listeners could tune in to broadcasts from New York and Chicago, where African American bandleaders and soloists were all the rage. It wasn't until the later 1940s that local radio significantly integrated its musical menu. The big, brassy, and predominately or exclusively white swing bands of Benny Goodman (1909–1986), Paul Whiteman (1890–1967), Tommy Dorsey (1905–1956), and Glenn Miller (1904–1944, with Fort Worth's own Gordon Lee "Tex" Benecke on tenor sax) were broadcast staples, alongside indigenous string-based western swing. But postwar stations embraced

Vintage Philco portable radio, model 46-350, *c.* 1946.

more ethnic programming, including "race music" and Tejano, a hybrid born of Mexican and Spanish musical traditions and Texan folk and "country" sounds, including the polkas and waltzes popular among the state's European (Czech, Polish, German) communities. A brief survey of Fort Worth radio helps illustrate the sonic and social ambiance of Ornette's youth.

One of the first and most enduring local stations was WBAP, founded in 1922 by Amon G. Carter (1879–1955), a quintessential Texan who left a lasting impact on his adopted hometown. Known as "Mr. Fort Worth" because he ran so much of it, Carter was born in a log cabin in Crafton, Texas, and proud of his humble beginnings. An admirer of circus showman P. T. Barnum, who warned that "you cannot afford not to advertise," Carter became the advertising manager of a local paper, the *Fort Worth Star*, in 1906 and by 1925 had purchased and consolidated three smaller papers into the *Fort Worth*

Star-telegram, a leading news provider until the present day. Like other white-owned dailies of the era, black community news was conspicuously absent from the pages of Carter's publication unless an African American was accused of a crime. Carter had meanwhile anticipated radio's encroachment on print media. "If this radio thing is going to be a menace to newspapers, maybe we had better own the menace," he reportedly told his circulation manager before starting WBAP.[42]

Carter envisaged the future of aviation in America and laid the groundwork for Fort Worth's prominent role in the defense industry. In 1928 he was a director and part owner of American Airways, soon to become American Airlines, with Fort Worth as its headquarters. Carter was influential in convincing airplane manufacturer Convair, later General Dynamics, to establish a production complex in Fort Worth in time for the Second World War boom. The mile-long plant that churned out thousands of B-24 "Liberator" bombers created 38,000 local jobs, of which only the most menial were assigned to black citizens.[43] Having purportedly dug ninety dry wells, Carter struck oil in New Mexico in 1935, then again in 1937 in the massive Wasson oil and gas field in West Texas.

Long-time president of the Fort Worth Club, bastion of Texan oil wealth and Washington lobbying power, Carter also directed the Southwest Exposition and Fat Stock Show, famed for its rodeo even now. His close friend Oklahoman Will Rogers (1879–1935), homespun humorist, vaudeville cowboy, and film star, introduced him to painters Frederic Remington and Charles M. Russell and their elegiac portrayals of the American West. Carter became an avid collector and provided in his will for the establishment of a museum in Fort Worth in his name. Lauded for his philanthropic endeavors, Carter's contributions to Fort Worth's African American community were among his less expansive. These included a "public park for Negroes" in Lake Como, a black neighborhood on Fort Worth's west side, and a $250 bequeathal to the African American woman who had served his family for much of her life.[44]

In its early years WBAP shared its frequency with two other radio stations, and the switch between them was famously announced with a cowbell. One was Dallas-based WFAA, the first regional station to present an African American swing band, the Alphonso Trent Orchestra, whose performances were broadcast live weekly from the Adolphus Hotel (1925–6), despite threats from the local branch of the KKK.[45] In 1932 WBAP became a "clear channel," one of the first that could be heard across America. Perhaps its most popular live-broadcast band was Milton Brown and his Musical Brownies. Born in Stephenville, Texas, vocalist and bandleader Brown (1903–1936) moved to Fort Worth as a teen, where he acquired his reputation as the "father of Western Swing," a style that emerged from the Jazz Age and matured in the midst of the swing era (1930s–mid-1940s) when "rural influence, traditions and instrumentation were encountering and aspiring to big city modernity." Milton Brown is credited with "transforming hillbilly music in Texas," smoothing its "barn dance" edges into a more urbane form embracing blues and jazz.[46]

Brown's originally five-piece band (upright bass, two violins, guitar, and banjo) could play a fast and furious blues interspersed with his shouts, hollers, gospelesque cries of "yeah" and "uh-huh," and the occasional jazzy scat. He was best known for relaxed, bluesy ditties like his 1930s hit "Fan It," whose lyrics ran, "if this song's too hot / you got to fan it / and cool it / honey till the cows come home." When Brown died following a car accident, former bandmate Texan fiddler Bob Wills (1905–1975), leader of the Texas Playboys, assumed his mantle. Wills and Brown started out in the early 1930s in the renowned fiddle band the Light Crust Doughboys, a group that was also broadcast by WBAP and another local station, KFJZ.[47]

Established in 1939, KFJZ's motto, "from Beethoven to boogie," suggested rather more variety than its programs delivered. These included wholesome live broadcasts of local and regional talent, and recordings of Guy Lombardo and his Royal Canadians and film star and crooner Bing Crosby.[48] Some early Fort Worth stations targeted a religiously inclined audience, as KFBQ, whose call letters stood for "Keep Folks Quoting the Bible," did. When the wartime ban on radio towers was lifted, a flock of fresh stations took to the local and regional airwaves. Fort Worth's KWBC, which began broadcasting in December 1946, announced a "variety/ethnic program" and was the first area station to air a Spanish-language program. But KVET (founded by Second World War veterans) out of Austin, the state's capital, made greater strides in this direction.

KVET first aired on October 1, 1946, offering a Spanish-language news and music show (*Noche de Fiesta*) and, beginning in 1948, targeting African American audiences with "The Jives of Dr. Hepcat" hosted by DJ Albert Lavada Durst (1913–1995).[49] Enlisting a black DJ was a bold move, owing to the substantial number of Texans who considered such a presence in their homes, however disembodied, an intrusion. According to Durst,

> If you were black, you had to get back. If you delivered mail, you had to deliver it at the back door. The radio station was the white man's property only . . . [future Texas governor] John Connally [who spearheaded the station] put his political career on the line, letting the black on the radio station, but I think they hit a gold mine, because the station became very popular.[50]

The success of "ethnic broadcasting" was, however, more than financial:

> Radio broadcasting helped break down the barriers between races because Jim Crow could not dictate what kind of music a person listened to . . . Many white listeners got their first introduction to R&B on [the radio] . . . Black DJs became that friendly voice between songs to their regular listeners, the first "black friend" many whites had.[51]

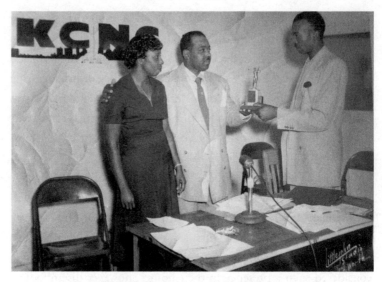

James "Pappy" Clemons (center), Fort Worth, *c.* 1949.

"A celebrity with local white college students" in addition to his following in the black community, Durst was a self-taught pianist who started out playing church music. Among his several recordings was "Hattie Green" (Peacock Records, 1950), a blues named for the madam of a brothel in Abilene, Texas, which he rapped rather than sang.[52] Durst also wrote the best-selling spiritual "Let's Talk About Jesus," recorded by a group of seven Austin singers called the Bells of Joy, for which he received neither credit nor royalties, "because I was in the blues business and [church] people might not like it."[53]

Durst opened his program with Duke Ellington's "Things Ain't What They Used to Be," and "went out with the blues." In between he played a mix of R&B and jazz artists, including T-Bone Walker and xylophonist and bandleader Lionel Hampton.[54] Although Durst is cited as Texas's first black DJ and undoubtedly contributed to a wider appreciation of jazz and R&B, it seems that other Texas stations put African American radio hosts on the air before him. Fort Worth's KCNC (sign-on date February 1947) gave James "Pappy" Clemons (1915–1990) a fifteen-minute spot in its daily broadcast, but the date of his hiring is uncertain.[55] Dallas station KLIF, however, began broadcasting black DJs as of its November 9, 1947 sign-on.

One of the first "frequency modulator" (FM) broadcasters, KLIF reached for wider audiences through programs as diverse as *Hillbilly Round-up* and *Harlem Hit Parade*.[56] An ad in the *Dallas Morning News* for the station's debut said that listeners could look forward to "a Negro Disc Jockey team, Red Calhoun and Buster Smith."[57] Henry Warren "Red" Calhoun (1905–1965) was a popular alto sax player and bandleader in Dallas in the 1940s–50s. With his Royal Swing Kings, he opened the Rose Ballroom in 1943, and later headlined at the Carousel Club owned by the notorious Jack Ruby, the man who shot Lee Harvey Oswald.[58] Red Calhoun was admired as a player and a bandleader who gave younger musicians a start, but his KLIF companion Buster Smith had a hand in jazz evolution, not least for having mentored saxophonist Charlie Parker (1920–1955).

THE LIFE OF Henry "Buster" Smith (1904–1991) mirrors that of many musicians of his generation whose musical legacy was inherited by innovators like Parker and Ornette. Born in Alsdorf, Texas (40 miles, or 64 km, south of Dallas), Smith was seventeen when he bought his first instrument, a clarinet, in a pawn shop for $3.50 he'd earned in the cotton fields, at 75 cents per hundred harvested pounds:

> The blues was all around, growin' up, pickin' cotton up in Collin County. There's where I was born, 1904. I heard them work songs, church hymns. I tried that blues on my Uncle's pump organ in Ennis [Texas], but my mother disapproved.[59]

By age eighteen, Smith was proficient on clarinet, organ, guitar, and, most famously, alto sax. Like other young musicians who needed work and wanted to travel, he signed up for a medicine show, those itinerant theatrical presentations of the post-bellum Southwest designed to attract customers for "cure-alls." It is uncertain which one he joined, but nearby Fort Worth was a favored stopover for shows touring the Southwest, each with a different configuration of musicians and performers. In the dusty outposts of central and west Texas, the entertainment that medicine shows delivered was warmly welcomed, as were their products, "wonder cures . . . mostly vegetable oil, plus a little bit of whiskey; that's where the wonder came from." Guaranteed to relieve ailments such as "weak gizzard, fallen arches and limp liver," some nostrums contained opium, an effective pain-killer that had the added advantage of ensuring return customers.[60]

In the 1920s Buster Smith graduated from medicine shows to playing clubs in the quarter of Dallas known as Deep Ellum. Located on Elm Street near its intersection with the Houston and Texas Central Railroad, Deep Ellum began as a string of shops established by European immigrants who were happy to serve African American customers. There were grocers, tailors, second-hand clothes stores, and pawn shops that did a brisk business at a time when banks shunned African American clients. Black-owned businesses eventually sprang up along a section of the railroad that became known as Central Avenue or Central Track. By the 1920s Deep Ellum had theaters showing films and vaudeville acts and dance-halls like the Green Parrot, the Tip Top, and the Pythian Temple. Aside from gambling joints and bootleg liquor, Deep Ellum's greatest attraction was music, which was everywhere, even in the streets.[61]

Buster Smith got his real start when the Blue Devils came through Dallas and hired him.[62] The Blue Devils were perhaps the best known of at least a hundred African American "territory bands" that played in dancehalls throughout the Mid- and Southwest and were headquartered in major cities including Dallas, Houston, and Kansas City. Based in Oklahoma City, the band comprised groundbreakers such as tenor saxophonist Lester Young, of Kansas City; Dallas trumpeter Oran "Hot Lips" Page; pianist Bill (later "Count") Basie from New Jersey; Oklahoman vocalist Jimmy Rushing; and

Texan guitarist Eddie Durham. Author Ralph Ellison recalled a circa 1930 performance of Smith with the Blue Devils in Oklahoma City's Slaughter Hall:

> [People did] a dance step called the "two and one." It was a brisk rhythm in which they would dance with and against the rhythm of the bands. There was a lot of improvisation going on on the dance floor, and these Negroes would go into quite a series of steps that carried them very rapidly from one end of the hall to the other, almost in one huge sweep of feet and bodies in motion. Then they would turn and come back down just as fast as they had gone.[63]

Ellison remarked that Smith's "strange, discontinuous style," traces of which were later evident in Charlie Parker's playing, may have originated in Smith's reaction to the dancers' movements.[64] When the Blue Devils broke up in 1932, Smith, Basie, and Durham joined Bennie Moten, a ragtime pianist and leader of another prototypal territory band, the Kansas City Orchestra. With its six-member horn section, banjo, guitar, piano, and accordion, Moten's band played "jump blues," said Smith, "which was a cleaner sound than that cotton patch blues . . . Jump blues was more like jazz."[65]

Throughout the 1920s and '30s territory bands served as ambulant music laboratories whose strength lay in their openness and flexibility. On tour, they picked up musicians whose talents reshaped the ensemble, as did the response of audiences in dozens of small towns where their arrival was cause for celebration. Traveling (and often sleeping) in trucks and buses, territory bands covered the sparsely populated region extending from the immensity of Texas in the south to Nebraska in the north, east to St. Louis, and west to Denver.[66] Like traders carrying goods from town to town, they created demand for their musical wares and inspired locals to produce their own versions. It was a way of life

Musicians touring with John Robinson's Circus, Breckenridge,
Texas, *c.* 1920s; photograph by Basil Clemons.

conditioned to change and this accounts for the fluid personnel of some of the bands and the appearance of the same musician in many different [ones] . . . the ability to work with other jazzmen from the general area helped create a common musical language. Change, tolerance for catch-as-catch-can living and eating arrangements, adversity . . . all seem to have combined to create in the Southwestern jazzman a musician of unusual originality, endurance and self-reliance, and this spirit, in keeping with the character of the plains country, is reflected in the musical style.[67]

It was tough going, especially for the leaders responsible for arranging bookings, travel plans, and room and board under pervasive Jim Crow constraints. But music meant mobility and the chance for adventure that many young musicians—including Ornette Coleman, who joined a touring outfit after high school—were more than willing to take.

When Bennie Moten (1894–1935) died of a botched tonsillectomy, Count Basie (1904–1984) picked up his baton. Buster Smith, nicknamed "Prof" for his composition and arrangement skills, contributed material to the Moten and Basie bands, including "One O'Clock Jump" (1934), which became Basie's theme song.[68] In describing a Basie recording of Smith's composition, "The Blues I Like to Hear" (1938), musicologist Gunther Schuller remarked upon the sense of place that it evokes:

how much further to the southwest Buster's Texas-based style was rooted, compared even with the somewhat peppier "smarter" Kansas City idiom . . . one cannot fail to note its distinctive sound . . . its "crying" blues-drenched harmonies. Clearly, it has a totally different feel: simple and uncomplicated, earthy low-down blues with a heavy rocking beat.[69]

Buster Smith recorded only one album as bandleader, much later in his career. But with his satiny tone and explorative riffs that transcended the blues idiom in which they were typically couched, he wielded considerable influence on saxophonists, among them Charlie Parker, whom he met in Kansas City, Parker's hometown. In a 1982 interview, Smith described their relationship:

> [Parker] was a slow reader [of music], and he hung around me all the time. He liked my playing, said I was the king. And I'd tell him he was the king. So I hired him to play with me at Lucille's Paradise [Kansas City], and he'd follow me everywhere I'd go . . . He wanted to do everything I did. I was like his daddy, and he was like my son.[70]

When jobs grew scarce in the Midwest, Smith moved to New York, and in 1939 Parker "hoboed [out there]" to join him. Parker was broke and Smith put him up. "My wife and me let him stay in the bed in the daytime and we'd stay in it at night." When Parker began playing with composer, arranger, and trumpeter John Birks "Dizzy" Gillespie (South Carolina, 1917–1993) in 1943, first in the Earl Hines and Billy Eckstine bands and finally in Dizzy's combo (1945), his career took off and bebop was born. "He liked to play a lot of solo horn," said Smith, explaining how Parker had tired of swing with its elaborate arrangements, and was about to leave his teacher, whose lessons he had absorbed, behind. "I like that big band sound," said Smith, who stuck with it even though its days were numbered, as smaller bebop ensembles took its place. In 1943 Smith left New York. "I seen what it was comin' to," he said. "I had my time, and I was ready to go home [to Dallas]."[71]

Smith hosted the aforementioned KLIF radio program and led a series of bands, mentoring young players, notably Dallas tenor saxophonist David "Fathead" Newman (1933–2009), a gifted, influential musician who recorded over one hundred albums with his

Charlie Parker, Carnegie Hall, New York, 1947;
photograph by William P. Gottlieb.

own and other groups. Newman described Buster Smith's "huge
sound on the alto":

> And his execution was superb; he could get over the instru-
> ment really fast—he knew it backwards. His phrasing and
> harmonic concept were modern, ahead of its time. He was a
> self-taught musician with perfect pitch, and he could sit and
> write arrangements while we were riding up and down the
> highways—he wouldn't have to be anywhere near a piano.[72]

In 1959 Smith was in a car crash and could no longer play sax, but he took up electric bass and performed until he was eighty years old. His modesty, resilience, and willingness to share his knowledge were the hallmarks of musicians who "came up the hard way" and whose explorations of the old forms from which jazz was derived blazed a path to the new.

MUSICIANS CAN OFTEN recall the circumstances surrounding their first hearing of particular songs as palpably as a first encounter with a lover, and a single song could inspire the intention to learn an instrument or launch a career. For Ornette, it was probably "Flying Home" (1942), recorded by the Lionel Hampton Band and featuring a solo from Houston tenor saxophonist Jean-Baptiste Illinois Jacquet (1922–2004).[73] Delivered with effortless exuberance, it was as if the nineteen-year-old Jacquet had distilled the very essence of being young and alive into song. His solo created a sensation; subsequent tenor players with the Hampton band reproduced it nearly note for note. Malcolm X, who heard "Flying Home" at Harlem's Savoy Ballroom, wrote, "I have never seen such fever-heated dancing."[74] Born in Louisiana and raised in Houston, Jacquet started singing and dancing in the family band with his father and brothers when he was three: "Oh everybody played, and that's what you did every day, just like you eat every day, that's what you eat, the music. And it becomes a natural thing, and it's still that way."[75] Musical nourishment in the form of inspiration and influence passed from player to player in an unbroken chain. Jacquet acknowledged Buster Smith, and tenor saxophonists Herschel Evans (Denton, Texas, 1909–1939) and Buddy Tate (Sherman, Texas, 1913–2001) as contributing to his formation, some of the same musicians Ornette admired and emulated in his youth.

Herschel Evans started out in a territory band, modeling his big-bodied sound on the luscious tenor of Coleman Hawkins (soloist

Illinois Jacquet, New York, *c.* May 1947; photograph by William P. Gottlieb.

with the New York-based Fletcher Henderson Orchestra during its heyday in the 1920s and early 1930s) but retaining his bluesy southwestern sound. In his brief career cut short by a heart attack, Evans played and recorded extensively with Count Basie, soloing on compositions arranged by his cousin the guitarist Eddie Durham, in addition to recording with Lionel Hampton and others. He was replaced in the Basie band by Buddy Tate, also associated with a Texan sound, described as "a straightforward, simple, heartfelt statement."[76] Dallas's Budd Johnson (1910–1984) was another tenor saxophonist of the same landmark generation. His career path intersected that of Buster Smith and Eddie Durham and led him to New York, where recordings with Dizzy Gillespie placed him at the forefront of the bebop movement.[77]

Ornette came to music at a time when homegrown talent was super-abundant and consequential for the history of jazz. Texas had produced popular, innovative geniuses since the turn of the century, notably pianist composer Scott Joplin of Texarkana (1868–1917), the "king of ragtime" whose "Maple Leaf Rag" (1899) was the first sheet-music song, in those pre-radio and record player days, to sell over a million copies. Joplin's father was enslaved in South Carolina and his family was one of many that came to East Texas after the Emancipation to work on the railroads that in turn fueled the lumber industry. His fifty published rags were a synthesis of forms: work songs, spirituals, shouts and hollers, call and response, in addition to the popular European waltzes, quadrilles, and polkas introduced by Texas's German and Eastern European settlers. "An incomparable fusion of folk music and learned music, of prairie and town," Joplin's syncopated rags laid the groundwork for early jazz.[78]

As for the blues, a signature element in jazz chemistry, Texas had a long, rich tradition. Perhaps the earliest written reference found there was a stark single-stanza song called "Nobody There" (1890): "That you, Nigger man, knockin' at my door? / Hear me tell you, Nigger man, nobody there."[79] Blues verses were documented in 1901 in the Mississippi Delta, another cradle of the form, but they were no doubt being sung long before someone started writing them down. In distinguishing Delta and Texan blues, music critic Robert Palmer observed that the former, with its references to "hoodoo" or black magic,

> has a potent mystique—hellhounds on your tail, blues and the devil walking side by side, selling your soul to the dark man at the crossroads . . . a kind of sacred music, opposed to the church yet espousing its own African-rooted spiritual values.

By contrast, Texas blues was "above all music for entertainment and dancing or for chronicling the ups and downs of day to day experience . . . unapologetically secular, sensuous, even carnal—like rock and roll."[80]

Archetypal bluesman Henry "Blind Lemon" Jefferson (1893–1929), born in Coutchman, East Texas, sang of loneliness, love and betrayal, lust and death, of trains, rural life, and the prisons where African Americans were being confined in great and disproportionate numbers.[81] His guitar served less as an accompaniment than a sidekick, thanks to comment-like riffs, short repeated phrases that became a building block of jazz. Jefferson's vocals were similarly inventive; he "howled and squealed," sometimes imitating the sound

Blind Lemon Jefferson, *c.* 1926.

"Lightning" Washington, singing with his fellow prisoners in the wood yard at
Darrington State Farm, Texas, 1934; photograph by John A. Lomax.

of "a wolf or a possum or a coon." Excused from fieldwork owing to his blindness, Jefferson played for Saturday night parties called "breakdowns" in neighboring farm communities, sometimes accompanied by a fiddle.[82] He also played the chock houses of the 1920s rural southwest, improvised nightclubs serving a rotgut brew named for its inventors, the Oklahoma Choctaw. "That's what you call a 'good time house,'" recalled Buster Smith, "you'd hear that slow blues and there'd be fightin."[83] Jefferson traveled widely by train, settling for a time in Deep Ellum where his protégé T-Bone Walker assisted him in moving from club to club. In 1925, while in Chicago, he attracted the attention of a talent scout from Paramount Records who signed him to the label. Jefferson's sales rivaled those of the "Empress of the Blues" Bessie Smith (who began recording in 1923) and his stylistic innovations passed through direct heirs like T-Bone Walker to subsequent generations of musicians.[84]

Many who contributed to the development of jazz came from remote towns that were nonetheless connected to the greater world by their appetite for music. Born in San Marcos, Texas, a town of a few thousand souls surrounded by ranchland, Eddie Durham (1906–1987) shaped the sound of big band swing with his compositions and arrangements, while his experiments with amplification helped define the guitar's role in jazz. Durham's mother was part African American, part Mohawk. His father, Joseph, was an Irish-Mexican fiddler, farmer, and bandleader of the Durham Brothers Orchestra. Between them, the five brothers played nine instruments; Eddie played guitar and trombone and the youngest sang. Joseph made his own fiddle using a cigar box for the body, cedarwood for a neck, catgut strings, a horsehair bow, and a finishing touch, recalled Durham, that involved hunting rattlesnakes:

> [My father would] get the rattles and he'd bring them back and dry those rattles for about four days. When they dry out, [he'd] drop them in the fiddle. When you hit the fiddle,

boy, them rattles would sound—that fiddle would sound like an amplifier.[85]

As a boy, Eddie shot snakes and sold their rattles for a quarter apiece to fiddle players less handy with a rifle. In the early 1920s he joined a traveling rodeo and circus called the 101 Wild West Ranch Show Band, which was "bigger than Ringling Brothers . . . they had three or four tribes of Indians . . . [that] would ride out on the horses . . . with arrows."[86] He was soon arranging pieces for the show's fifteen- and nine-piece bands, earning a substantial $25 per week. Durham toured America with the 101 and then, in 1928, worked for a while with Oklahoma City Blue Devils, followed by the Bennie Moten Band. Durham met Moten in Kansas City, the musical capital of the Midwest, where "bands came off the stage at eight and nine in the morning [in time] for people to go to work."[87]

To help his guitar's volume compete with Moten's brass section, Durham "made a resonator with a tin pan [inserted in an acoustic guitar] . . . and when I hit the strings the pie pan would ring and shoot out the sound." Experiments with amplification continued when Durham joined the Jimmie Lunceford Orchestra at the peak of its popularity in the mid-1930s, when it replaced Cab Calloway as the Cotton Club's house band in Harlem: "I tried converting radio and phonograph amplifiers and even drilled into the body of the guitar. With that rig I used to blow out the lights in a lot of places. They weren't really up on electricity like they are now."[88]

In addition to his guitar playing, Durham composed and arranged for the Count Basie Band (which he joined around 1937) and for other signature swing bands of the prewar era, including Glenn Miller's. Towards the end of a long, prolific career, he said, "It's hard for me to remember all the bands and arrangements . . . [I played] with more musicians than I can count."[89] But he recalled that Lunceford "had some three hundred numbers in his repertoire. And I never pulled my book [of chord changes] out, never."[90] Mnemonic prowess was and

The Glenn Miller Orchestra, *c.* 1940.

remains a skill prized, if not possessed, by all musicians. Durham's achievements as a composer and arranger have overshadowed his talent as a player, despite his presence on numerous recordings, but his contemporaries, fellow Texan guitarists T-Bone Walker and Charles Edward Christian, are still referenced by musicians across the blues, R&B, and jazz genres.

Aaron Thibeaux "T-Bone" Walker (Linden, 1909–1975) started off as "lead boy" for his mentor, Blind Lemon Jefferson, accompanying him through the streets and saloons of Deep Ellum. Walker's mother was "full-blooded" Oklahoma Cherokee, his father played bass, and the banjo Walker strummed as a child in the family band was made from that most protean of recyclables, the cigar box (which also served as a receptacle for tips). In his early teens, Walker sang and danced at a Dallas soft-drink stand called Eddie's Drive-In, near a hotel whose customers complained of the noise. "We'd start work at seven, and by nine . . . the wagon would come—the whole band would be in jail every night."[91] Walker was nineteen when he started touring with a medicine show, traveling and sleeping on a truck that also served as the stage where he danced and played guitar. "Of the fifteen dollars I got [per week]," he recalled, "I sent ten back to Mama."[92] Along the way, Georgian blues singer Ida Cox (1888–1967) spotted Walker and enlisted him in her vaudeville show where his act, as he described it, consisted of tap-dancing "35 or 40 choruses of 'Tiger Rag' with a table in my teeth and the banjo on the back of my neck." The table's size is uncertain but it was presumably large enough for effect. "Never had a toothache in my life," Walker said.[93]

T-Bone Walker's career unfolded at a time when music doubled as carnival-like entertainment and competing club owners were avid for novelty. He and tenor player Buddy Tate worked a club outside Dallas called "The Big House," whose "gangster" owner had them perform "dressed up in prison uniforms."[94] Before he was twenty, Walker had toured the South and Southwest and made his first country blues recording à la Blind Lemon Jefferson ("Wichita Blues," 1929) on acoustic guitar. While retaining Jefferson's riffing style, Walker embraced the upbeat swing-inspired tempos that characterized early rhythm and blues. Like Jefferson, Walker played his instrument held almost flat out in front of him as if writing on a clipboard, but his sound, recalled Buddy Tate, "was jazzier," his vocal phrasings relaxed and nuanced. In the mid-1930s, around the time Walker frequented Ornette's childhood home, Fort Worth's African American-owned Jim Hotel made his group their house band, his first decent job. But his big break came later in Los Angeles, where he recorded "Stormy Monday" on electric guitar (released November 1947), an instant blues classic.

According to Illinois Jacquet, who performed with T-Bone at a club in Watts, Los Angeles, "he played guitar and it was almost like a conversation. Then he would sing. Like two people."[95] Beyond the themes of heartbreak and disappointment typically associated with the blues, Walker's running guitar commentary communicated irony, humor, and hard-won wisdom with the eloquence of a rhetorician.

T-Bone sang, but his guitar did the talking. At the 1966 edition of Jazz at the Philharmonic, he took his place onstage with Dizzy Gillespie, Coleman Hawkins, and other preeminent jazzmen, introduced by impresario Norman Granz. "If it appears at first to be an anomaly to have a singer of this type with the show," said Granz, "don't think it. Because . . . all jazz comes from the blues."[96]

T-Bone Walker brought jazz phrasing to electric blues guitar, and Eddie Durham experimented with amplification in a swing band context, but it was Charlie Christian (1916–1942) who reinvented the guitar as a center-stage jazz instrument. Born in Bonham, Texas, and raised in Oklahoma City, Christian played ukulele, then guitar, and by age fifteen was performing in Deep Deuce, Oklahoma City's equivalent of Deep Ellum. From his youth, Christian listened to and often jammed with western swing bands, which were the first, in the mid-1930s, to record songs featuring electrically amplified standard and steel guitars.[97] In 1939 he auditioned for Benny Goodman and was soon the star of Goodman's band. His style, wrote Gunther Schuller, relied on "clean uncluttered lines, often in arching shapes— his favorite phrase contour; his flawless time; his consistently blues-inflected melodic/harmonic language."[98] Critic Martin Williams called Christian "*the* major guitarist and a major soloist regardless of instrument."[99] Although his career lasted little more than a decade, Christian was inducted into the Rock and Roll Hall of Fame in 1990 as "an early influence," an honor awarded to T-Bone Walker in 1987. Christian died of tuberculosis in 1942, the year that Illinois Jacquet soloed on "Flying Home." The song, coincidentally, was first recorded by the Benny Goodman Sextet in 1939, featuring Lionel Hampton on vibraphone and the 23-year-old Charlie Christian on guitar.

ORNETTE COLEMAN WAS heir to this lineage and repertoire of sounds, the fund from which jazz borrowed its themes and memes. Nearly all the Texan musicians played Fort Worth and mostly knew one another, had met on tours, worked together in different bands, and in some cases were relatives. These interactions, spread over many cities and the small towns in between, created a musical frame of reference whose parameters were constantly being redefined in performance. The accompanying narrative of camaraderie and conquest (of audiences and fellow players) meanwhile enhanced the attraction of the musical profession. More than trendsetters, whose speech, clothes, and haircuts were imitated alongside the idiosyncrasies of their sound, musicians were heroes, possessed of the power to capture and carry a crowd, to tell a story with sensation instead of words and to be loved for it. No wonder Ornette chose music: he believed in his individuality, and music was the surest means of both expressing it and getting paid. By the time he picked up his sax, Texas had produced a bumper crop of musicians whose hybrid styles, derived from homegrown influences, alloyed with those encountered on the road, were like currents of a mighty river flowing to the sea of jazz.

The initial stages of Ornette's music career were less physically arduous than those of his predecessors. Instead of farm or ranch work, he held a series of part-time jobs including shoe shiner and busboy at downtown Fort Worth's Blackstone Hotel. He was around fourteen when his mother, to whom he rendered his earnings, condoned the purchase of a gold-plated Conn alto. "I used to play one note all day," he said.[100] Like others of his generation, Ornette found his way around his instrument by listening to the radio or records, using focus and desire to translate hearing into playing. Formal schooling was something he distrusted from the start: "My teacher spanked me once because I told her she was wrong. But I was right and I believe that to this day. I learned quickly in school that all you had to know was the answers."[101] Ornette's early musical instruction confounded him, and it was perhaps with church bandleader William Fowler that he encountered his first difficulty. It began when he mistook the first seven letters of the alphabet as the standard concert scale, which instead of A B C D E F G ran C D E F G A B, as Ornette explains:

I thought my C that I was playing on the saxophone was A, like that, right? Later I found that it did exist thataway only because [on] the E-Flat alto, when you play C-natural it is [concert] A [transposed]. So I was right in one way and wrong in another—I mean, sound, I was right.[102]

The bandleader who discovered Ornette's error told him he'd never make it as a saxophonist.

Ornette found further proof of teachers' fallibility around age fifteen, when he visited an aunt in New York, whose husband arranged a lesson with a saxophonist who played with the Cotton Club's star bandleader, Cab Calloway. "[He] had me look in the mirror and play for an hour," Ornette recalled, "that was my lesson." Ornette held his cousin James Jordan (1931–2018), who played alto and baritone sax, in higher regard, no doubt owing to his patience and support. Jordan

The Blackstone Hotel in downtown Fort Worth, *c.* 1920s–30s.

I. M. Terrell High School, Fort Worth, rectangular building at top left, in 1939.

gave Ornette lessons and remained a close companion and professional advisor throughout much of his life. "I always wanted to earn respect from Jordan because he went to [college] and I didn't," Ornette remarked, while noting that "Jordan had to know exactly what the thing was all about before he did it," whereas Ornette felt no such constraints.[103] His penchant for experimentation got him into trouble, conflicts with authority that defined his character and career.

Like his cousin James, Ornette attended Fort Worth's I. M. Terrell High School (1944–8), an imposing edifice built in 1938 on a hillock by the Trinity River.[104] Grudgingly funded by municipalities who paid black teachers less than white ones, high schools like I. M. Terrell were found only in larger cities, meaning students poured in from dozens of outlying communities, creating a nexus of talents and energies. I. M. Terrell was a highly respected institution; music was an integral aspect of its curriculum, and its marching and concert bands earned statewide awards for excellence. Jazz was not a study topic, but students acquired the fundamentals of music literacy and were familiarized with classical European forms. It has been said that if it wasn't for God and football, there would be no jazz, since the church's tradition of sponsoring bands was iterated in high schools, where football's pregame and halftime rituals provided their *raison d'être*. Young musicians learned discipline and cooperation by playing in the smartly costumed and well-rehearsed orchestras, large and loud enough to resound from turf to bleachers. Many jazz musicians of Ornette's generation started out this way, some of them forming collaborative friendships that lasted a lifetime.

Admission required preparatory lessons and passing muster with the bandleader. George A. Baxter was in charge at I. M. Terrell; he was a man who "would not let you escape from what he considered to be perfection" and who "seemed to be always at Ornette," perhaps for the way he dressed.[105] Ornette affected an overcoat even in warm weather and wore his hair long and conked (straightened and pasted down with a pomade called Konkoline) beneath a porkpie hat. Whether or not his clothes were at fault, Ornette vexed Baxter and vice versa. The tale of how Baxter expelled Ornette from the band for improvising in the midst of Sousa's "Washington Post" belongs to the jazz annals.[106] But in the version still circulating Fort Worth, the song Ornette chose to interfere with was no less than "The Star Spangled Banner," "the sacred hymn, you know, of the world," remarked an I. M. Terrell alumnus with only mild sarcasm.[107] Ornette swore it wasn't he who diverged from the score that day while admitting he may have done so on other occasions. But the story of his wayward riffing gained currency because it confirmed the generally held perception that he was different, an outsider, and a rebel—in other words, in some counterintuitive way, a true Texan.

Attendance at I. M. Terrell dropped off during the Second World War as students enlisted or else were obliged to choose jobs over school. When Ornette was in his freshman year in 1944, the graduating class was congratulated for completing their studies despite war-related pressures, and "home front responsibilities" formed the substance of the class president's speech.[108] Fort Worth was nonetheless in party mode. There were jitterbug contests on the Southside and talent shows where kids, including Ornette, competed for cash prizes.[109] Bands played in dozens of white- and black-owned establishments, from the down and dirty dive to the deluxe dancehall. Aside from high-caliber local talent, Fort Worth attracted the biggest names in jazz and rhythm and blues. In black neighborhoods, where people dressed up to step out on weekends, the wartime music scene was described as a "southwestern version of the Harlem Renaissance."[110] And with adult musicians in diminishing supply, young men began replacing them on the bandstands. By age sixteen, Ornette belonged to the Black Musicians' Union and was dividing his time between school and gigs.[111]

Clubs and restaurants catering to the black community advertised in the *Fort Worth Mind* (whose slogan was "Read the Mind"), one of several African American-owned local publications operating in the 1930s and '40s.[112] With a banner proclaiming itself "Fort Worth's largest circulated Negro newspaper, fearless and independent: a champion of race development," the *Mind* filled the gaps left by a mainstream (white) press that largely ignored the affairs of black citizenry. It covered national and local news, notably voter suppression and discriminatory prosecution practices. In addition to sports, church news, club news (social and charitable clubs), and a "world of women" column, there was a society page highlighting the activities of doyens and debutantes and a section covering "nightlife, screen and drama." A few white-owned businesses, including Leonard's Department Store, advertised in the *Mind*, but the publication was kept afloat through the support of small African American enterprises.

Among these were dozens of cookeries that doubled as beer and juke joints, like the Gay Paree on the east edge of downtown not far from where Ornette lived, an area with a number of black-owned restaurants and nightspots called the Ninth Street Strip. The Dixie Tavern (E. 3rd Street) was famous in the war years for its "hotcha floor show." The spacious assembly room of the black Masons' Prince Hall Mosque (E. 1st Street) was rented out for live bands and dancing.[113] Jazz greats such as Count Basie and Duke Ellington visited the Greenleaf Café (on 9th Street) when they played Fort Worth, accompanied by James Luther "Pappy" Clemons, African American DJ and impresario.[114] In 1943 Clemons was managing the Egypt Nightclub, a 9th Street hotspot whose name was apparently inspired by the day job of its owner, a mortician who taught at the Texas College of Embalming. "Jump for Joy," read the club's October 1943 ad, "doors open at 7 o'clock for clean entertainment."

James Clemons was a protégé of William Madison "Gooseneck" McDonald (1866–1950), the black community's answer to Amon Carter, "probably the richest Negro in America" according to *Ebony* magazine. A stirring speaker and Republican Party chairman, McDonald leveraged his political and Masonic connections into the 1912 creation of the Fraternal Bank and Trust, the area's first financial institution serving African Americans. As a real-estate developer, Macdonald helped transform the Southside from "the ragged edge of nowhere" into a flourishing, albeit segregated, middle-class black neighborhood.[115] In the late 1920s he made a lasting contribution to Fort Worth's music scene: the two-story, fifty-room Jim Hotel. Located near Ornette's childhood home, the Jim had a nightclub, the College Inn, where from the mid-1930s to the early 1950s an array of now legendary musicians performed.[116] In 1946 McDonald financed James Clemons's first big nightclub venture, the Rainbow Terrace ("Fort Worth's Nitery [*sic*] of Splendor"), which held Sunday-night jam sessions and presented out-of-town talent.[117] Dallas tenor saxophonist Budd Johnson was a big draw, as was T-Bone Walker, whose "capers on the stage are equal to a cast of entertainers," according to an ad in the *Mind* for a January 1947 engagement.

Along with Downtown's 9th Street, the Southside's Rosedale Avenue was "on fire" in the 1940s, with clubs like the Aristocrat Inn, the China Doll, the Bombay Room (known for its large aquarium), the Zebra Lounge, the Famous Door, and the Paradise Inn.[118] Many clubs were converted houses whose success relied as much on the quality of their cooking as on their musical attractions. At least one was purpose-built, the Zanzibar, with a retractable roof that "rolled back so you could dance beneath the stars."[119] Its proprietress, Lucille Wallace, was a glamorous Creole who "finished college, but never took to that side. So she opened the Zanzibar, built it herself . . . and jazz was played in there."[120] The Zanzibar was later purchased by Quentin Crenshaw, but his daughters Nadine, Theodora, and Betty Jean reportedly ran it and maintained the tradition of regular jam sessions. The Bluebird, in the predominantly black neighborhood of Como, west Fort Worth, was also owned and operated by women. When Viola and Vlastine Grant acquired it in the late 1930s it was an abandoned streetcar, painted blue and repurposed as a juke joint. The wood-frame building the sisters built in its place hosted musicians touring the Chitlin' Circuit and remained (under subsequent ownerships) a fixture of Fort Worth's night life until the early 2000s.[121]

When Ornette was in high school, everyone was listening to singer, saxophonist, and bandleader Louis Jordan (1908–1975), the "king of the jukebox," whose danceable songs were major hits. Jordan played Fort Worth with his group the Tympany 5 more than once, and his 1946 hit "That Chick's Too Young to Fry" occupied the top slot on the "Music Lover's Popular Chart," a regular feature of the *Fort Worth Mind*, while his "Choo Choo Ch'Boogie" was number three. Ranked with Duke Ellington and Count Basie as one of the most popular African American recording artists of his time, Jordan was the first to achieve a significant crossover audience, appearing on both Billboard's rhythm and blues "race" charts and mainstream (white) pop charts. Known for his floorshows with acrobatic dancers, Jordan, who started out in fellow Arkansan Alphonso Trent's territory

Louis Jordan (with sax) and his band Tympany 5, New York, 1946–8;
photograph by William P. Gottlieb.

band, was an accomplished alto saxophonist. "You learned a lot just
listening to how he got around on the instrument," recalled Bobby
Bradford, then a member of Dallas's Lincoln High School band. "If
you could play the latest Louis Jordan record that was your audition,"
Bradford said.[122] Ornette's first group, the Jam Jivers, which included
I. M. Terrell schoolmates Charles Moffett (trumpet) and Prince Lasha
(vocals), covered Louis Jordan hits for school dances and soon moved
on to clubs.

In his sophomore year Ornette broke his collarbone playing sand-lot football, an accident resulting in an imperfect mend that exempted him from military service and enabled him to convince his mother to let him trade his alto for a tenor sax, claiming the doctor said it was less strenuous.[123] The real reason was that the family needed money and tenor players were in greater demand in local clubs. Rhythm and blues was popular, as were the performers who helped define the idiom, including Illinois Jacquet, Arnett Cobb (Houston, 1918–1989), and Cecil James "Big Jay" McNeely (Los Angeles, 1927–).[124] Ornette's early role models were "honkers," tenor saxophonists who could whip audiences into a frenzy with their relentless riffing, repeating a note "past any useful musical context, continuing it until [they] and the crowd were thoroughly exhausted physically and emotionally."[125] Alongside a virtual sound assault, honking involved physicality and direct audience contact. Abandoning bandstand etiquette, Big Jay McNeely would move into the crowd and get down on the floor, horn raised to the heavens. Likewise, Ornette literally bent over backwards to heighten the excitement and please the crowd. According to Charles Moffett, when the Jam Jivers started playing Fort Worth clubs, "he was dancing quite a bit . . . with that tenor saxophone on top of tables and everything else . . . He was enjoying himself and making everyone else enjoy themselves."[126]

Kinetic excitement was built into the music; freed of the church setting of its origins rhythm and blues reveled in carnality, and the moans and grunts of heated honking attracted predictable censure. Describing Arnett Cobb's style, a commentator remarked that "in full flight, [his] is one of the most rhythmically exciting sounds in the music, although the excess of vulgarity inherent in much of his work hides this fact."[127] Rhythm and blues was rooted in the sweat and blood of collective experience; "[its] very vulgarity assured its meaningful emotional connection with people's lives," wrote LeRoi Jones. Honking's appeal to Ornette and others was precisely its defiance of social and musical niceties:

Lionel Hampton (with drumsticks) and Arnett Cobb, the Aquarium, New York, 1946; photograph by William P. Gottlieb.

The point, it seemed, was to spend oneself with as much attention as possible and also to make the instrument sound as unmusical, or as non-Western as possible. It was almost as if the blues people were reacting against the softness and "legitimacy" that had crept into black instrumental music with swing.[128]

Ornette once said he didn't listen to "older blues" so they were never an influence, probably referring to the "country" or "cotton patch" blues of the rural South.[129] But playing freewheeling rhythm and blues at the intersection of swing and break-out bebop, he experienced its power. "Sometimes you can be playing that tenor and I'm telling you, the people want to jump across the rail," he said, "especially that D-flat blues."[130]

I. M. Terrell classmate John Carter, whose later compositions, like Ornette's, challenged accepted jazz norms, considered himself "a Texas blues person," stating, "I couldn't change that if I wanted to . . . what I write now . . . is still grounded in that."[131] Likewise Dewey Redman, another I. M. Terrell alumnus, affirmed, "I couldn't get rid of that Texas sound if I wanted to." Neither could Ornette, who, music critic Howard Mandel observed, "had the blues, existentially."[132] As Texas bluesman Samuel "Lightnin'" Hopkins (1912–1982) put it, "when you born in this world, you born with the blues," rather like original sin. But while the blues expresses the pangs of the human condition, it also relays against-all-odds striving. Fort Worth vocalist Robert Ealey (1925–2001) referred to "something inside the blues that makes people start wondering."[133] This was what lingered in Ornette's music, the yearning for that which is ever slightly out of reach.

Despite his contributions to the household income, Ornette's mother was unenthusiastic about her son's choice of profession. "I'd say 'Mom, listen to this' and she'd say 'Junior, I know who you are.'"[134] But his sister Trudy (Truvenza) made up for it, helping Ornette's group find engagements and making sure they got paid. Trudy Coleman was ten years her brother's senior, though she liked to say they were about the same age. She attended I. M. Terrell but for some reason transferred and graduated from a high school in Waco (90 miles, or 145 km, south of Fort Worth). Rosa Coleman, who by then held a clerical job, was surely proud of her daughter, especially when Truvenza enrolled at Prairie View A&M College. And she was certainly disappointed that despite her hard work to support her daughter's education, Trudy dropped out before obtaining a degree because of music.

While still in school Trudy started booking a "band of chums" who convinced her to join them as vocalist, which meant she'd earn more. The band was soon renamed Trudy Coleman and her Orchestra.

Truvenza Coleman (second from left) and friends: guitarist Sumter Bruton (third from left); T-Bone Walker (seated with guitar); Fort Worth press writer Pete Kendall (seated, far right), Fort Worth, *c.* 1970.

Trudy sounded like a female version of her friend and mentor Joseph Vernon "Big Joe" Turner (Kansas City, 1911–1985), who sang a jazzy, urbane blues. Also known as "the Boss of Blues," Big Joe nicknamed Trudy "the boss lady"; she was an imposing woman by all accounts.[135] Trudy was tougher than Ornette. She knew her way around Fort

Worth, and by the time her brother was ready to work she was there to protect him. "Ornette wouldn't hurt a fly, sweet as he can be," said Marjorie Crenshaw. "Now his sister Truvenza might give you some trouble, 'cause she'd bless [euphemism for "cuss," or curse] you out real good."[136] Trudy was grounded in the blues and attached to Texas, whereas Ornette was looking outward. But they had music—and Rosa—in common. She was "very strict," said Trudy, "and to get away, we played." Years later Ornette wondered if Truvenza, not Rosa, was his real mother.[137]

Trudy helped Ornette form his first musical alliances. Trumpeter and drummer Charles Moffett (1929–1997) started working clubs at age thirteen with his Como neighbor John Carter. Both played in the high school band but didn't get to know Ornette until Trudy heard them at the Bluebird and suggested they work together.[138] Moffett's friendship with Ornette would blossom into a creative collaboration as adults, but he and John Carter were music-loving friends from childhood. Together they stood on boxes piled beneath nightclub windows to hear groups play and hid in dressing rooms so they could meet the musicians before the management sent them home. With Ornette their explorations deepened, guided by an alto sax guru named Charlie Parker, whose records they devoured.[139] According to John Carter, he, Ornette, and Moffett "were all stone boppers" gathering regularly "to work on [their] bebop repertoire and at the same time develop [their] individual styles."[140] Likewise, in Dallas, trumpeter Bobby Bradford belonged to "a little clique" with fellow Lincoln High School band members David "Fathead" Newman, James Clay (tenor), and Cedar Walton (piano):

> We bought Charlie Parker records, exchanged ideas and prac-
> ticed at each other's houses . . . There were six or eight of us
> boppers, we wore our little dark glasses and used the bebop
> slang . . . but that was just based on our love and thrill of this
> new music . . . and we were kind of outsiders, of course we

loved that too, you know, in the same way Charlie Parker and Dizzy Gillespie were outsiders, the idea of being a hip outsider meant a lot. But what attracted us all was the music . . . god, when I heard the boppers [at age fourteen], man, the top of my head came off.[141]

The sound that captured the imagination of Ornette and his friends was jarring to ears accustomed to laid-back blues, lyrical swing, or danceable R&B. It was unromantic, wrote Jean-Paul Sartre in 1947, "no way to take the hand of the girl beside you, to make her understand with a wink that the music reflects what is in your heart." Bebop was "dry, violent, pitiless," Sartre continued, yet "it fascinates, you can't get your mind off it."[142] Comprising intriguing techniques like contrafacts, new melodies obliquely built atop the chord changes of established standards, bebop was more brainy than emotional. Musicians had to think on their feet, simultaneously acknowledging and reinventing the old songs.

Instead of big, lavishly orchestrated bands, bebop favored tight ensembles—bass, drums, piano, and a couple of horns—small enough to squeeze onto a small stage in a packed club. Bebop was "full of splintered phrasing and astringent sounds, [its] rhythm was angular and complex, queer, off-center, yet riveted to some atavistic rock." It was big in New York and in Chicago, where an ad for Fox Brothers Tailors read: "Order YOUR Leopard Skin Jacket as worn by Dizzy Gillespie / BOP IN AND LET FOX BUILD YOU A CRAZY BOX!"[143] But in Fort Worth and Dallas rhythm and blues still held sway, and bebop was a fugitive music; it wasn't on the radio and black clubs weren't hiring musicians to play it.

Throughout high school Ornette worked wherever he could, whether with the Jam Jivers, his sister, or in other configurations, often in places where gambling was going on in some backroom. Clubs weren't allowed to sell hard liquor, but for a small fee clients could bring their own bottles and were supplied with glasses and ice.

People danced as hard as they drank in a charged ambiance that encouraged both. One night a white woman ambushed Ornette in a club kitchen and straightforwardly began to undress, an experience he found "frightening," ostensibly because interracial couplings were forbidden.[144] But the erotic energy he could command with his horn

Dizzy Gillespie, New York City, 1947; photograph by William P. Gottlieb.

also amazed and alarmed him. Fort Worth summers were long, the nights hot and muggy. Fights sometimes broke out, whether over a woman or a throw of the dice. Ornette saw people stabbed and shot and was convinced the music was responsible. His earnings were substantial but it started to seem like blood money. Nor did R&B feed his intellectual curiosity; although gratifying in some respects, it was all release and rebuke. His aspirations were increasingly at odds with the music and his surroundings, where tides of inchoate emotion at times threatened to overwhelm him. "Wherever I was playing the blues there were plenty of people without jobs who did nothing but gamble their money," he complained. Bebop was more reasoned, less "connected to a certain scene." It could "exist in a more normal setting," said Ornette, who saw bebop "as a way out."[145]

Ornette had his first taste of bebop in 1945, seeing Dizzy Gillespie in New York City while visiting relatives. That same year, he heard Charlie Parker's recording of "Now's the Time" and soon afterwards befriended tenor and alto saxophonist Red Conner, who encouraged his bebop inclinations. A student at I. M. Terrell, Conner was less than a year older than Ornette and his fellow boppers but "much farther along" musically, according to John Carter.[146] Ornette was taken with him. Conner introduced the fashion of longer, straightened hair that Ornette copied.[147] He attended a "holy [holiness] church," Ornette recalled, "and that became my church."[148] Born in Fort Worth, Thomas William "Red" Conner (1929–1957) lived on the Southside, recalled a neighbor,

> in a house near the grocery store on 1400 block of Evans. My mother used to send me to the store and wonder why it took me so long to get home. I was listening to the music. Red sat out on the sidewalk and taught the young ones. He was what you call a person with innate talent. Nobody really had to teach him, it was just there.[149]

The only known photograph of Thomas "Red" Conner (center right)
and fellow I. M. Terrell alumnus "King" Curtis Ousley (center left),
Fort Worth, *c.* late 1940s–early 1950s.

Conner's father, John, was a Pullman porter who died of pneumonia
six months before Red was born. His mother was Helen Griffith
(1901–1955) of Denison, Texas, and he had a half-sister named Eva.
On the eve of his 28th birthday, Red Conner was struck dead by a
cerebral hemorrhage. Little else is known, except that he dazzled
everyone who heard him. Ornette saw Conner sit in with the masterful Lester Young in Fort Worth and thought that Red outplayed
him.[150] Dewey Redman called Conner's sound "tremendous" and
placed him on a par with John Coltrane.[151] Conner made a lasting
impression on Como-born vocalist and flautist Prince Lasha, who
wrote a song about him, "Red's Mood" (1962). David "Fathead"
Newman, who performed with Conner in Fort Worth and Dallas,
underlined his individuality, noting, "he didn't particularly pattern
himself on any of the forerunner tenor players."[152] Conner reportedly
recorded with Houston pianist Amos Milburn, who brought him to
California, but it is uncertain whether the tapes or records survive.

A single photograph has surfaced in which Conner appears onstage playing alto, handsome in a light-colored double-breasted suit, with his hair slicked back and a slight moustache.[153]

Conner and his band apparently made a point of slipping bebop compositions into their sets; Ornette said he heard them play "every bebop tune that was recorded" and that it humbled him. "They were really playing *music*," he said. "I was getting all the praise around town, but I wasn't making any contribution." He'd wearied of honking, as had Illinois Jacquet and Buddy Tate, who called it "a gimmick, a novelty" and had moved on. Ornette set his tenor aside, returned to alto and expanded his repertoire. "Anything that was melodically complicated," he said, "I thought I had to learn." He developed a talent for listening and assimilating his discoveries, like the inner logic of the contrafact; "I thought that was the greatest thing since Bach," he said.[154] Ornette tried his hand at composing this way and, playing alto one night with Red Conner's band, he had an epiphany.

It was 1948 in an all-white club, the first of many where Ornette found work. According to Bobby Bradford, white audiences liked "sentimental music," songs they were familiar with from radio and records, "[the latest] Broadway show tunes and songs by Dinah Shore or Bing Crosby." They also wanted to dance, which meant bebop was out of the question.[155] Red's band was playing "Stardust," that most standard of standards, and Ornette was about to take his solo, dutifully improvising on the melody, when he had a change of heart:

> I was dragged because I could hear all these other notes I could play to the [chord] changes of Stardust. The people were out there just slow dragging . . . so I just started playing all the things I could think of to the changes without touching the melody. And then a guy hollered out, "Get on the melody, get on the melody!" And then I realized . . . I was already playing the melody [from the outside] and this guy didn't know it.[156]

To free himself of chord progressions, Ornette first had to own them. A typical solo was challenging: "like having to know the results of all the chord changes before you play them, compacting them all in your mind," he said. But with "Stardust" that night, having done the compacting, he "literally *removed* it all and just *played*."[157] The "slow dragging" dancers stopped in their tracks and at the end of the set the club owner fired him. But Ornette had found the frontier territory that became his field of action.

Opportunities to pursue his investigations were rare in the clubs he played for money, but the College Inn at the Jim Hotel advanced Ornette's education. It was the place to be, to listen and be heard. "All the musicians from the rich hotels would finish work and go jam at the Jim," said Ornette, "the rich, the blind, the prostitute—everybody would come there after midnight."[158] The Jim's owners were Levi and Oscar Cooper, who bought it from Gooseneck MacDonald in 1934 and made of it a minor dynasty. A former chauffeur, Levi started a cab company in 1917. Brother Oscar owned the Greenleaf Café and "one of most well-orchestrated bootleg operations in Tarrant County." Ornette said the Jim could get rough and thought it doubled as a brothel but while it might have had its shady side, musically speaking it was hallowed ground. A list of visitors from the mid-1930s to the 1940s reads like a jazz hall of fame: Louis Armstrong, King Oliver, Bennie Moten, Cab Calloway, Fats Waller, Count Basie, Lester Young, Billie Holiday, Ella Fitzgerald, Louis Jordan, and many more. The big names who came through town were usually guests in the homes of the Southside's well-to-do but their band members stayed at the Jim. The jam sessions that lasted well into the morning were open to players of every race and musical proclivity. Disgruntled white club owners complained to the police that the Jim was stealing their clientele and attempted, unsuccessfully, to shut it down.[159]

In 1947, following a $12,000 refurbishment, the Jim called itself the city's "Hotel of Comfort, Distinct Reflected Beauty, Economy and Excellence." It had a barber shop, a beauty salon, a taxi service

(Cooper Rent Co.), and hosted the office of Musicians' Local No. 292. Visitors could look forward to "Food, Drinks, Comfortable Rooms and Spicy Entertainment" in the "spacious College Inn."[160] The Jim offered the best accommodation for African Americans available in Fort Worth, but downtown's white-owned hotels were monumental by comparison, with dance halls big enough to swallow half its fifty rooms. The Hotel Texas (est. 1921) had 13 floors, the Worth Hotel was 19 stories high and the 23-story Art Deco Blackstone (est. 1929), where Ornette used to shine shoes, boasted "tub and shower, running ice water [and] radio in every room."[161]

For a small city, Fort Worth had a supersized entertainment scene catering largely to its white population, beginning with the Deco-style Will Rogers Memorial Complex (1936), which included a domed coliseum (the first and largest at the time), a 3,000-seat auditorium, fairgrounds, and facilities to support the annual rodeo and livestock show. It was built as a gauntlet thrown by Amon Carter to arch-rival Dallas when the latter was appointed host of the 1936 Texas Centennial Celebration instead of Fort Worth. Not to be outdone, Carter obtained federal funding for the 20-acre (8 ha) "entertainment and cultural complex" to host an alternative "Frontier Centennial" with help from his White House friends, Texan VP John Nance Garner and President Franklin D. Roosevelt. Aside from outdoing Dallas, the Frontier Centennial's somewhat conflicted mission was to "present an authentic picture of frontier life" and portray Fort Worth as a "city of the future."[162]

To advance these aims Carter hired Broadway producer Billy Rose, who proposed the creation of Casa Mañana ("House of Tomorrow"), a gargantuan outdoor dinner theater (capacity 5,000) with the world's largest revolving stage (diameter 130 ft, or 40 m; weight 17,000 tons). The Dallas Centennial may have boasted "twenty million bucks of machinery," but Fort Worth had "girls—pelvic machinery," said Rose. Casa Mañana showcased hundreds, all 6 feet tall even without their towering headdresses. One of the

headliners was burlesque queen Sally Rand, who dressed exclusively in "a sort of plaster" and danced with a gigantic weather balloon.[163] In the prewar years Casa Mañana welcomed thousands of customers nightly, "some in diamonds, others in overhauls" for either sit-down steak dinners at linen-clad tables or 30-cent beers at "the world's longest bar."[164] A reviewer ranked it alongside the Grand Canyon as one of the "two things that come up to the claims of their press agents."[165] The only African Americans who saw the inside of this manmade wonder were the people who worked there, including some 250 waiters.

The war effort derailed Casa Mañana's festivities but the Will Rogers Auditorium, which remained a concert venue throughout the 1940s, was also strictly Jim Crow. Black impresarios and civic groups could book it only when white ones did not want to, and were sometimes bumped from the schedule to accommodate them at the last minute. There was nonetheless a significant white audience for famous African American performers. In 1946 Duke Ellington ("the

Chorus girls in gold cowgirl costume at the
1936 Casa Mañana Fort Worth Centennial.

Aristocrat of Jazz") played the Will Rogers Auditorium, where the
announced "special section reserved for whites" meant the best seats
in the house.[166] Blacks had a separate entrance that led directly to their
customary place of exile, the balcony, referred to in the vernacular as
"nigger heaven." The same was true of the Northside Coliseum (123
East Exchange Street), originally built to house the Southwestern
Livestock Exposition (1908) and rodeo. Although larger than the
Will Rogers Auditorium, the Coliseum was more rustic, with acoustics better suited to its Monday-night wrestling matches than music.
Capitalizing on its size, promoters booked it for big-name acts like
Ella Fitzgerald ("First Lady of Song") and Dizzy Gillespie ("King of
the Modern Trumpet, Creator of Be Bob [*sic*] Music"), who appeared
there together in 1946.[167]

A combination ballroom and amusement park, the Lake Worth
Casino (northwest Fort Worth) booked nationally known white

Ella Fitzgerald, New York, November 1946;
photograph by William P. Gottlieb.

bandleaders like Tommy Dorsey, Artie Shaw, and native son Tex Beneke, and on Sundays offered 50-cent "bargain dances."[168] But indigenous nightlife was best represented on the Jacksboro Highway, aka "Thunder Road', a 3.5-mile (5.5 km) stretch of State Highway 199 dedicated to clubs, restaurants, liquor stores, and "no-tell" motel brothels, a latter day Hell's Half Acre. Gambling was a favorite pastime in Fort Worth; parents took their kids to cafes to play slot machines and purchased miniature versions to give them as toys.

The Jacksboro Highway was a rawboned mini-Las Vegas frequented in the 1940s by defense plant workers, meatpackers, and the odd West Texan "oil-field roughneck." "They weren't all killers," an habitué recalled, "they just loved to fight."[169]

Brawls were so common that the owners of the Four Deuces (2222 Jacksboro Highway) estimated the night's take based on the number of ambulances required to transport the wounded—the more the merrier. "If it was [just] a three-ambulance evening, money was a little tight," a manager said.[170] Black musicians working in white venues were understandably wary; trumpet player Willie Crenshaw, who sometimes accompanied Trudy Coleman at a Jacksboro institution called the Rocket Club, said he "always got himself by the door so when the fighting started he could get away." Some proprietors protected musicians from flying bottles with a chicken wire fence strung across the bandstand; on one occasion, musicians used a microphone stand to break a window behind the stage to make their escape.[171] The Jacksboro's *pièce de résistance* was the Skyliner Ballroom (Louis Armstrong once played there), with rose-tinted mirrors encircling a burgundy laminated dance floor where five hundred couples could dance the conga. Both black and white audiences were welcome at the Skyliner, only never on the same night.[172]

"Oh Ft. Worth was definitely racist back then," said boogie-blues guitarist and singer Ray Sharpe (1938–) referring to the late 1940s. "White boys used to ride up and down the street [on the Southside] just kind of terrorizing people," said Sharpe, who was eight or nine years old when he saw his aunt "chased down . . . and literally run over."[173] Ornette had seen more than his share of violence in the familiar confines of black neighborhoods by age eighteen, but the danger of playing white venues extended from his person to his self-esteem:

This fellow came up to me and said "Say, boy, you can really play saxophone. I imagine where you come from they call you mister don't they?" He couldn't see me with my [long]

Effigy of an African American found in Fort Worth's
Trinity Park following a federal court order calling for the
integration of an all-white local high school, summer 1956.

hair and beard coming from Texas; Negros don't go around
looking like that. So I said, no this is my home. "I want to
shake your hand," he says. "It's an honor to shake your hand
because you're really a saxophone player—but you're still a
nigger to me."[174]

From the time he became interested in music Ornette had adopted hairstyles and clothes like other adolescents, to reflect his affinities and stand at a distance from the crowd. He became a vegetarian, which in Texas amounted to sacrilege, as if his beard and straightened hair weren't enough. But looking and thinking differently were no longer sufficient; the distance had closed and he found himself attached to a society he both feared and held in contempt. "I couldn't really think what it would be like to leave Texas, or how to go about it," he said.[175]

Leaving home required decisions, not least about college, which his mother no doubt wanted him to attend. His cousin James Jordan and other high school classmates were intent on continuing their education, but Ornette saw little point in the investment. Music, he'd learned, could be a relatively lucrative profession, and a degree, then as now, did not guarantee a living. "Even the principal where I went to school worked in the summer in the hotel where I [used to be] a bus boy," he said. "I didn't have respect for him."[176] With Red Conner and others he'd heard proof that achievement is not calculated in money or fame, but Ornette was still proud of his earnings. Whether owing to maternal disapproval and the social expectations he'd failed to meet or pride in his self-determination, he was always defensive in his attitude towards school, saying he was offered a scholarship at Sam Houston College in Austin, but recoiled from what he perceived as pretention:

> I grew up with all these little black kids, their asses hanging out, they're starving and on welfare and all, but when I got to the college, they all acted like they're Einstein, like they'd never been hungry, like their asses was never out—and I said, "Oh, I don't want this influence . . . I want to teach myself whatever it is to become an adult . . . "[177]

Being an adult meant earning a living, but there was nothing respectful about having to coax his pay out of drunken club owners at the end of the night. Ornette was, however, working steadily enough to forestall decisions. "I'd go and play in a white nightclub and two nights I'd go over in a black nightclub then go over and play in a Spanish Mexican place," he said. He worked sometimes with his sister, who arranged for him to back Big Joe Turner during a protracted Fort Worth gig. "He was very cooperative with me," Trudy said; "he played the music he had to play here, but he didn't enjoy it."[178]

Ornette would often associate his hometown with a sense of fatality, recalling it as "the city where all the packing houses are . . . I could see the cattle going to be slaughtered and turned into steaks."[179] The tension to leave was mounting, even though he didn't have a plan. In spring of 1949, Fort Worth was struck by the worst floods in decades, rendering hundreds of residents of low-lying black neighborhoods homeless. But Ornette was gone by then; out of the blue he'd made his move, lied to his mother that he was going to Dallas, and, like many before him, joined a traveling band.

"Had he been a more glib musician," wrote A. B. Spellman, "Ornette might have found a seat in somebody's reed section, and [been] exposed to the kind of first-rate musicianship that would have saved him years of isolation." As it was, whether by default or as some penitential initiation, he joined Silas Green of New Orleans, a run-down vaudeville tent show. There were "shake dancers" and comedians; the band played anachronistic ragtime and Dixieland, and Ornette took a tenor solo on a single blues each night. They went to Oklahoma, Arkansas, Louisiana, and Georgia, which only impressed him by their squalor. "I thought I had played some rough places in Fort Worth," he said, "but the scenes we had in that minstrel group were something else." He was the sole Texan in a band that didn't like him or the way he played. He tried to practice bebop with another horn player who complained to the bandleader and he was fired in Mississippi. "Then the law decided I didn't look right, these white cracker cops . . . they knew I wasn't from [around there]," so they ran him out of town. Ornette found work with a rhythm and blues group that got him as

The flood of May 1949, Fort Worth.

far as New Orleans, where he was once again marooned without job
or instrument. He'd been badly beaten in Baton Rouge outside a club
by audience members who disliked him so much that they also
demolished his sax.[180]

Ornette had a friend in New Orleans, clarinetist Melvin Lassiter,
who restored his spirits. Melvin let Ornette use his brother's alto and
was an enthusiastic practice companion. Ornette worked yard jobs
by day and by night went to clubs where he listened and sometimes
sat in. His six months in New Orleans were significant, not least
because he met drummer Ed Blackwell, who became one of his closest
collaborators, and clarinetist Alvin Batiste, who shared his penchant
for experiment. He learned something that both disappointed and
encouraged him. New Orleans may have been a cradle of jazz, but
the child had grown up and moved on. Local musicians were not as
open as he might have hoped and unwilling to try new things. His
sound "had a lot of Charlie Parker in it," wrote A. B. Spellman, but

Ornette "approached the 'head' of the tune from a harmonic angle that sounded dissonant to the rest of the group" and his solos played havoc with the chords.[181] When he joined jam sessions, some players stalked off the stage, but with the support of Lassiter, Blackwell, and Batiste, he grew a thicker skin. That few were willing to bend the rules was clear. Rather than rejection, Ornette began to see it as natural selection.

On his return to Texas in 1950 Ornette landed a four-month job in an Amarillo nightclub and formed a band with Charles Moffett (drums), his cousin James Jordan (baritone sax), and Fort Worth bassist Aurelius Hemphill.[182] They played nearby towns and after-hours jam sessions in Amarillo's La Hoya Hotel, "a bad old place out in the Flats," a black neighborhood on the muddy shore of a shallow playa lake. The white-owned La Hoya offered otherwise upstanding white citizens a place to gamble discreetly and a rare opportunity for local western swing musicians to interact with jazz and rhythm and blues players.[183] Integrated jams were atypical in

Photograph by Walker Evans of a poster advertising Silas Green's traveling minstrel show, Demopolis, Alabama, 1936.

Texas, but a racially mixed band, such as that assembled by Fort Worth western swing guitarist Sock Underwood with Ornette on alto, was an anomaly.

A high school football star enamored of Milton Brown and his Musical Brownies, Oliver "Socko" Underwood (Hearne, 1917–1994), was bassist with Houston's Modern Mountaineers, and then guitarist with Fort Worth's Crystal Spring Ramblers. While working as a radio cowboy singer promoting a local dairy farm, Underwood longed to play the "jazzed-up string band music" of groups like Houston's Village Boys, whose repertoire included both "hoedowns" (square-dance music) and Benny Goodman, Duke Ellington, and Louis Armstrong compositions. His chance came in 1941, recording two sessions with Bill Mounce's Sons of the South, featuring pioneering electric steel guitarist Bob Dunn (formerly with Milton Brown) and nineteen-year-old electric standard guitarist Jimmy Wyble, who later performed with Benny Goodman and other jazz notables. After serving in the army, Underwood returned to Fort Worth (1950) and started a band with Chubby Crank (trumpet), Buddy Wallis (electric mandolin and fiddle), and C. B. White (steel guitar), all white, Texan musicians with a bebop tilt.

From its blues-inflected beginnings, western swing had more or less followed jazz's lead, however mindful the musicians may have been of their audience's folksy expectations. To some, western swing was a subterfuge, a way of playing black music in a white world, "one of the few outlets for white people to express the affinity they felt for the musical styles (and other artistic and social aspects) of African American culture."[184] Whenever possible, Underwood jammed with black musicians, who seemed more open towards western swing players than their "mainstream pop and jazz white counterparts, who looked down their noses at the 'hillbillies.'" After hearing Red Conner and Ornette play together, Underwood invited them to join his band for a gig at a friend's after-hours joint. He loved their sound, particularly Ornette's, and when the engagement ended continued to find opportunities to have him onstage, to the extent that, according to Buddy Wallis,

> it became a source of irritation to the rest of the band because . . . none of them really liked playing with Ornette . . . they just thought he was too far out . . . they didn't hear what Sock heard in Ornette. He thought Ornette was a genius.[185]

It must have heartened Ornette to discover that the interests of musicians traveling diverse paths could nonetheless converge. Nor was he immune to the charms of western swing, its playfulness, the languorous lyrics, the honeyed tones of the steel guitar, and the jaunty, drawling, or bickering strings. When he started playing violin around a decade later, Texas could not have been far from his mind. Western

Square dance, Fort Worth, 1938.

swing also presented a certain technical challenge, since it was played in keys notoriously difficult for horn players.

Across the south and Midwest, integrated jam sessions probably occurred often enough to occasion a degree of cross-fertilization, and some black musicians grew up listening to western styles and came to R&B or jazz that way. One of them was trumpeter Kenny Dorham (1924–1972) of Post Oak, Texas, who worked on cattle drives as a teen and wanted to "yodel and sing songs like the horsemen of the West." Yodeling became the cowboy singer's stock and trade thanks to country singer Jimmie Rogers (1897–1933), who wed the hypnotic, pitch-shifting Alpine version to downhome blues. Dorham studied music at Wiley College (Marshall, Texas) and subsequently "traded his bridle for bebop," replacing Miles Davis in Charlie Parker's ground-breaking 1948 quintet. Aside from a "fleet fingered . . . running style," he developed a knack for quotations, melodic phrases from other songs interjected into solos like asides in an actor's monologue. Dorham's genre-bending quotes of everything from English folk tunes to orchestral suites demonstrated both his musical erudition and the "all-encompassing nature of jazz, its openness to all sources."[186]

Sometime around 1951, Ornette joined singer and guitarist Pee Wee Crayton's band, which had played Fort Worth often and was headed to Los Angeles. An "old style Kansas City blues shouter," Connie Curtis "Pee Wee" Crayton (Rockdale, Texas, 1914–1985) often appeared in "music battles," sometimes with his mentor T-Bone Walker, where paired singers, guitarists, or sax players fought to upstage one another and win the loudest applause. John Carter saw Crayton in a "cutting contest" with Big Joe Turner: "[they] would stand up and sing one verse after another, oft times just making verses up as they went along."[187] Crayton's 1948 hit, "Blues After Hours," launched his career playing upbeat western-flavored blues (also known as rockabilly). But arriving in Los Angeles with his band in tow, after a grueling cross-country series of one-nighters, Crayton learned their engagement had been cancelled.

Cast adrift yet again, Ornette might have turned back but instead found cheap lodging at the Hotel Morris (5th Street and Ruth), a formerly well-appointed establishment where his New Orleans friend Eddie Blackwell was coincidentally also staying. Favored by hard-up musicians, the Morris was located in comfortable proximity to "the Nickel," a red-light district along 5th Street with clubs where race and sexual preferences were not an issue. Segregation was less regimented in Los Angeles than in Texas or other places Ornette had known. It offered greater opportunities for work and interaction with musicians, but there was also more competition: occasions to jam were hard to come by, much less paying gigs. When Ornette could no longer afford the Morris, a woman who ran a nursery hired him to help her in exchange for a room in the back of her garage. He was broke, and his mother was sending him food from Fort Worth by mail. Her eldest son had died in LA and it wasn't long before she sent Ornette a bus ticket to come home.

Ornette spent a year or so in Texas in career limbo; work was easy to find and the financial pressure was temporarily relieved. He jammed at the Jim Hotel, where local and internationally acclaimed musicians, inducing Red Conner, Fathead Newman, Ray Charles, and Stanley Turrentine, still showed up.[188] He had a reputation in Dallas from his honking years and on May 2, 1953, played Deep Ellum's famed Empire Room (formerly the Rose Ballroom). "The 20th Century Progressive Club presents big MUSIC BATTLE," read the poster for the event. Ornette had top billing but the organizers misspelled his name: "Arnett Coleman Sextette vs. Stan Johnson's Band."[189] That was the last Texas heard of him for a while.

Ornette knew he had to go to New York eventually and, following his unique inner compass, returned to LA, where he would advance his "investigative tampering" with music and further his education in adulthood by marrying and having a son.[190] At 23 Ornette was a musical omnivore. He'd come up in the midst of a veritable feast and had an unerring ear that could, in Texas parlance, "find a whisper in a whirlwind." He had seen a fair bit of life and knew that only death was permanent. He was thin and wiry, seemingly meek but fiercely in love with an outlaw music that he could hear but didn't quite yet know how and with whom to play.

Apollo 11 launch: on July 16, 1969, the 400-ft-tall (110 m)
Saturn v rocket launches the Apollo 11 mission from Pad A,
Launch Complex 39, Kennedy Space Center, Florida.

Part Two: Ignition

FIRST OF ALL, we think the world must be changed.
GUY DEBORD, Situationist manifesto, 1957

If New York had a tutelary deity it would have to be Hermes. From the moment the transatlantic post tethered it to London and beyond, New York was America's thrumming brainstem, shepherding the nation's flow of information. Newspapers and wire services started there, the publishing and recording industries, radio networks, television stations, and conversations in countless languages. In short, ever since the first beaver skins and glass beads changed hands, New York was devoted to the marriage of communication and commerce and to their offspring, money, which as everyone knows can talk. Many New Yorkers are convinced their city is the center of the universe and for a while, especially for artistic types, it was. It was here that the borders of the acceptable and categorically known were daily trespassed on the bandstand, stage, and canvas, and in pen and print. The disciplines of music, painting, dance, theater, photography, film, and literature drew strength from one another, each in its way looking back, whether to integrate or annihilate the past, and forward, towards the possibilities of an interplanetary future, the ultimate avant-garde.

Ornette arrived in 1959, the year the microchip was patented, NASA selected its first astronauts, Frank Lloyd Wright's cylindrical Guggenheim opened in New York, and the Russian spacecraft *Lunik 3* photographed the far side of the moon. Thanks to Barney Rosset of the Grove Press, the obscenity ban on *Lady Chatterley's Lover* was lifted, and France's Olympia Press published William S. Burroughs's *Naked Lunch*, hailed as both a work of genius and a piece of filth. The old artists were innocuous "household names" but the new, true ones were transgressors. Of the many present in Manhattan at the dawn of the 1960s, Ornette gave voice to the moment. Sometimes called "free jazz" or "the new thing," his was the sound of a changing world.

Ornette's music was emblematic of what Brian Eno called a *scenius*, "a whole ecology of people, groups and ideas that give rise to good new thoughts and good new work."[1] Nowhere had the old been so thoroughly trampled as in post-atomic New York, with creative individuals of every persuasion converging from around the planet to improvise on the theme of explosion. More than a city, New York was a portal for Ornette to other artistic dimensions, the place from which he would travel, return, and call home. Above all it was a point of encounter with people with whom he shared the understanding that life was what you made it, ideally an art in itself whose effects were observable in the outcomes of individual and group projects. Offering cheap rent and a convivial lifestyle that favored experimentation, show and tell, and debate, New York wasn't paradise, but it was where Ornette elaborated the meta-quality defining every great artist: a world view.

Before crossing that threshold, Ornette had another flaming hoop to jump through, namely Los Angeles. Despite a more varied and vibrant music scene, mid-1950s Los Angeles was not entirely unlike Texas. You spent a lot of time driving or walking to get from place to place, it was hot, living arrangements were tight, and while whites were more tolerant towards non-whites, the police considered an upright bass in a car's backseat reason enough to pull black drivers to the curb and brandish their weapons, figuring the instrument was stolen. Ornette was once obliged to assemble his sax and play it to prove them wrong. Work was scarce; you needed friends to survive and Ornette had good ones, beginning with drummer Edward Blackwell from New Orleans and nineteen-year-old Dallas trumpeter Bobby Bradford, who met Ornette the year before (1953) in Texas and ran into him on an LA streetcar wearing "a beard down to his breast bone and his hair in a *crocignole.*"²

Blackwell (1929–1992) was a few months older than Ornette and for a while they shared an apartment; Bobby, the only one with a car, ferried everyone around. Both respected Ornette and believed that together they were making real music if not real money. In Blackwell's drumming Ornette discovered "one of the most musical ears of playing rhythm of anyone I have heard," a musicality that fueled his growing conviction that rhythm, melody, and harmony were of equal

Ed Blackwell at Don Cherry's *Where Is Brooklyn?*
(Blue Note, 1969) session, Van Gelder Studio, Englewood Cliffs, NJ,
November 11, 1966; photograph by Francis Wolff.

value and every instrument could serve them equally well.[3] As for Bradford, Ornette considered him "one of the best trumpet players alive," and he took Ornette just as seriously. "[Ornette's] music," Bradford said, "was conceived to hit you right between the eyes."[4]

Ornette's most intimate friend was Sallie Jayne Richardson (1934–2012), whom he married in 1954 and who would later be known as the "secular priestess of the [1960s] Black Arts Movement" owing to her work as theater director, poet, and civil rights activist.[5] Ornette had always had a strong woman in his life, whether as antagonist or champion, and in Jayne Cortez (as she renamed herself, evoking her Filipino maternal grandmother) he found both. Her father was an army man and she was born in the Huachuca Mountains of Arizona, just north of the Mexican border. Her family moved to San Diego on the Pacific coast, where the reek of the canneries replaced the rarified air of her early childhood, "a smell that was embedded in the skins of [the] workers," Jayne recalled.[6] Then came Los Angeles, where the family settled in Watts, a largely black neighborhood on the city's south side whose population burgeoned in the wake of the Second Great Migration, when African Americans came in search of defense industry jobs.

Jayne's parents loved jazz and collected records, so she grew up listening to Duke Ellington, Count Basie, Jimmie Lunceford, Billie Holiday, and Ella Fitzgerald. Following the path of many young intellectuals, she "fell in love" with bebop at age thirteen. Jayne was a reader and at fourteen wrote her first short stories. She studied piano, tap dance, modern dance, and ballet, played bass and cello, and took music theory courses in high school, in addition to painting and drawing classes. She was also a fighter. Her high school, John C. Fremont, was integrated but "miserable . . . they taught such lies about Africa," she said, "when a white kid called me 'nigger' I had to jump up and beat the hell out of him or her. And I did that constantly."[7] Jayne was articulate, outspoken, and outraged by racism and injustice whatever its guise; the poems she later wrote were scathing in their indictments. When Ornette met her, probably at one of the clubs where he or her friends were playing, she was doubtless the most exceptional young woman he'd come across, and besides that, she liked his music. Jayne also had style; she made her own clothes and before long she was making Ornette's.

Bobby Bradford helped move the newlyweds to a flat above a garage in Watts and interceded with his employer to hire Ornette as a fellow stock boy at Bullock's Department Store in downtown Los Angeles, a bastion of the white bourgeoisie. The only steady music gig Ornette found was also galling, playing the old R&B at a Mexican dance club, albeit alongside a friend, tenor saxophonist James Clay, Bradford's former bandmate from Dallas's Lincoln High. Although he sometimes worked the clubs on Central Avenue with Bradford, Blackwell, and others, they were more often jamming for next to nothing. Future jazz giants played the LA clubs in the mid- to late 1950s and while Ornette was not the only experimentalist in town, he was easily the most maligned.

"Nobody wanted to play with him," said Ed Blackwell. Bebop tenor Dexter Gordon regally ordered him off the stage; drummer Max Roach and trumpeter Clifford Brown toyed with him, making him wait until the set's end to join them and packing up their instruments when he did. The white plastic sax he'd acquired in 1954 (more afford-able than a new metal alto) was considered hokey. "People would laugh when his name came up," said another musician.[8] Ornette was an easy target, soft-spoken and slight of stature. Nicknamed "Nature Boy" for his hirsute appearance and "raw" sound, he was unfashionable, at least by West Coast standards.[9]

"Cool jazz" was LA's latest thing, a studiedly blasé bebop deriv-ative associated with a group of musicians (none of them from California), notably Miles Davis (1926–1991), the trumpet prodigy who replaced Dizzy Gillespie in Charlie Parker's band in 1947; bari-tone saxophonist Gerry Mulligan, who recorded on the 1949–50 sessions issued as Miles's celebrated *Birth of the Cool* (1957); and

Don Cherry, recording *Where Is Brooklyn?* (Blue Note, 1969),
Van Gelder Studio, Englewood Cliffs, NJ, November 11, 1966.

trumpeter Chet Baker (1929–1988), who played in Mulligan's quartet.
"Ornette's music arouses aggressiveness in people who can't understand it," observed Blackwell, who was at times "infuriated" by his
"meekness" and concluded "he just doesn't anger that easily."[10] But it
was pride that prevented Ornette from confronting his critics. He was
patient and stubborn; "no matter how much you get rejected," he told
trumpeter Don Cherry, "you put that much more study and work
into it so that you can produce more."[11]

Donald Eugene Cherry (1936–1995) heard about Ornette through
Jayne, whom he called "my guru, the one who would turn me on to
the latest records and books." He played a pocket trumpet (cornet)
that he referred to as his "tonsil," and was part Choctaw, thin as

a blade, and musically precocious.[12] When he was four, his family moved to Watts from Oklahoma City, where his father, also a trumpet player, had run a nightclub called the Cherry Blossom. He grew up with music, jitterbugging to the record player and singing in church on Sundays. Watts district teens went to Fremont High, but Cherry lied about his address in order to attend Thomas Jefferson High, known for its progressive jazz band. Led by pianist and educator Samuel Rodney Browne, Jefferson's bands attracted musicians from around Los Angeles and, like Fort Worth's I. M. Terrell, produced outstanding alumni.[13] After graduation, Cherry worked as a delivery boy for Schwab's drugstore in Hollywood and at night played with musicians who considered Ornette *infra dig*: Clifford Brown mentored him; Dexter invited him to sit in. Don Cherry's meeting with Ornette in the summer of 1956 was the start of a symbiotic musical relationship.

Jayne had just given birth to their son, Denardo, and Ornette spent most of his time woodshedding, the jazz term for a musical retreat, a group of men holed up in a garage like astronauts in a space station. The core group comprised Blackwell, Bradford, James Clay, and pianist George Newman, another friend of Jayne's and the garage owner. When Bradford and Clay were drafted to the Korean War, Cherry and his Jefferson High bandmate, drummer Billy Higgins, stepped in, with Blackwell tutoring young Higgins until leaving for a job with singer and pianist Ray Charles. "Swing" in Ornette's parlance was not a kind of jazz but what he referred to as "the light in the rhythm," a quality that illumined Higgins's playing.[14] Cherry and Higgins (1936–2001) were part of a bebop group called the Jazz Messiahs, but Ornette's approach marked a turning point in their development. Ornette needed to work with musicians who were not set in their ways and whose fresh responses kept him alert. Attention and flexibility were his weapons in a war on musical entropy, that is, playing from habit or adhering to a particular style, for example executing speedy arpeggios in a display of technical brilliance, as was

Billy Higgins at Dexter Gordon's *A Swingin' Affair* (Blue Note, 1964) session, Van Gelder Studio, Englewood Cliffs, NJ, August 29, 1962; photograph by Francis Wolff.

common among bebop players. Ornette was not interested in dazzling anyone with his footwork. "My playing is spontaneous, not a style," he said; "a style happens when your phrasing hardens."[15]

When Newman's garage was unavailable, Ornette and his mates rehearsed at Cherry's place or at his apartment, where Jayne presumably looked after the baby, and he wrote everything they played. "He didn't write fluff so you had this stuff to work with, deconstruct, reconstruct, expand," said Bobby Bradford.[16] Ornette treated his compositions less as songs than experimental matrixes, attacking them differently from day to day, drilling with his band for a show-down that showed little sign of materializing whether in the form of a gig or a recording date. Between money pressures, fatherhood, and the need to literally blow his own horn, Ornette was a burning fuse, and his relationship with Jayne was suffering.

As artists, he and Jayne shared formative ideas about working in creative groups. Ornette's emphasis on the focused listening and interplay between musicians was mirrored in Jane's approach to theater. Author Stanley Crouch later worked under Jayne's direction in a production of Jean Genet's *The Blacks* for the Watts Repertory Theater (which she cofounded in the early 1960s):

> The basic thing that all of us there learned from Jayne was that each individual has to be responsible to the cast and to support everybody else and she was very emphatic about that. If someone was not paying attention while somebody else was giving a soliloquy or something she'd say "hold it"—because paying attention was part of your role as a supporting actor— there is no front or back when you're onstage.[17]

The years Ornette and Jayne spent together were few but life-changing, certainly for Jayne, to whom the task of raising their child would largely fall. While Ornette occasionally alluded to his private life in later years, Jayne never answered questions about their marriage and stared down interviewers who dared to ask. According to Crouch, she took exception to a dismissive remark that Nat Hentoff attributed to Ornette in an *Esquire* article about the LA years, implying

Bobby Bradford, September 17, 1976; photograph by Mark Weber.

that she didn't understand or support her husband. She told Crouch that Ornette would never say such a thing.[18] But the lack of sufficient work and money, and his constant absence or else presence with the entire band in their small apartment, may have strained the relationship, and perhaps their son's birth altered it in ways for which they were unprepared. For whatever reason, although they would remain lifelong friends, by 1958 their marriage in terms of cohabitation was over while Ornette's career was coincidentally about to take off.

Thanks to the intercession of friends and a successful audition, Ornette signed his first recording contract with LA-based Contemporary Records and sold its owner, Lester Koenig, seven songs at $25 apiece.[19] *Something Else!!!! The Music of Ornette Coleman* (1958), was the first of a series of exclamatorily titled albums that, unlike others of its time, was comprised wholly of original compositions, including "Jayne," a cheerful tune with a wry Tejano lilt and Ornette's plastic alto trailing notes like words in a lost argument.[20]

Writing about the record for the New York-based *Jazz Review* (est. 1958), which featured articles authored by musicians and composers, LA trumpeter Art Farmer was nonplussed by Ornette's willingness to abandon a song's melody or chords in his solos: "It doesn't seem valid for me somehow . . . for a man to disregard his own tunes." Ornette's penchant for playing a quarter-tone off pitch, indeed "his whole attitude," Farmer wrote, "is different from what I'm used to."[21] But lettered critics Martin Williams and Nat Hentoff (*Jazz Review* founders) were in Ornette's corner from the start. So, by and large, was *DownBeat*, America's most prominent music magazine, whose reviewers tracked new talent and covered performances and record releases at home and abroad. In August 1958, a *DownBeat* critics' poll nominated Ornette as an "Alto Saxophone New Star" and lauded Lester Koenig for having the "courage and foresight" to record him.[22] A pattern was established: music critics and composers were apt to sing Ornette's praises while musicians found him suspect—with, however, some notable exceptions.

While working for Contemporary, Ornette befriended tenor saxophonist Theodore Walter "Sonny" Rollins (1930–), who grew up in Harlem. Although the same age as Ornette, Rollins was famous, having recorded nineteen albums on labels including Prestige, Blue Note, and Contemporary. Grounded in bebop, Rollins was tall, imposing, and considered "rough, street and unconventional." He was so admired in Los Angeles that once, when "one of his fans was in the middle of losing a fist fight, he called out [Sonny's name] . . .

Sonny Rollins, San Francisco, 1982; photograph by Brian McMillen.

as if [he] would appear . . . and vanquish his opponent."[23] He had just recorded the deftly executed *Freedom Suite* (Riverside Records, 1958), which Ornette must have noticed consisted of reinterpreted standards and just one original composition. Others had begun defying "chordal hegemony" before Ornette, including Thelonious Monk, Miles Davis, and Rollins himself. But in Ornette, Rollins saw someone anxious to go further. Ornette challenged his preconceptions as he would those of other musicians; together they drove to the Pacific coast and played duets out to sea, with the pounding waves as their rhythm section.

Ornette's circle of supporters was growing. Billy Higgins was playing at the Hillcrest Club with Canadian pianist Paul Bley's band and arranged for Ornette and Cherry to sit in. After the first set, Bley invited them to join the band for the balance of the October 1958 engagement. Bley (1932–2016) was profiled in *DownBeat* when he was 21, and a name draw in Los Angeles. Like Ornette, he was a seeker, attempting "to define an approach . . . [uniting] tempo and non-tempo, tonality and non-tonality, written and improvised [music]," and in Ornette's playing and compositions he found a viable formula. The Hillcrest's predominantly black, working-class audience was, however, unenthusiastic, as Bley recalled:

> If you were driving down Washington Blvd. past the Hillcrest Club you could always tell if the band was on the bandstand or not. If the street was full of the audience holding drinks in front of the club, the band was playing. If the audience was inside, it was intermission.[24]

Bobby Bradford put it plainly: "Ornette's music wasn't intended for poppin' your fingers and getting drunk. You had to sit down and listen."[25] Ornette's first decent gig in Los Angeles lasted less than a month before the Hillcrest's owner "realized he could no longer afford having an atom bomb go off in his club every night."[26]

Ornette had meanwhile established a lasting rapport with Bley's bassist, an eerily gifted Iowan seven years his junior. Charlie Haden (1937–2014) grew up singing and playing country music in the Haden Family Band and was around thirteen when he heard Lester Young and Charlie Parker in a Jazz at the Philharmonic concert in Nebraska. "I didn't know what jazz was but I knew I liked it," he said. With money earned selling shoes, Haden moved to LA to study music, but dropped out to work the clubs. On his first visit to Ornette's flat, Haden recalled, "we started playing music that I'd never heard in my life . . . to play with Ornette you really had to listen to everything he did because he was playing off the *feeling*."[27] Haden grew devoted to Ornette, and while they were separated for years at a time owing to Haden's struggle with heroin addiction, they shared an intensity of purpose. Haden spoke of the ability of some musicians to improvise "'beyond category', playing so free and deeply, at a level, I call it, with your life involved."[28]

Ornette had another eleventh-hour encounter in LA, with conservatory-educated composer and arranger John Lewis (1920–2001), whose jazz pedigree was established in the 1940s playing piano with Dizzy Gillespie, Charlie Parker, and Lester Young before cofounding the Modern Jazz Quartet in 1951. The MJQ proposed jazz as a high art, "chamber jazz" to be played in concert venues by tuxedoed musicians. Lewis was an early proponent of Third Stream music, which combined aspects of jazz with classical references and composition techniques, a form whose detractors included Miles Davis, who misogynistically compared it to "looking at a naked woman you don't like."[29] Lewis was nonetheless a "consecrating figure" in the jazz community whose endorsement of Ornette held weight.[30] Cofounder (in 1957) of the Lenox School of Jazz in Massachusetts and artistic advisor to the Monterey Jazz Festival (started in 1958), Lewis arranged invitations for Ornette to both and convinced the MJQ's record producer, Nesuhi Ertegun, to sign him on Atlantic, the label that launched the careers of John Coltrane, bassist and composer Charles Mingus, and others.

The Lenox program lasted four summers (1957–60), uniting musicians and composers of an experimentalist bent in an upscale Berkshire Mountains woodshed where the line between faculty and student was lightly drawn. Ornette and Don Cherry spent August 1959 there on Atlantic's tab. At Lenox, Ornette met composer and pianist George Russell, author of a treatise on jazz theory (*The Lydian Chromatic Concept of Tonal Organization*, 1953), and the two became fast friends. It was his first encounter with Third Stream composer and jazz historian Gunther Schuller (1925–2015), who played early jazz and blues records for Ornette that, Schuller said, "were a revelation

The Modern Jazz Quartet at Schiphol Airport, Amsterdam, 1961;
L–R: drummer Connie Kay, vibraphonist Milt Jackson, pianist John Lewis,
and bassist Percy Heath; photograph by Harry Pot.

to him about his own heritage." Ornette met a living piece of that heritage, Texan trumpeter and former cowboy Kenny Dorham, who played with Max Roach and had just recorded the soundtrack for Roger Vadim's *Les Liaisons Dangereuses* (1959) with its composer, Thelonious Monk.

Ornette also spent time at Lenox with Jimmy Giuffre (Dallas, 1921–2008), a composer, clarinetist, and saxophonist who had been part of LA's cool jazz scene from the early 1950s. Like Ornette, Giuffre grew up in a blues-drenched environment and had copied Louis Jordan records as a teen. But Giuffre had also studied music theory and composition and worked with the Boyd Raeburn Band, whose arrangements of jazz standards were re-tooled with the likes of Stravinsky, Bartok, and Debussy in mind.[31] Ornette "needled" Giuffre "for being too structured" and according to Schuller, the older Giuffre was game. The two played "like wounded animals," Schuller said, "until a state of utter exhaustion had been reached."[32] Giuffre, who later worked with Paul Bley, shared Ornette's goals of "complete freedom and expressiveness," noting in a 1961 interview that "fusion or the meeting of minds is essential to the success of this music."[33]

A rare recording of the Lenox class of 1959 performing in various configurations communicates the exuberance of the endeavor, with Ornette playing several of his own compositions with Don Cherry and others.[34] Ornette had two of his own albums awaiting release on Contemporary by then, having edited the tapes for the second at Lenox. *Tomorrow Is the Question!* (recorded January 16, February 23, and March 9–10, 1959) was still an approximation of his ideal ensemble: *sans* piano (an instrument that remained absent from most of his subsequent ensembles), with Shelly Manne on drums and two bassists, Percy Heath (of the Modern Jazz Quartet) and Red Mitchell, all highly respected musicians. But it wasn't until his first Atlantic album that Ornette's LA incubation period was brought to term.

The Shape of Jazz to Come (recorded May 22, released October, 1959), with Charlie Haden, Billy Higgins, and Don Cherry, sprang onto vinyl like Athena in battle gear from Zeus' forehead. In his liner notes, music critic Martin Williams predicted that Ornette would "affect the whole character of jazz music." *DownBeat* reviewer John S. Wilson noted his "formidable" ability to render the human voice though his horn, and the "creativity, in strong concentrated waves" emanating from an album that would fulfill the promise of its title. "There was urgency and dead seriousness in Ornette's music," remarked Bobby Bradford, "that said things weren't going to be about Jim Crow, or a resigned black man or West Coast Cool anymore."[35] Ornette's brief appearance at the Monterey Jazz Festival in October 3, 1959, alongside tenor elders Coleman Hawkins and Ben Webster was a kind of ordination. That same week he recorded his second album for Atlantic, to be released the following year. But the best of 1959 was yet to come. On the recommendation of Martin Williams, Ornette's Quartet was invited to debut at New York's Five Spot Café and with girded loins, he entered the arena.

THE JAZZ CLUB deserves a place alongside temple, amphitheater, and cathedral for not just conveying higher values but generating them, night after night, dissolving the arbitrary boundaries separating individuals from a shared experience of the present moment. "Jazz is like bananas—it has to be eaten on the spot," wrote Sartre, evoking the spontaneous creation occurring live onstage by an act of communion.[36] Transmitting emotions and moods with dizzying directness, jazz was conceived as a participatory and, above all, ephemeral art; for every record that exists there were thousands of unrecorded sessions where players laid bare their souls to an audience that returned the favor in a blaze of intersubjectivity. It didn't happen everywhere. The vibe was important, the baseline excitement of a place derived from an acquired reputation, amplified by the anticipation of those who sought it out. When it did occur, the exhilaration was at once intellectual, emotional, and physical, like an *au point* round of repartee in a pre-revolutionary Paris salon crossed with some cathartic tribal dance around a bonfire.

Of Harlem's storied clubs—Monroe's Uptown House, the Showman Bar, Small's Paradise, Connie's Inn, the Baby Grand, the Apollo Theater, the Audubon and Renaissance Ballrooms, to name a few—Minton's Playhouse, in a remodeled dining room of the Cecil Hotel, "was to bebop what Zurich's Café Voltaire was to Dada."[37] Saxophonist Henry Minton was its owner; the first black delegate of the American Federation of Musicians (New York Local 802), he knew that musicians were usually broke and fed them when they came to work, seated at linen-covered tables bearing vases with fresh flowers. House bandleader Thelonious Sphere Monk (1917–1982) set a high bar with his jabbing, probing improvisations. A large man with a thick beard, he would sometimes rise and do a jig around the piano because he'd played or heard something too good to be taken sitting down. The drama was enhanced on "celebrity nights," weekly jams that were part talent show, part jazz coliseum. According to Miles Davis, "if you got up on the bandstand at Minton's and couldn't play, you were not only going to be embarrassed by people ignoring you or booing you, you might get your ass kicked."[38] Charlie Parker, Charlie Christian, and Dizzy Gillespie were frequent players and keen listeners. A seventeen-year-old Jean-Louis "Jack" Kerouac, one of the few non-black regulars, reportedly smoked his first joint at Minton's while soaking up the sound that would seep through his improvisational "bop prosody."

Midtown Manhattan was another jazz zone—52nd Street— bathed in the neon flash of clubs like the Three Deuces, the Famous Door, the Carousel, and the Onyx. Dexter Gordon said that for musicians, the stretch between Fifth and Sixth Avenues was "the most exciting half-block in the world," albeit not always for the right reasons.[39] Shortly after his 1959 release of *Kind of Blue*, one of the best-selling records in jazz history, Miles Davis stood outside of Bird Land (a block west of 52nd Street) for a between-sets break. When

Thelonious Sphere Monk, at Minton's Playhouse, New York, 1947; photograph by William P. Gottlieb.

a cop told him to keep moving, he pointed to the marquis bearing his name. In response, the cop administered his nightstick to Miles's skull, splattering his white suit with blood and calling to mind poet Langston Hughes's remark that the word "bebop" came from the sound of "police beating Negro heads."[40]

In the 1950s, a new jazz epicenter developed downtown in an altogether different neighborhood where dark, smoky atmospheric clubs like the Village Vanguard (est. 1935), Café Bohemia (1955), the Half Note (1957), and the Village Gate (1958) were booking top talents, while other kinds of hangouts were attracting unusual crowds. Lower Manhattan was rundown and multiethnic, its obsolete sweatshops steadily transmogrifying into artists' lairs. In the Bohemian stronghold of Greenwich Village, what places like the Cedar Tavern or the San Remo lacked in live music, they made up for in "the feeling that everything [had] become an open question that everybody [was] trying to answer at once."[41] Co-owned by a butcher and a window washer, the Cedar was to Abstract Expressionism what Minton's was to bebop. Depending on his mood, Wyoming-born Jackson Pollock (1912–1956) might regale the clientele by snatching a tablecloth from beneath the bottles and glasses, or else trash the place in a volcanic rage over a disagreement with fellow artists Willem "the Dutchman" de Kooning or Pennsylvanian Franz Kline. Another habitué, German Hans Hofmann (1880–1966), who ran an art school on West 8th Street, critiqued Pollock for subtracting nature from his paintings, to which Pollock replied, "I am nature."[42] He might as well have said "I am American," which at that time meant to be vital to painting. Having subsumed the talents and energies of European exiles in its postwar vortex, New York easily outpaced art's old world

The Village Vanguard, New York, 2007; photograph by Jimmy Katz.

capitals in painting as in other vehicles of creative expression, and was the undisputed king of the road.

Dramatist Judith Malina (1926–2015), whose family fled Germany when she was three, described the tone of the Greenwich Village taverns as "strictly macho," the boot camps of what Kerouac dubbed "the Beat Generation."[43] Malina met Kerouac and Allen Ginsberg at the San Remo (on the corner of Bleecker and MacDougal), along with William S. Burroughs, Tennessee Williams, Gore Vidal, and poet Gregory Corso, who lived across the street. Composer of silence John Cage showed her how to consult the I Ching, the ancient Chinese oracle that, like artistic experiments then in vogue, enlisted chance (six throws of three coins) to access destiny. Malina said that the Living Theater, cofounded with her husband Julian Beck (1925–1985), was born in the San Remo, inspired by the work of Bertolt Brecht and Edwin Piscator whose "epic theater" was conceived in 1920s Berlin to unpick the knots in an increasingly complex reality.[44]

In 1955 Malina was arrested and jailed for protesting the choreographed hypocrisy of the u.s. Atomic Energy Commission's Operation Alert, nationwide drills where schoolchildren ducked beneath desks and men were advised to shield their eyes from radiation by lowering the brims of their hats. Ginsberg was writing *Howl* that year, a rallying cry to all comrades in arts straddling the contradiction between possible annihilation and all possibilities. In 1955 Living Theater performed Pirandello's *Tonight We Improvise*, a play about staging a play, signaling the ensemble's wish to breach the borders between art, life, and politics. They "shook up the notion of what theater should be," said *New York Times* culture editor John Rockwell, "less scripted, more improvisational, more the expression of a lifestyle."[45] The lifestyle in question was communal, engaged, everyone dreaming aloud, "the actual exercise of 'free speech'—of free citizens reading and thinking and hearing and saying whatever they wanted—hurtling much closer to the concept's ideal," indeed as close, in the late 1950s through the 1960s, as it had ever been.[46]

Atomic bomb test, Nevada, 1951.

Practitioners of every art form were breaking with convention, including Swiss-born Robert Frank, who moved to Greenwich Village in 1947 and employed photography in a previously unessayed, declamatory style. With the help of a Guggenheim grant, he bought a black Ford Business Coupe and toured the country in 1955, recording 27,000 images, 83 of which were published as *The Americans* (1959), a book that challenged the nation's gilded self-image and the sentimentality and aesthetic formalism of contemporary photography. A friend of Ginsberg and Kerouac, Frank admired the improvisational aspect of their writing, whose rhythm and musical flow he tried to replicate in the acts of both taking and presenting his photographs.[47] Shot from the hip, on the move, in factories, dime stores, and parks, at lunch counters and drive-ins, and on front porches, Frank caught America in the act of being. Ravaged by critics, accused of hating America and, worse, of being a communist, Frank did for photography what Ornette Coleman would soon do for jazz, turning it back on itself to confront its possibilities.

The counterculture was meanwhile expanding east of Broadway where rents were lower and the Five Spot Café, located on the frontier

Cecil Taylor's *Unit Structures* session, Van Gelder Studio, Englewood Cliffs, NJ, May 19, 1966; photograph by Francis Wolff.

of the new territory (5 Cooper Square), shone like a beacon amidst the flophouses of the Bowery.[48] When owners Joe and Iggy Termini opened their storefront bar "No. 5," the street was a fetid tunnel moldering in the shadow of the Third Avenue Elevated Train. The train's 1956 removal brought a breath of air to the neighborhood, encouraging the brothers to literally jazz their place up and reopen it as the Five Spot Café. The first officially booked band—the Cecil Taylor Trio (November 1956–January 1957, with bassist Buell Neidlinger, percussionist Denis Charles, and, later in the engagement, Steve Lacy on soprano sax)—set the club's new tone.

Although a native New Yorker, Cecil Taylor (1929–2018) was considered a jazz outsider, "so overlooked," commented record producer Michael Cuscuna, "he could have robbed a police car in midtown Manhattan without getting arrested."[49] Taylor studied piano from the age of five and graduated from the New England Conservatory, where he launched his assault on the conventions of song form. The most common reaction to his music, wrote critic Howard Mandel, was "bafflement edged with effrontery," but some were captivated by its improvisational "density and dynamism . . . tempests and longeurs," and a physicality that on at least one occasion sent the ivories of the Termini's old upright flying off the keyboard. "I try to imitate on piano the leaps in space a dancer makes," said Taylor, who claimed he would have danced had he not been a musician.[50] His performances were a siren's song to the art crowds at the Cedar and San Remo, who began drifting east for the music. Thelonious Monk's Quartet came in 1957, featuring tenor saxophonist John Coltrane and cementing the Five Spot's reputation as the place to hear real music; "the sawdust came off the floor, the prices went up," and the Terminis hired a hatcheck girl.[51]

It was a long narrow room with a bar on one side, tables down the middle and a slightly elevated stage at the far end opposite a wc that reportedly emitted eye-watering fumes. When full, the Five Spot held around 75 people:

a fairly wild looking crowd of jazz aficionados. College girls
in shorts . . . long haired painters in mottled dungarees.
Village girls in leotards, men in sweaters and leather jackets
. . . dark glasses . . . sailors, cadets and the Madison Avenue
cool crowd . . . [52]

The space was large enough to be interesting but small enough to
keep audience and musicians close. "You could see and hear anywhere in the room," wrote music critic Whitney Balliett; "as a result it
was intricately awash with music and reaction, reaction and music."[53]

Ornette may not have known much about the Five Spot before
he got there but owing to his recent record releases, New York musicians had heard plenty about him and were wondering if he deserved
all the fuss. *DownBeat*'s December issue was on the newsstands with
a review of *The Shape of Jazz to Come*, when Ornette, Don Cherry,
Charlie Haden, and Billy Higgins hit town. To translate the buzz
into business, the Terminis organized a press preview night and,
perhaps as insurance should Ornette fail to deliver, they booked the
Jazztet to share the bill. Cofounded earlier that year by Art Farmer
and tenor sax player Benny Golson ("a sextet that sounds like a big
band," as per an ad in the *Jazz Review*), the Jazztet's members were
respected locals.[54]

Ornette's kickoff (November 17, 1959) attracted "the largest collection of VIPs the jazz world [had] seen in many a year," including
music producer and civil rights activist John Hammond, musicologist and jazz historian Marshall Stearns, Hsio Wen Shih, cofounder
of the *Jazz Review*, Ornette's bosses at Atlantic Records, Nesuhi
and Ahmet Ertegun, influential jazz DJ Symphony Sid Torin, critics
from Germany and the UK, and members of the music elite.[55] It was
a formidable bunch, but Ornette had champions in the audience,
including his Lenox School mentor Gunther Schuller, LA bandmate
Paul Bley, and Jayne Cortez, who made her first trip east with son
Denardo to cheer him on.[56]

As opening nights go, Ornette's is probably the most widely reviewed, referenced, and recollected in jazz history, eliciting some of the most colorful and contradictory descriptions in the annals of premieres at large. "He arrived," wrote A. B. Spellman, "a walking myth, a small bearded man striding out of the woods of Texas into New York's usually closed jazz scene."[57] The choice of the Jazztet to trade sets with Ornette proved fateful, creating an aural contrast so pronounced, it registered like a slap in the face. Paul Bley described the effect:

> The week before Ornette came [the Jazztet] sounded like a very modern, Horace Silver-type arranged band; beautiful aesthetics, with all the rough points ironed out, slick, smooth. Ornette played one set and turned them into Guy Lombardo.[58]

British critic John Craddock agreed that "in juxtaposition with the earthy crudities of Ornette Coleman this very excellent band sounded bland and insipid."[59] Ronald Sukenick compared the audience's response to "Parisians being shocked out of the Belle Époque by Stravinsky's *The Rite of Spring*."[60] *DownBeat*'s George Hoefer gathered audience reactions:

> "He'll change the entire course of jazz." "He's a fake." "He's a genius." "I can't say, I'll have to hear him a lot more times." "He has no form." "He swings like HELL." "I'm going home to listen to my Benny Goodman trios and quartets." "He's out, real far out." "I like him, but I don't have any idea what he is doing."[61]

Visually, the band made an impression, not least because its members were quite young. Ornette, at 29, was four years Cherry's senior, while Higgins and Haden were just 22 and 21. They wore dark suits and ties with white shirts beneath vests that Ornette had designed for the occasion (and that Jayne had probably sewn). People were struck by the witchery of the Quartet's attunement, how they stopped and started without exchanging a glance and how solos emerged organically in no pre-arranged order. Gunther Schuller queried Ornette and Cherry on the matter, ascribing it to the extensive rehearsal time they spent together, but Cherry said "we can do it with strangers, too," and Ornette explained that it was related to an awareness of their own and each other's breath as a means of keeping the music "natural."[62]

Higgins grinned while playing "as if his drums were telling jokes to the rest of the band."[63] Don Cherry, with his "newly fashioned midget trumpet," somehow reminded British critic Stanley Dance of "a shoulder holster and the villain in a western"; another British reviewer compared him to a lithograph by Toulouse-Lautrec.[64] Charlie Haden swiveled around his bass like a contortionist, while Ornette, neck muscles bulging over his shirt collar, blew his white plastic sax, "practically biting [it] and fighting with the music as if in a rage."[65] Hearing Ornette was "a distressing experience" for *Jazz Journal* (UK) reviewer John Craddock: "the listener cannot fully appreciate Coleman without divorcing from his mind all ideas as to how modern jazz *should* sound." Stanley Dance expressed similar frustration: "it all began to seem to us like a musical kipper," he wrote, "a hell of a lot of bones, but get what you can out of it, for some of it is good."[66]

Ornette was cast as antagonist as critics hastened to declare fealty, whether to what they thought he stood for or the status quo he stood against. Not all musicians disliked him on first hearing but most regarded him skeptically. Trumpeter Roy Eldredge said, "I think he's jivin' baby." In a rare concession for the jazz maestro, Miles Davis sat in with Ornette, commending him "because he doesn't play clichés," but he soon revised his opinion. "Hell, just listen to what he writes and how he plays," Miles scoffed, "the man is all screwed up inside."[67] Alpha-drummer Max Roach reportedly followed Ornette home one night and challenged him to a fight, and Charles Mingus harassed him onstage. Mingus (1922–1979), who played the Five Spot before

Ornette, was known to deliver political tirades from the bandstand, to insist his audience remain silent, and on one occasion to smash his upright bass in a fit of pique. According to one Five Spot regular, the painter, poet, and trumpet player Ted Joans, "[Mingus] came on stage and started clomping on the piano. Ornette took his horn down . . . and stopped and sort of looked at him . . . Don Cherry was taking a solo and just ignored him."[68]

Musicians like Miles, Roach, and Mingus had broken considerable experimental ground before Ornette stepped up and were vexed by the messianic praise Ornette garnered, not only from critics but from high-profile audience members such as New York Philharmonic conductor Leonard Bernstein, the lord almighty of New York's moneyed music establishment, who rose to his feet, shouting, "this is the greatest thing ever to happen to jazz!"[69] The impact of Ornette's premiere was not unlike that of Alfred Jarry's play *Ubu Roi*, which began with the farcical despot screaming "MERDRE! [*sic*]," and prompted audience member William Butler Yeats to remark, "What more is possible? After us the Savage God."[70]

The animosity Ornette inspired was visceral, territorial. To musicians who had paid their dues in New York (that is, worked the clubs, recorded albums, defined the criteria by which they judged themselves and their fellows), Ornette was at worst a usurper, at best a greenhorn whose vox humana Texas edge was considered "country" and uncouth. Tellingly, one of his most self-righteous detractors was Dallas-born pianist Red Garland, who started out in territory bands before moving to New York in 1946, recording with John Coltrane and eventually joining Miles Davis's Quintet: "Nothing's happening . . . Coleman is faking. He's being very unfair to the public."[71] Ornette might have been dismissed as a charlatan had he not been taken so personally. Don Cherry noted that some musicians "really loved [the music], the growth and the spirit of it," while others "felt it was jeopardizing their position in life."[72] Buell Neidlinger said musicians were "scared to death that Ornette was going to be the thing and that they

Charles Mingus, Lower Manhattan, July 4, 1976.

couldn't make it."[73] An unnamed Jazztet member remarked, "Well, I guess I'm out of date now."[74]

Simply put, Ornette was breaking the rules jazz modernists had taken pains to codify and master. Author Francis Davis, former critic for the *Village Voice*, described the departure from convention:

> Coleman regarded a chord sequence as just one of many options for advancing a solo . . . [the] decision to dispense with a chordal road map also permitted him rhythmic trespass across bar lines. The stealthy rubato of Coleman's phrases and his sudden accelerations of tempo implied liberation from strict meter, much as his penchant for hitting notes a quarter-tone sharp or flat and his refusal to harmonize his saxophone with Don Cherry's trumpet during group passages implied escape from the well-tempered scale . . . Perhaps the trick of listening to his performances lies in an ability to hear rhythm as melody, the way he seems to do, and the way early jazz musicians did. Some of Coleman's comeliest phrases . . . sound as though they were scooped off a drumhead.[75]

Likewise, Ornette encouraged the bass and drums to explore melody and harmony, rather than just playing their role as rhythmic backbone, carrying the chords and keeping time. Martin Williams, Ornette's "leading lay interpreter," saw his approach as a natural progression:

> What he has done, like all valid innovations, [is] basically simple, authentic and inevitable . . . if you put a conventional chord under my note, you limit the number of choices I have for my next note; if you do not, my melody may move freely in a far greater choice of directions . . . As several [recent] developments have shown, no one really needs to state all those chords that nearly everyone uses and . . . if someone does . . . he may end up with a harassed running up and down scales

at those "advanced" intervals like a rat in a harmonic maze. Someone had to break through the walls that those harmonies have built and restore melody.[76]

The most concise explanation of Ornette's method and the reason musicians resented it was ad-libbed by tenor saxophonist and Living Theater actor Jackie McLean (1931–2006): "You spend your life making a three-piece suit that's incredible, and this guy comes along with a jumpsuit, and people find that it's easier to step into a jumpsuit than to put on three pieces."[77]

McLean's metaphor implies an expediency that was absent from Ornette's music, which demanded rigorous practice, listening, and constant recalibration in performance. But by conceiving the three pieces—harmony, melody, and rhythm—as equal, blurring the lines between them, Ornette put the jump in the suit. Rather than diminishing the music's requisite virtuosity, he proposed an alternative means for its expression, namely as an intimacy with one's instrument and fellow instrumentalists, as extensions of oneself.

When John Coltrane (1926–1967) heard Ornette at the Five Spot, he said, "Well, that must be the answer," and the two became fast friends. "He would grab Ornette by the arm," recalled Charlie Haden, "and they would go off into the night talking about music."[78] Coltrane was famous, having already recorded some twenty albums, including *Soultrane* (Prestige, 1958, where Ira Gitler's liner notes memorably described his music as "sheets of sound") and the landmark *Giant Steps* (Atlantic, 1959). Yet Coltrane approached Ornette as a teacher, spending several months studying his playing and writing; "he was really sincere about growing," Ornette said. In the summer of 1960 Coltrane recorded an album with Ornette's band members featuring several Coleman compositions, called *The Avant-Garde* (Atlantic, 1966).[79] Paul Bley was one of many musicians who saw Ornette as a trailblazer:

When someone unravels a solution which leads a peer group from chasing its tail, and points it in a direction which gives it validity for another ten years, that's not just somebody playing well. That's somebody instructing the peer group on the way forward.[80]

Ornette was often compared to Charlie Parker, the gold standard of jazz innovators, with some saying he'd surpassed him and others that he wasn't even close. But the more musicians heard Ornette, the more they listened to him. Charles Mingus offered a frank assessment to music critic Leonard Feather in one of his "blindfold tests," where Feather played records for a given musician who had to guess who it was and share his or her thoughts. In this case, Feather did not play Ornette but Mingus had something he wanted to get off his chest:

John Coltrane arriving at Amsterdam's Schiphol Airport, October 26, 1963; photograph by Hugo Van Gelderen.

Now, [Ornette] is really an old fashioned alto player. He's not as modern as Bird [Charlie Parker]. He plays in C and F and G and B-flat only . . . Now aside from the fact I doubt he can even play a C scale in whole notes . . . in tune, the fact remains that his notes and lines are so fresh. So when Symphony Sid played his record [on the radio] it made everything else he was playing, even my own record that he played, sound terrible . . . It doesn't matter about the key [Ornette's] playing in— he's got a percussional [*sic*] sound, like a cat with a whole lot of bongos. He's brought a thing in—it's not new. I won't say who started it. But whoever started it, people overlooked it. It's like not having anything to do with what's around you, and being right in your own world. You can't put your finger on what he's doing. It's like organized disorganization, or playing wrong right.[81]

Alongside the debate over what has been described as the "eldritch wrongness" of Ornette's sound, discussion often centered on whether his music was old or new.[82] Jazz critic and historian Dan Morgenstern thought that while it was "being presented as something very new," it was "more closely rooted to the jazz mainstream."[83] Musician and music critic Robert Palmer later wrote that Ornette's compositions and performance

looked ahead with its polyrhythms, geared to exploration rather than to predetermined patterns . . . [and] looked back through the jazz tradition with its collective improvisations and its personal, speech-like approach to intonation and phrasing, so much like the ensemble and solo styles of the early Southern and Southwestern blues and jazz musicians.[84]

Texas aside, Ornette was permeated with music; as he put it, "when you hear me, you probably hear everything I've heard since

I was a kid."[85] Reconciling the old/new dichotomy, he was at once "revolutionary and atavistic" and firmly positioned in a resonant now.[86]

Had Ornette arrived in New York any sooner, before he and others had planted signposts, he would have been as ostracized as he had been elsewhere. Had he come any later, he would have been taken for granted, so swiftly were conventions in music, as in all the arts, being shredded and scattered like confetti. As it was, the timing was perfect and Ornette was an overnight underground sensation. The Five Spot run was extended from two weeks to the end of January 1960 and reprised April–July with Ed Blackwell replacing Higgins on drums. It attracted the curious, the doubtful, and the reverent,

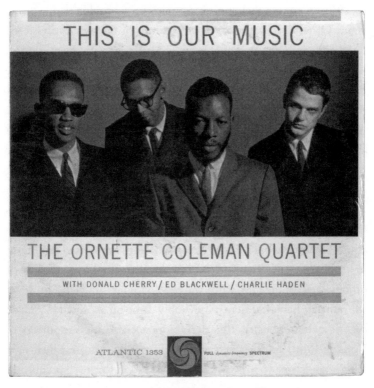

Cover of *This Is Our Music* (Atlantic, 1961),
recorded July 19, 26, and August 2, 1960.

among them painters Franz Kline and Texan Robert Rauschenberg, writers James Baldwin and LeRoi Jones, a steady stream of musicians, sundry beatniks, and eventually news reporters from *Time* magazine.[87] Lionel Hampton reportedly sat in one night and one wonders if Ornette recalled the days of "Flying Home." It was the longest club date he'd had since Texas, time for the band to relax and dig in. By the end they were making $682 per six-night week, the best money they'd ever had, and, wittingly or not, they were making history. "First came the Sumerians, then Jesus, then the Magna Carta, then the Bill of Rights, then Ornette's gig at the Five Spot," wrote friend and producer John Snyder, one of many commentators who felt epochal terms were called for.[88]

Whether or not they approved of him, critics couldn't stop writing about Ornette. It was more than a matter of taking a professional stand or describing something for their readers: as with the musicians, it was personal. In *The Subterraneans* (1958), Kerouac has Charlie Parker onstage, looking "directly into my eye, looking to search if I was really that great writer I thought myself to be." This was Kerouac wondering if he could measure up to jazz, a question that hovered above the pen of many a critic describing Ornette's music. The music writers belonged to their era: they were "high modernists, looking for originality, influence, a certain toughness of self-expression in their heroes."[89] In other words, they were looking for the qualities they either ascribed to themselves or wished to possess. Writing about Ornette, whatever the determination, amounted to a statement of character. To appreciate him was to align, superficially or otherwise, with the new, while those who found him facile, however substantial their arguments, inevitably came off as "square." Placed on the defensive, Ornette's detractors accused his supporters of "forcing [him] on the jazz world" and "touting [him] for their own self-aggrandizement."[90] Either way, as critic John Rockwell points out, "a scene happens when the critics pay attention" and Ornette was like a red flag to a bull.[91]

Ornette's chance to address a querulous public came on February 7, 1960, via an interview with Gunther Schuller broadcast on WBAI, the famed New York affiliate of the Pacifica Radio Network, established by a group of conscientious objectors in 1949. The listener-funded voice of the counterculture and town crier throughout the civil rights, anti-war, and women's liberation movements of the 1960s, WBAI's programming included jazz, poetry, theater, literature, and a show called *Existentialism for Young People*. From the WBAI studio in a deconsecrated church near the Queensboro Bridge, Ornette thanked Gunther, and began by saying in a soft, lisp-moistened voice:

> The music we are trying to play is no more abstract than most modern paintings . . . it's just music in which we have tried to get together and play and use our emotion and intelligence . . . [as] far as we could carry it . . . I have tried my best to become as—maybe you can use the word "free"—I really call [it as] complete [as possible] . . .[92]

Ornette refined some of the ideas from this interview in his liner notes for the Coleman Quartet's second Atlantic release, *Change of the Century* (recorded in October 8–9, 1959, issued June 1960), which read more like a manifesto:

> Some musicians say, if what I'm doing is right, they should never have gone to school. I say, there is no single *right* way to play jazz. Some of the comments made about my music make me realize though that modern jazz, once so daring and revolutionary, has become, in many respects, a rather settled and conventional thing. The members of my group and I are now attempting a break-through to a new, freer conception of jazz, one that departs from all that is "standard" and cliché in "modern" jazz . . . Today, still, the individual is either swallowed up in a group situation, or else he is out front soloing

. . . one knows pretty much what to expect. When our group plays . . . we do not have any idea what the end result will be. Each player is free to contribute what he feels . . . Ours is at all times a group effort and it is only because we have the rapport that we do that our music takes the shape that it does . . .[93]

Ornette seemed surprised that emotional intelligence, a quality he possessed, was less abundant in others. "Many people apparently don't trust their reactions to art or music unless there is a verbal *explanation* for it," he wrote; "in music, the only thing that matters is whether you *feel* it or not. You can't intellectualize music . . . [to do so] is to reduce it to nothing very important."[94] The interplay between intellect and emotion held a lifelong fascination for Ornette, who later summarized his work by saying: "How do you turn emotion into knowledge? That's what I try to do with my horn."[95]

By way of introducing *Change of the Century*'s compositions (all his own), Ornette compared their throughline, which he described as "a continuity of expression, certain continually evolving strands of thought," to "something like the paintings of Jackson Pollock." It was an apt, if oblique, reference to the paradoxical density and spaciousness characterizing both his sound and Pollock's canvases, whose rhythmic chaos must have seemed to Ornette like a musical score.[96] Had he lived to hear it, Pollock probably wouldn't have liked Ornette's music; he preferred pre-bebop jazz and when he wasn't painting, he played his records "until the house would shake."[97] But like Ornette he had withstood both ridicule and lavish praise, and he too was interested in how intellect and emotion served art. "You know more," he once told de Kooning, "but I *feel* more."[98]

While Ornette was at the Five Spot, a joke made the rounds: a waiter drops a trayload of drinks and a man says to his lady-friend, "Listen honey, Ornette's playing our song." Hearing it now, the Quartet on *This Is Our Music*, recorded just after the Five Spot gig, sounds charged and adventurous but structured and hardly cacophonous.

Ornette, however, was just getting started. In December 1960 he assembled two quartets, one for each ear, to perform *Free Jazz: A Collective Improvisation* (Atlantic, 1961), released in 1961 with Jackson Pollock's painting *White Light* (1954) on the cover.[99] To Ornette's admirers, the music was like Pollock's painting, described by an art critic as "bedazzlement . . . the atomic bomb transformed into myth."[100] As for the critics, *DownBeat* felt obliged to publish a "double review" to cover the mixed reactions. One reviewer thought that *Free Jazz* "might stand as the ultimate manifesto of the new wave of young jazz expressionists." The other asked, "Where does neuroses end and psychoses begin? The answer must lie somewhere within this maelstrom."[101]

With its "cross-hatched strains of melody," *Free Jazz* sounds opaque to some listeners, but Ornette reveled in aural complexity.[102] He had "a phenomenal ear," remarked Gunther Schuller, able to track patterns and parallels as they unfolded in performance.[103] Ornette never much liked the term "free jazz" for the lack of discipline it implied, but his *Free Jazz* album was nonetheless a declaration of independence. Composing and playing what he wanted with whom he wanted and, at least for the moment, where he wanted, he was a free man in New York.

IN 1960, ORNETTE began taking the city in, spending time at the museums, going for long walks,

> seeing people do things they know how to do. I don't care what it is—sports or a craft—so long as a man is showing delight in a skill he's developed. It's relaxing to watch a man express himself, and what is usually called art is far from the only medium of self-expression.[104]

He spent time with painter Bob Thompson, a jazz enthusiast he met at the Five Spot. In 1958 Thompson (1937–1966) moved from

Kentucky to New York, rented a studio on Rivington Street, and was a part of a salon-like circle that included Cecil Taylor, LeRoi Jones, and A. B. Spellman. Thompson's work gained currency during the Black Arts Movement of the late 1960s.[105] He died young, in Rome of an overdose, but in those halcyon days on the Lower East Side, Thompson dedicated a painting to Ornette, an earth-toned dance of women and trees encircling the face of a man.[106] "There was a lot of openness between various people," recalled painter Emilio Cruz, studio-mate of Bob Thompson. The artists' community was relatively small and people either knew one another or else were easily met:

> When you would walk down the street . . . you would look
> at somebody and you would recognize them instantly as
> artists, and you would immediately find you had some kind
> of rapport . . . and politically there was a sense of hope, that
> America could arrive at a higher moral state . . . so racism
> . . . in that world was frowned upon.[107]

Another of Ornette's painter friends was Larry Rivers (born Yitzroch Loiza Grossberg, 1923–2002), a fixture at the Five Spot, where he organized poetry readings on Mondays, the musicians' night off. A student of Hans Hofmann, Rivers's painting was often soft-toned, figurative, dashed off with graphic ease. He was also an accomplished reedman (tenor, baritone sax, and clarinet) who had attended Julliard, where Miles Davis was also studying, courtesy of the GI Bill. Ornette acquired works from Rivers and Rauschenberg, frequented the downtown galleries, many of them artists' co-ops, and started to experiment with painting himself.

More than exhibition spaces, galleries were hangouts and performance venues, like the Reuben Gallery (Fourth Avenue) that opened with Allan Kaprow's *Eighteen Happenings in Six Parts* (October 1959). Born in Atlantic City, New Jersey, Kaprow (1927–2006) studied painting with Hofmann and music with John Cage. He admired

Bob Thompson, *Ornette*, 1960–61, oil on canvas.

Jackson Pollock, who, he wrote, "left us at the point where we must become preoccupied with and even dazzled by the space and objects in our everyday life."[108] Kaprow filled a room with things—some ordinary, some incongruous—and called it an "environment," a collage to inhabit instead of view. Happenings, by extension, were collective artworks, interactive *mise en scènes* whose outcomes were unforeseeable and unique.

The fluid interplay of expressive forms meant that "young artists of today need no longer say 'I am a painter' or 'a poet' or 'a dancer,'" wrote Kaprow, "they are simply 'artists.' All of life will be open to them."[109] And as an all-enfolding artistic process, life demanded the readiness and attunement embodied in jazz, which was central to the scenius. "The whole point of modern poetry, dance . . . performance, prose," wrote Allen Ginsberg, "was the element of improvisation and spontaneity . . . and jazz was a model for almost everybody . . . and partly a parallel experiment [on behalf of each discipline] in free form."[110] To paraphrase Walter Pater, all art was aspiring towards the condition of jazz, and Ornette was at the heart of that experiment.

In 1961 Ornette shared a loft above a broom factory on 52 Gold Street with a painter from San Francisco named Eve Griffin. "[Eve] had a shower and a gas stove and a room divider," recalled Bobby Bradford, who came from Texas on Ornette's invitation to replace Don Cherry for an upcoming gig at the Five Spot. Bassist Jimmy Garrison replaced Charlie Haden, who was struggling with drug problems; the gifted young Scott LeFaro, who would have been Ornette's next choice, had recently died in a car crash. Like Cherry, Ed Blackwell was playing elsewhere and as if on cue, Charles Moffett arrived with wife and kids in tow, having quit his job teaching music in Fort Worth (where, he told Ornette, he played *Change of the Century* for his students). "He unloaded his drums right there," said Bradford, "gave Ornette a big hug and said, 'the Lord sent this to us both.'"[111] After the Five Spot, the Quartet played the Jazz Gallery and the Village Gate, but however fruitful Ornette's reunion with his old bandmates, Jimmy Garrison (Georgia, 1934–1976), the odd man out, had trouble adapting:

> Ornette writes phrases the way he feels them; if it comes out three and a half bars [instead of four], then that's it. His playing sometimes leaves you hanging the same way . . . leaves you thinking, "is there anything else to come?" But it just means it's the end of the phrase and he's moved on . . . you can only go so far with his music without knowing about it, and one night I just exploded.[112]

Garrison left Ornette amicably and while they continued to work and record together, from 1961 to 1967, he was a pillar of John Coltrane's monumental quartet (with McCoy Tyner on piano and Elvin Jones on drums).[113] Ornette replaced Garrison with classically trained concert bassist David Izenzon (Pittsburgh, 1932–1979), who sat in one night at the Five Spot, his first time onstage with a jazz ensemble. Alert, adept, and self-assured, he was a perfect fit.

Having accumulated enough material for several more Atlantic releases, Ornette accepted an October 1961 concert date in Cincinnati, Ohio.[114] He reassembled his double quartet (this time with Bradford and Cherry on trumpet, Art Davis and Jimmy Garrison on bass, Moffett and Blackwell on drums and Eric Dolphy on bass clarinet) and ventured boldly forth from New York. Cincinnati was not exactly at the vanguard of the music scene; the wording on the marquee announcing Ornette read: "Free Jazz Concert," and Cincinnatians took it literally. When told they had to buy tickets, the crowd refused, causing a ruckus that might arguably have been worse had they paid and been treated to an atomic myth's-worth of improvisation. Realizing there would be no door receipts and therefore no pay, Ornette and the band slipped out a side exit, a no doubt chastening experience.

Nor were club dates as plentiful as they might have been in New York in 1962, had Ornette not tripled his price. He'd noticed that pianist Dave Brubeck's quartet earned larger fees and was unconvinced that Brubeck's hugely successful album *Time Out* (Columbia, 1959), with its hit single "Take Five," was adequate justification. "Music and money got nothing in common," observed Billy Higgins, and Ornette's business sense seemed at times to form a negative correlation with his musical one. But he was taking stock, legitimately weighing the effort versus the reward while trying to maintain artistic clarity. "I'm not sure but what I lose more than I gain by working every night," he complained, wishing for a shorter week playing longer sets: "I get so tired I don't have the enthusiasm to write or rehearse during the day

. . . sometimes I go to the club and I can't understand what I feel. Am I here? How will I make it through tonight?"[115] When the Newport Jazz Festival offered Ornette $1,500 for an afternoon appearance (a fair sum, considering what he made at the Five Spot), he said, "that's all right for me but what about the rest of the band?"[116] He had a series of managers whose job was to negotiate acceptable fees but none were able to persuade him to do much of anything he didn't want to.

In April 1962, the Quartet played a one-off gig for a conference of the American Institute of Architects, a gathering whose connotations appealed to him as he expanded his interests and fields of reference.[117] He had recently helped animation wizard and composer John Whitney Sr. conduct an experiment in "digital harmony," conceived as a meeting point between aural and visual stimuli, composing a soundtrack to accompany the first presentation of analog computer-generated graphics.[118] Around the same time, Ornette set to work creating a concert in his own image and on his own tab at Town Hall, a highly respected venue. He was tired of jazz clubs, whose music and liquor-fueled energy he equated with a sordid past. "The jazz scene hasn't really changed since it left the New Orleans whorehouses," he said; "the nightclub is still built on the same two things: whiskey and fucking."[119] Had club owners paid what he felt he was worth he may have played for them more willingly, but Ornette was in the process of reinventing himself. Asked the irksomely frequent question as to whether or not he could read (music), Ornette replied: "'Only the newspaper.' So after that, write-ups always picked up on that quote . . . I realized that my image was sort of 'cornpone musician,' this illiterate guy who just plays, so I started writing classical music."[120] Hypersensitive to critique about his lack of formal musical training, Ornette turned to composition as both a vehicle of expression and a means of validation that, like his Town Hall concert, was intended as a caution to whoever dared underestimate him.

A midtown Manhattan landmark built by suffragists in 1921, Town Hall was designed to reflect the principles of democracy, with no elitist boxes and a clear line of sight for all 1,500 audience members.[121] Ornette probably knew that Thelonious Monk had played there in 1959 and he would have heard about the concert of Stravinsky conducting a piece with four pianists that same year.[122] Monk had producers for his concert; Stravinsky had the full weight of the music establishment behind him. Ornette was obliged to take a do-it-yourself approach. He rented the hall, wrote the music, rehearsed the musicians, put up posters around town, and hired someone to record an event that demonstrated his self-determination and multidimensional musical stance. At Town Hall he performed in trio format (with Moffett and Izenzon) for the first time; it was also the debut of "Dedication to Poets and Writers," his first composition for string quartet. Enlisting a rhythm and blues trio to join him on "Blues Misused" was Ornette's way of saying, "yes, this too." From the sound of the enthusiastic applause, at least several hundred people attended, but however riveting the music, the concert apparently did not generate much press. This may help explain Ornette's dour recollection of what was, in fact, a landmark achievement:

> I'll never forget, it was 1962 December 21, and that night there was a subway strike, a newspaper strike, a taxi strike, I mean everything was strike, even a match strike, know what I mean? Not only that, I hired a guy to record it for me, and [later] he committed suicide. I could tell you lots of tragedies that happened, but that was called [as released on ESP Records] *Ornette at Town Hall*.[123]

It was the last time Ornette performed publicly for two years.

As a kind of musical reboot, he took up trumpet and violin (bowing with his left hand), to flush out anything mechanical or perfunctory that had crept into his playing. He was a tinkerer and enjoyed repairing his instruments. He studied music notation with Gunther Schuller and was dedicating more time to composing, beginning to think of himself more as a composer than a performer. "Performance is the shell of the peanut," he told John Snyder. "Composition is the peanut."[124] He decided to open his own nightclub to provide a conducive ambiance for musicians, found a space, and was about to redecorate when he discovered that residential zoning laws forbade such establishments. He took steps to establish a music publishing company to protect musicians' copyrights but it never got off the ground. His mild demeanor prompted Nat Hentoff to call him "Buddha-like," but Ornette was paddling furiously beneath the surface to maintain that swanlike glide. Robert Frank, who met him around this time, described him as "a hard critic" who "didn't like many things."[125] He developed stomach problems he later ascribed to ulcers provoked by the "horrible things" detractors had written about his music, as if he'd been cursed. Yet admiration for his work was widespread and growing, as was his influence.[126] In his first novel (*V*, 1963), Thomas Pynchon rechristened Ornette as McClintic Sphere, a pivotal figure whose motto was "keep cool, but care."

Ornette was trying. He played informal, explorative sessions with Cecil Taylor and tenor saxophonist Albert Ayler (1936–1970), who shared his opinion that "conventional jazz [had] become a joke."[127] New to the city, Ayler was staying with an aunt in Harlem after five years abroad, several of which were in the army. He had much in common with Ornette, whom he deeply admired.[128] He came from a religious family in Cleveland, Ohio, grew up with church music, played R&B as a teen, graduated to bebop, and later sought to distill from his experience a purer, simpler form of jazz. His sound was raw, reaching, redolent of Baptist hymns and New Orleans threnodies yet technically audacious; in the liner notes for one of Ayler's albums, Michael Cuscuna called him "the folk musician of the avant-garde."[129] Ayler met and played with Cecil Taylor in Copenhagen, and when he returned to America, Taylor invited him to join his band for a high-profile Lincoln Center concert where Coltrane's group also performed, on December 31, 1963. Coltrane

Ornette Coleman's *The Empty Foxhole* session, Van Gelder Studio, Englewood Cliffs, NJ, September 9, 1966; photograph by Francis Wolff.

became Ayler's mentor and friend, lending him money when club dates weren't enough to keep him going.[130]

Coltrane and Ayler were openly spiritual and viewed music as a means of accessing higher values. Coltrane had overcome a harrowing heroin addiction, he believed, thanks to a greater power that he addressed and arguably channeled in his album *A Love Supreme* (Impulse!, 1965). "In order to play a truth, a musician has to live with as much truth as possible," said Coltrane, a sentiment echoed by Ayler:

> We are the music we play. And our commitment is to peace, to understanding of life. And we keep trying to purify our music,

to purify ourselves so that we can move ourselves—and those
who hear us—to higher levels of peace and understanding.[131]

A current of Eastern philosophy ran through the scenius, a compatible
cut-up of Hindu, Confucian, and Buddhist concepts urging an
enlightened inner and outer life.[132] In 1965 Coltrane recorded *Om*
(Impulse!, 1968), incorporating portions of the Bhagavad Gita and
the Tibetan Book of the Dead, chanting with tenor saxophonist
Pharoah Sanders (1940–), another close friend of Ornette's, who had
perfected the art of circular breathing.

Aside from his 1968 recording "Buddha Blues," Ornette showed
no partiality to Eastern schools of thought, with which he nonetheless
had an affinity.[133] But he experimented with religion and at one point
considered dropping music to study it full time. In LA he'd been
baptized a Jehovah's Witness but when he learned their Texas churches
were segregated, he dropped them, remarking that "the church needs
god, just like the people."[134] He attended a conference of the Nation
of Islam, whose militant, separatist message of black pride he found
too full of hate. He tried the Rosicrucians and "various 'metaphysical'
groups." Wary of organized religion, Ornette thought of himself as
a "spiritual freelancer" who, like Ayler and Coltrane, saw music as a
form of communication that both expressed and transcended the
human condition.[135]

An interviewer once asked what Coltrane hoped to be in five
years, and he said, laughingly, "a saint."[136] His death of liver cancer
(at age forty) was a kind of beatification; the African Orthodox church
founded in his name in San Francisco the following year still holds
services revolving around his music and philosophy.[137] One of
Coltrane's last requests was that Ornette and Ayler play at his funeral,
which they did in separate configurations.[138] During the performance,
Ayler took the sax from his mouth and let out a prolonged, gut-
wrenching wail. He too would be dead within three years, found
floating in the East River, an apparent suicide. John Coltrane, Albert

Ayler, and Eric Dolphy (dead at 36 of diabetes)—all prodigiously talented, all linked to Ornette's early career and lifelong endeavor—there's no telling how their art might have matured. Ornette outlived and consequently outplayed them. At a time when most musicians were plagued by some combination of poverty, prejudice, illness, and addiction, survival was a triumph in itself.

When Ornette finally decided to play his trumpet in public he did so in Coltrane's supportive presence, sitting in briefly with his group at the *Half Note* in 1964. His divorce came through that year. He was still on hiatus, listening, practicing, and at age 34, monitoring a scene he'd helped create, showcased at a five-night, free jazz event called "the October Revolution," which attracted around seven hundred people to the Cellar Cafe. Jimmy Guiffre was on the bill, as were Paul Bley, David Izenzon, Cecil Taylor, Sun Ra, and other lesser-known musicians. Although he didn't play, Ornette's work was echoed in that of the younger players. Covering the event with Dan Morgenstern for *DownBeat*, Martin Williams saw it as proof of his prediction that free jazz was the way forward. "The new music is here. And any jazz journalists who don't like it can lump it," he wrote. Nonetheless, as Dan Morgenstern pointed out, "the two fountainheads of the new jazz—Cecil Taylor and Ornette Coleman—are not working steadily or hardly working at all." Morgenstern called for government or institutional subsidies for musicians experimenting with jazz, who deserved it as much as "painters, poets, classical musicians and writers who are now among the recipients of such aid."[139] Decent-paying gigs were getting harder to find as audience sensibilities shifted towards pop, rock, and Motown. Some musicians called the Beatles' 1964 arrival in town "the beginning of the end" for jazz.[140] Slowly but surely, club clienteles were shrinking, leaving owners unwilling to book risky music.

In society, as in the arts, the status quo was under fire. Antiwar demonstrations protesting America's involvement in Vietnam began in earnest in 1965, with university students leading marches nationwide. "My saxophone is like a machine gun in the hands of the Viet Cong," said Archie Shepp, one of many musicians who took a political stand, especially as the peace movement overlapped with and lent momentum to the fight for civil rights.[141] Jazz was inherently political, charged with rebellion, wrote Stanley Crouch:

> The musicians themselves [represented] a way of saying no to everything that held you down . . . [they were] the blood on the knife of the music . . . specialized in the wounds that men had to live through and that were somehow conquered and simultaneously purged if expressed in all their anguish and anger.[142]

On July 2, in the midst of a long struggle, President Lyndon Johnson signed the Civil Rights Act, outlawing discrimination on the basis of race, creed, religion, sex, or nationality. It was a hollow victory for black citizens still denied the vote, subjected to hate crimes, police aggression, and prejudice both at home and abroad as members of the armed forces, defending a nation that refused them full citizenship. "Many among us want to kill," said Charles Mingus, "because we were treated like animals and fascistic methods were used against us."[143] The ink had barely dried on Johnson's new law when riots broke out in Harlem, sparked by the murder in broad daylight of a fifteen-year-old African American by New York City Police.

In September, Martin Luther King, leader of the nonviolent civil rights movement, visited Cold War Berlin to deliver a speech for the city's "Culture Week" (comprising the first Berlin Jazz Festival), underlining the connection between the music and the fight for human dignity:

> It is no wonder that so much of the search for identity among American Negroes was championed by Jazz musicians. Long before the modern essayists and scholars wrote of racial identity

Harlem protest in support of African Americans who marched
in Selma for the right to vote and who were run down and beaten
by police on horseback, March 1965. Photograph by Stanley Wolfson
for the *New York World Telegram and Sun.*

as a problem for a multiracial world, musicians were returning
to their roots to affirm that which was stirring within their
souls. Much of the power of our Freedom Movement in the
United States has come from the music. It has strengthened
us with its sweet rhythms when courage began to fail. It has
calmed us with its rich harmonies when spirits were down.[144]

King had given his "I Have a Dream" speech the previous year, speaking out against oppression from the steps of the Lincoln Memorial
to 250,000 Americans of all colors.

In January 1965, Ornette ended his performance hiatus to play
the Village Vanguard with Moffett and Izenzon, occasionally trading
his sax for the trumpet or the violin. The *New York Times, Newsweek,*
and *Time* magazine were on hand for his comeback, and the critics
were kind with regard to his new instruments. But Ornette needed

money, not compliments. Nor could he ignore the hypocrisy he experienced as a black musician, lauded in the press but underpaid or unemployed in real life. "In jazz, the Negro is the product," he said, "so if it's me they're selling, the profits [can't] come back to me, you dig?" Sounding a Marxist note, he continued:

> The people I recorded for and worked for . . . have been guilty of making me believe I shouldn't have the profits from my product because they own the channels of production . . . They act like I owe them something for letting me express myself with my music, like the artist is supposed to suffer and not to live in clean, comfortable situations.[145]

Although less vehement than some black musicians, Ornette never hesitated to express his views on the racism he'd experienced throughout his life. "A white American can wake up in the morning without having any past on his mind," he said, "but I can't, at least not yet."[146] America's discord was deepening in February 1965, when forty-year-old black resistance leader Malcolm X was gunned down in Harlem.[147] In March, African Americans were trampled and beaten by mounted police while demanding their right to register for the vote in Selma, Alabama, further heightening racial tensions across the country.

Following the example of Don Cherry and Ed Blackwell, who were already touring widely, Ornette was considering an escape to Europe, where musicians were finding work and appreciative audiences in a more tolerant, creative environment. He needed money to get there and in May, Conrad Rooks (1934–2011), heir to the Avon cosmetics fortune, handsomely commissioned Ornette to compose the music for a film based on his experience with addiction. A heavy drinker from the age of fifteen, Rooks befriended jazz musicians and other members of the underground while ingesting copious amounts of coke, smoke, heroin, and hallucinogens. When he decided to clean up, he entered a Swiss clinic for "the sleep cure," which involved being knocked out with anesthetics until the agonies of withdrawal had passed. *Chappaqua* (1966) is Rooks's detoxifying dream, a filmic pinwheel spinning zeitgeist colors from Freud and the Café Flores to 42nd Street and the Fugs. Rooks produced, directed, and played himself in the movie, beautifully and audaciously shot by Robert Frank in locations in New York, Paris, and elsewhere. There's a walk-on (or rather sit-on) from Allen Ginsberg and a more substantial contribution by William Burroughs, wearing a top hat and resembling Abraham Lincoln's recently exhumed evil twin. Ornette also makes an appearance, cast in the unlikely role of a "peyote eater" who administers Rooks a healing dose.

Ornette was never really into drugs. He smoked the odd cigarette, didn't mind the occasional joint, and had taken LSD several presumably beneficial times. He tried heroin more than once but didn't like it. He'd seen what it had done to his friends Ed Blackwell, Billy Higgins, Charlie Haden, and a host of other musicians. He lent them money when they asked for it, forgave them when they missed or were late for gigs, and had "no moral thing" against users.[148]

Martin Luther King and Malcolm X, March 1964;
photograph by Marion S. Trikosko.

Ornette's pragmatism and sense of self-preservation shielded him from addiction. "The problem [with heroin]," he said, "was you never got anything done, you just sat around feeling good about yourself."[149]

Ornette recorded Rooks's score in June with Moffett, Izenzon, Pharoah Sanders, and an eleven-piece orchestra conducted by cellist Joseph Tekula of the Modern Jazz Quartet. When he finished, he went to Los Angeles, where he met with a pianist to discuss a project that never materialized. Visiting Jayne and Denardo was probably the main reason for Ornette's journey west. He was about to leave America, intending to stay in Europe as long as he could, and he wouldn't be seeing them for a while.

DURING THE COLD War, when America competed with the Soviet Union for moral ascendancy alongside military and technical might, it was obliged to acknowledge that racism gave its "liberty and justice for all" rhetoric the lie. A means of raising its tarnished profile was proposed by Adam Clayton Powell Jr., an African American clergyman and congressman representing several New York districts, including Harlem, where he was born. The Soviets had the Bolshoi Ballet, Powell reasoned, but America had jazz. In 1956 the u.s. State Department began sponsoring concerts worldwide, appointing Powell's friend Dizzy Gillespie as its first jazz ambassador and sending him to Pakistan, Lebanon, Yugoslavia, Turkey, and Greece. Duke Ellington was emissary to South Asia and Eastern Europe; Benny Goodman played his clarinet in Moscow's Red Square; Louis Armstrong visited the Congo and Cairo, where he was photographed blowing his horn for the Sphinx. Call it propaganda, but the musicians loved it, basking in the glow of multicultural welcomes while absorbing new music, rhythms, and sounds. Audiences everywhere rejoiced, as did u.s. diplomats. "You can't get as much good-will out of a tank as you can get out of Dizzy Gillespie's band," one wrote.[150]

American musicians had been gravitating to Europe since the 1920s, when Jazz Age trends in music, dance, and fashion swept the continent. Jazz bands were hugely popular, including Sam Wooding and his Chocolate Kiddies (featuring Texan Willie Lewis on clarinet), who were big in Paris in the 1920s, with aspiring local musicians joining their ranks. The 1930s brought giants like Coleman Hawkins, Benny Carter, and Louis Armstrong, who stayed for months or years, nurturing the indigenous jazz scene. The Second World War did not diminish Europe's love of jazz, despite the Nazis banning it from the radio and imposing strict conditions for performance.[151] What the Third Reich labeled "degenerate music" became a symbol of defiance and in the wake of Hitler's defeat it was Europe's victory song. Nor was the Iron Curtain impermeable; jazz thrived in Soviet-controlled Central and Eastern Europe, as it did in the Soviet Union. Born of adversity, it was the sound of overcoming, and the ensembles that played it represented an ideal society in microcosm, where individuals expressing their unique talents augment, rather than threaten, the common good. Improvisation was synonymous with freedom: more than the mere absence of constraints, it implied a skillful and responsive openness.

By the war's end jazz had laid down firm roots, with European musicians transfusing developments flowing from America with fresh frames of reference and direction. In the 1960s, American musicians began relocating to Europe in greater numbers, no longer as jazz ambassadors but jazz exiles, seeking work and a respite from racism, police violence, and the sinkhole of urban drug culture at home. Some, like Dexter Gordon, chose Denmark, where the living was easy and the audiences rapt. Walking the streets of Copenhagen, Gordon said he felt "like the mayor."[152] But London and Paris were the preferred destinations for many musicians who were quickly plugged into a progressive scene by colleagues, club owners, and concert producers.

Ornette arrived in London in July 1965 with no real plan but an excellent contact in Victor Schonfield (1940–), whom he'd met in New York the previous year. A London School of Economics graduate, Schonfield worked as assistant to Michael Horovitz and Pete Brown, cofounders of the Oxford-based literary journal *New Departures*, which had branched out into concerts and events. A jazz aficionado, Schonfield contributed to *DownBeat* and similar UK-based publications, and on his first trip to New York he sought out Ornette, whose career (and that of his sidemen) was closely followed by the British music press. They talked music for a while, then Ornette picked up the violin and played an impromptu twenty-minute serenade that triggered the 24-year-old's eureka moment. "I suddenly understood what free improvisation was about," Schonfield said; "it was the new world, and he opened it up for me."[153] A year later Ornette asked him to produce a concert to kick off his first European tour, a task for which Live New Departures (LND) was ideally positioned.

Between 1959 and 1965, London had become a center of the transatlantic avant-garde, thanks in no small part to *New Departures*. While a student at Oxford, avid jazz fan and poet Michael Horovitz

Louis Armstrong and his wife Lucille, Cairo, 1961.

(1935–) met William Burroughs and Allen Ginsberg in Paris to solicit material and found them more than willing.[154] Although aligned with the Beats, *New Departures* had a broader, more open-ended purview, mingling the perspectives of international writers, artists, dramatists, and composers of an experimental bent. The first issue (Summer 1959) appeared shortly after Britain's Obscene Publications Act was ratified and featured, among others, Samuel Beckett and William Burroughs. Within a year, Horovitz and friends initiated a series of roadshows combining jazz and new music with poetry readings and theater. The musical director was Cornelius Cardew, graduate of the Studio for Electronic Music in Cologne, the world's first high-tech, composer-led laboratory of sound (established in 1951). "Conceived in the name of an experiment," which Horovitz defined as "an act or course of action of which the outcome is unknown," Live New Departures produced hundreds of events at arts festivals, jazz clubs, colleges, galleries, TV studios, and civic halls countrywide, building audiences along the way.

Live New Departures' watershed year was 1965, when their "First International Poetry Incarnation" (June 11) attracted 7,000 flower-garlanded attendees, not to some park or repurposed movie theater but the orotund Albert Hall, which was packed to the rafters. Occupying the stage where Wagner, Rachmaninoff, Einstein, and other luminaries once stood, poets addressed the topics of sex, drugs, peace, and enlightenment in free verse. A benedictory Allen Ginsberg chanted tantric mantras and rang little bells; Lawrence Ferlinghetti, founder of City Lights Press, was there, as was British poet Adrian Mitchell, who read "To Whom It May Concern (Tell Me Lies About Vietnam)." Author and Arabist Robert Irwin was studying at Oxford when he attended the "iconic" gathering, wearing a cape and "brandishing a silver-topped cane." Impressed by the size of the young, flamboyant, and intoxicated audience, he realized, "we were the coming storm."[155] The crowd, the readings, and the rock concert ambiance of the ordinarily staid venue made the event "as instrumental in the creation of

Swinging London and the Summer of Love as any Beatles album."[156] A performance by Ornette was ideal for maintaining the counter-cultural momentum, and the recently opened 1,800-seat Fairfield Hall in southern London (Croydon) was secured for August 29.

There was a problem with the London Musicians' Union, which placed exchange quotas on foreign musicians. The jazz quota was full but not the classical one. Ornette disliked musical categories and took pleasure in demonstrating their arbitrariness. He set to work composing "Forms and Sounds for Wind Quintet," to be performed by London's esteemed Virtuoso Ensemble, and was duly registered as the UK's first African American "concert artist." Moffett and Izenzon were summoned from New York and were no doubt excited at the prospect of the job and the journey. The news from home was not good.

In early August 1965, Lyndon Johnson signed the Voting Rights Act to cancel the efforts of local and state lawmakers to prevent African Americans from exercising their constitutional right, as citizens, to vote. Instead of uniting the nation behind an affirmation of democracy, the act ignited the anger of both blacks, who knew legislation would not stop bigotry, and whites, who felt too great a concession had been made. Riots erupted in Watts, sparked by a roadside argument between the police and a black man they accused of drunk driving; 34 lives were lost that week (August 11–16). "Black people were tired of the contradictions, the inequalities, the mounting violations, police brutality, unemployment, lack of opportunity, lack of respect, and the amount of sacrifices made as a consequence of white domination," wrote Jayne Cortez, who was by then a leader of the Watts community.[157] Her safety and Denardo's surely weighed heavily on Ornette's mind that summer as he prepared for his Europe debut.

The show opened with a poetry reading by Horovitz, accompanied by a local jazz ensemble followed by Ornette's "Forms and Sounds," comprised of ten parts. Instead of waiting until the composition's end to show their appreciation, the public "greeted [each part] with applause in the true jazz concert manner, a meeting of two worlds which produced immense amusement in the gentlemen of the Virtuoso Quintet."[158] The main event was Ornette (on alto, trumpet, and violin) with Charles Moffett and David Izenzon. Perhaps the most remarkable piece they performed that night was "Silence," where the group's improvisation incorporated consensually determined random pauses. Ornette was surely familiar with John Cage, who had also worked with LND and was famous for using silence in his compositions. But by introducing it as an improvisational element "played" by the ensemble, Ornette one-upped him. In the midst of one of those silent intervals, recalled Mike Horovitz,

> A strident voice yelled: "Now play Cherokee," referring to Ray Noble's theme, which had become a classic bebop standard [famously recorded by Charlie Parker, 1942] . . . Ornette instantly whizzed into an immaculately faithful version, whose lightning variations prompted the first of the evening's extensive series of standing ovations. He said later: "I just wanted them to know I knew."[159]

While hailing Ornette as "the most vital and essential single force in contemporary jazz," Jack Cooke, reviewing the concert for the *Jazz Monthly*, was unimpressed with Ornette's foray into "straight" music with "Forms and Sounds":

> It's probably after all too much to hope that after showing the escape route to an entire generation of jazz musicians caught in their harmonic trap that he is going to revolutionize the entire Western academic tradition overnight.[160]

But Cooke had not calculated the concert's effect on Victor Schonfield, who had done most of the running to make it happen, including producing the printed program, where he made a more accurate prediction:

[Ornette's] vision stretches beyond the horizons of jazz as a specific, localised musical form to approach developments in contemporary academic music . . . [His] revolution will very probably be the last in the pure jazz tradition. From this time, jazz musicians will have more direct access to European musical culture.[161]

Schonfield started Music Now to serve as a platform for experimental music of all kinds. From 1967 to 1976, Music Now produced over eighty concerts of artists including the Velvet Underground and Soft Machine, Sun Ra, AMM (a British free jazz ensemble), Musica Elettronica Viva (an acoustic and electronic improvisation group started in Rome), John Cage and minimalist composer Terry Riley, greatly advancing LND's exploration of the art of improvisation as practiced in both free jazz and in "straight" or scored music, where it was referred to as "indeterminacy," the academic term for a more cautious version of the same process.

"Indeterminacy was understood to offer a kind of emancipation," wrote Cornelius Cardew, where musical notation acts "as more of a stimulus to the player's imagination, than a blue print," stressing that "performances of such pieces [require] a high degree of awareness . . . the ability to react spontaneously within situations that are familiar yet always fresh in detail is a skill to be acquired."[162] He and like-minded composers were arriving by a rather tortured, intellectual path at what for Ornette and practically every other jazz musician was a fact of life. More than a musical skill, the attunement Cardew described was a technique applicable to all the arts, one that Ornette had cultivated and Schonfield recognized as the new baseline criteria for the creative act, whatever its form.

Ornette did not linger in London after his concert, passing a leisurely September 1965 in Paris with just a short trip to the Lugano Jazz Festival, where the trio received a fifteen-minute standing ovation. In October, they played a festival in Barcelona and doubled back for a night at Amsterdam's Concertgebouw, the smaller Dutch equivalent of Albert Hall, renowned for its acoustics. The opening band that night (October 29) was led by Danish-Congolese altoist John Tchicai (1936–2012), who must have known Ornette from New York, where he lived for several years (1962–7), recording with Don Cherry, Coltrane, and Albert Ayler. Raised in Copenhagen, Tchicai was an accomplished and inventive multi-instrumentalist and composer who admired Ornette and led the free jazz contingency in northern Europe. Tchicai recalled the large enthusiastic audience and receiving "the best possible" treatment at the Concertgebouw event, one of the venue's earliest departures from traditional programming (soon to be followed by Led Zeppelin, Pink Floyd, and the Who) reflecting the counterculture's growing foothold in mainstream institutions across Europe.[163]

The night after Amsterdam, the trio appeared at the Berlin Jazz Festival, and the next day (October 31, 1965) in Copenhagen's Tivoli Gardens for an afternoon concert where Ornette had a chance reunion with Sonny Rollins, who was also on the bill.[164] Then it was Stockholm for a festival at the Johanneshov Ice Stadium, a combination music venue/hockey rink. That night (November 2), Ornette met Ake Abrahamsson, who booked him for a two-week engagement later in November at Sweden's best-known jazz club. The trio returned to France for a short set for the Paris Jazz Festival at the Maison de la Mutualité (November 4), where a full concert was scheduled for the coming spring. After a brief break, they were back in Stockholm to open at the Golden Circle, where Don Cherry had played with his own quintet a couple of weeks before.

The *Svenska Dagbladet* hailed the trio's engagement (November 22–December 4) as a "great cultural event," urging "everybody in Sweden's music world, from pop musicians to serious composers" to attend. The article equated those who found Ornette's music "grotesque, filled with anguish and chaos," with the philistines who "[objected] to Willem de Kooning's portraits of women or Samuel

Beckett's absurd plays."[165] If Ornette's whirlwind tour of Europe's capitals was any indication, free jazz was the thread running through them, a rallying point for kindred spirits aligned with the break-through arts.

Sometime in late 1965, Ornette met Thomas White, a 33-year-old American living in the bohemian bosom of Montparnasse. White had worked as an assistant to Roger Vadim and just shown his first fea-ture film as director at the Locarno Film Festival, where it essentially bombed. *Who's Crazy* was the improvisational product of his collabo-ration with a group of Living Theater actors who were marooned in a farmhouse on Belgium's North Sea coast awaiting the return of Judith Malina and Julian Beck, then fighting charges of tax evasion in New York City. Shot in black and white, the film's story of patients taking over the asylum was less successfully portrayed than the reality of broke but game and ebullient actors taking over the somewhat dere-lict farmhouse of a wealthy arts patron in the dead of winter (1964–5). White provided no particular direction; the film was a way for the troupe to pass some creative time when the pantry was bare but there was nonetheless, recalled White, "a lot of smoke in the room." The actors simply played with one another, doing improvisational exer-cises, frolicking in the snow, and producing a couple of set pieces (a trial and a wedding), all vigorously animated by a combination of joie de vivre and the need to keep warm. White showed the finished prod-uct to Malina and Beck when they returned to Europe in late 1965; they said it lacked the Living Theater's customary "energy vector."[166] The film needed a new soundtrack, White decided, enlisting, among others, classical guitarist Ramon Ybarra, a young British folk singer named Marianne Faithfull, and his new friend Ornette Coleman.[167]

Ornette, Moffett, and Izenzon recorded the music in Paris while watching footage projected on the wall. At some point, unbeknownst to Thomas White, someone else showed up with a camera. *David, Moffett and Ornette: The Ornette Coleman Trio* (1966), directed by Dick Fontaine, documents with rare intimacy the musicians at work and the makeshift situations under which lasting art was often produced. After White showed the new and improved *Who's Crazy* at Cannes in 1966, it vanished from sight until 2016 when it was screened in New York to critical acclaim, with special praise reserved for his inspired use of Ornette's soundtrack.[168] It was, coincidentally, the only fully realized film to use compositions that Ornette wrote and performed. *Chappaqua* was also screened in 1966, at the Venice Film Festival where it won second prize, but Ornette's score was absent as it was deemed too distracting. Rooks (and presumably Philip Glass,

Ornette Coleman, Charles Moffett, and David Izenzon at a photograph session for the cover of the trio *At the "Golden Circle"* (Blue Note, 1965), Humlegarden Park, Stockholm, December 1965; photograph by Francis Wolff.

who is credited as the film's music consultant) replaced Ornette's work with Ravi Shankar's tabla and sitar, a smattering of jazz, Native American chants, a Motown hit, and a spiritual from a Holy Roller funeral service.[169]

The same thing happened to the soundtrack Ornette, Moffett, and Izenzon recorded for *Population Explosion* (1966), an animated film highlighting the plight of the world's underfed majority. Due to the music's "controversial nature," Canadian director Pierre Hébert later reissued the film with John Coltrane's group replacing Ornette's.[170] Ornette probably shrugged such things off as all in a day's work. There were larger issues, as he told Dick Fontaine in their filmed interview:

> This is what I really would love to have in my music: presence, you know as long as I can live, I mean I don't care about nothing I played yesterday if I can go home right now and write some music that is a presence.[171]

With *Who's Crazy* in the can, Ornette focused on an upcoming broadcast for French radio and the trio's concert at the Maison de la Mutualité.

The French critics adored Ornette, how he played and talked and especially his free jazz premise. "Rupture with tradition, absolute liberty of expression: the point of departure and a trajectory without constraints," wrote Jean-Pierre Binchet, "[Ornette's] musical language encompasses a way of thinking." Ornette was a visionary, misunderstood in his own country and above all a freedom fighter, Binchet continued, "a terrorist comfortable with his insurgence, a 'Dynamite Ornette,' the titles of whose albums are explosions that do not submit but flaunt their intentions."[172] The correlation between free jazz and activism grew firmer in the later 1960s, against the backdrop of student revolts and Algeria's fight for independence. For a generation in search of "politically engaged art," the new thing "struck a near perfect balance between aesthetic transgression and political expression."[173]

In 1966, however, critics considered Ornette's Paris appearance as more poetic than political.

Despite the previous week's radio broadcast, the crowd for the March 5 concert at La Mutualité was small (around three hundred) but intense, judging by reviews. *Jazz Magazine*'s Jacques Réda described the trio's performance as "a hymn to a sort of pure academic beauty, a little Parnassian *happening*" but he wanted more:

> True freedom would be to publicly gather bass tubas, African xylophones made of gourds (balafons), little flutes, ancient sistrums, herbal cures, tall stories, things of no importance, maids in the key of "C" and Carolingian hunting horns, then everyone would play without discrimination or false shame, until the smoke of the orgy, the bacchanal, the feasts, rises to the noses of the reinvigorated gods, a testimony of human innocence restored in a brotherhood of noise.[74]

Writing for *Jazz Hot*, Michel Delorme hailed Ornette as a "paradoxical apostle and ancestor," describing his music as "the Dixieland of free jazz," referencing the group improvisations of early New Orleans bands. The concert was a "revelation" and a "miracle" for Delorme. As the trio performed, "in a state of grace that never faltered for an instant," he grasped "a clear and irremediable truth" and was compelled to rush backstage after the show to relate "the emotions [he] experienced, the happiness Ornette gave [him]," to which Ornette replied: "Well it wasn't perfect, maybe next time."

Others contributed to the *Jazz Hot* review, including an apologetic critic who suspected that the small crowd may have reflected "the pseudo-intellectual Parisian life, the nullity of its theater, its old-fashioned architecture, the hokey 'innovations' of its magazines," none of which, he wrote, could outweigh the redemptive fact that "Paris had Ornette." Another reviewer compared Ornette to a magician "pulling sounds from his saxophone like rabbits from a hat." Yet another was marked by "Ornette's blues and David Izenzon's tears at the end of a composition entitled 'My Master's Voice'," which the bassist dedicated to his wife for her birthday. "Anyone untouched by the beauty of this music," Nahman concluded, "will remain, throughout their lives, sinister BIRDS."[175]

Following an appearance at the San Remo Jazz Festival (March 27, 1966), the trio returned to London for a haymaking month-long gig at Ronne Scott's jazz club (est. 1959), which provoked a similar if more restrained response to the one the Quartet had received at the Five Spot. Perhaps with Victor Schonfield's assistance, the trio also played several concerts outside of London, and then appeared a second time at Croydon's Fairfield Hall. After nine dense months, having come full circle, Ornette's self-imposed exile was over. Author and photographer Val Wilmer interviewed him shortly before he left, remarking how his first Fairfield concert was already "practically a legend," but Ornette was characteristically guarded: "I'm happy about where my music situation is. I'll be happier when I have less financial problems . . . but I guess that will come in the future. I'm pretty contented to keep growing."[176] Ornette rarely expressed pleasure in his achievements or the adulation showered upon him, at least in public, often dwelling on what he lacked or was denied rather than on what he'd pulled together, like this highly productive European adventure. He might have given himself more credit. Having communed with a large and fervent free jazz diaspora, Ornette was returning to America riding a wave of his own making.

ON HIS SON's sixth birthday, Ornette phoned him in Los Angeles and asked what he'd like as a gift. Denardo suggested a toy gun but his father talked him into accepting a drum set. Jayne saw to Denardo's music lessons and he became a proficient reader; when Ornette visited LA, they played music together in the garage. As a child, Denardo knew nothing of his father's stature so perhaps didn't dwell on his promise that they'd record together when he returned from Europe. Shortly after Ornette's 1965 homecoming, the ten-year-old traveled to New York to join him and was back for school in September, the only kid in his class who cut an album for Blue Note Records on his summer vacation (*The Empty Foxhole*, 1966). The displaced Charles Moffett had probably encouraged Denardo's initiation: he later played and recorded extensively with his own multi-instrumental off-spring.[177] Izenzon bowed out of the trio, saying he was uncomfortable playing without Moffett. But Charlie Haden had beaten his addiction and was back on full form. Ornette was invested in the project; he chose one of his own paintings for the album cover art and wrote a poem for the back of the sleeve.[178]

Listening and responding to his father's magisterial alto (and trumpet) and Haden's rhythmic embroidery on upright bass, Denardo acquitted himself admirably, though not everyone thought so. Despite his respect for Ornette, drummer Shelly Manne (who played on *Tomorrow Is the Question*) called *Empty Foxhole* "unadulterated shit" and suggested Denardo might one day "make a good carpenter."[179] Others were more accepting, but Ornette expected a warmer response to what he viewed as both a creative and commercially viable proposition:

> The way Denardo is playing now would be a novelty for any other race of people. Someone would have gotten in and said "we can make lots of money with this father and son," the whole trip. Instead they put it down.[180]

Denardo wasn't always a pliant student. "Every time I wanted him to play for me, I had to damn near beg him," Ornette said, but he per-sisted in experimenting with his son's possibilities.[181] As a tabula rasa, without musical memory or mechanical habits, Denardo brought purity and directness to the ensemble. He may also have represented Ornette's chance to recover a more innocent state of mind unsullied

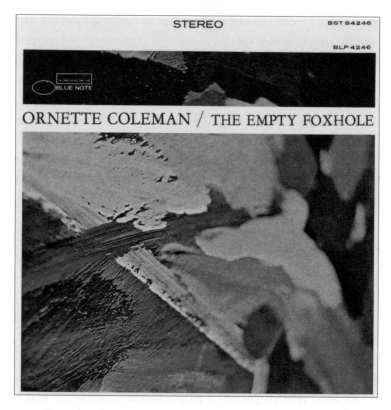

Sleeve of *The Empty Foxhole* (Blue Note, 1970), reproducing an oblique photograph of a detail from a painting by Ornette Coleman.

by adult regrets and resentments. "I felt the joy," he said, "of playing with someone who hadn't had to care if the music business or musicians or critics would help or destroy his desire to express himself."[182] Ornette's irritation with the music business was on display in an article he wrote for *DownBeat* in 1967, a *cri de coeur* addressed to his "musical brothers and audience" urging the acceptance of difference, the abandoning of commercialism, and the acknowledgment that musicians were often exploited. "I was once told by a very social record producer that a musician shouldn't expect to make a living from records," Ornette wrote, "yet *he* was making a good living from records that musicians had made for him."[183]

That Ornette saw his son's development as an extension of his own was apparent in the title of their second album together (with Haden), *Ornette at Twelve*, recorded in 1968, when Denardo was that age.[184] In the course of that remarkable year, father and son participated in Martin Luther King's Poor People's March, a six-week-long sit-in (May 12–June 24) for economic justice. Between rows of tents, Ornette laid a piece of plywood across the muddy path and performed with Denardo for the protest campers. A lanky youngster with a fair-sized afro and an unassuming way, Denardo also accompanied his father in the San Francisco premiere of a seven-part composition called *Sun Suite*.[185] In August, they played the Filmore West, with Denardo's name appearing alongside that of Dewey Redman, "Robert" Bradford and "Charles Hayden [*sic*]" on a poster designed by Dore, famous for his psychedelic graphics. The only child of a "free jazz prophet" and a firebrand poetess (he also performed and recorded with Jayne), Denardo's youth and musical education was unique and uniquely challenging.[186] Aside from appearing on eleven of Ornette albums (and many others), he later became his father's longest-serving manager, working with him onstage and off throughout his life.

Tenor saxophonist Dewey Redman (1931–2006) joined Ornette's musical family in 1967, as a result of a chance reunion with Ornette at a San Francisco nightclub. Born in Fort Worth, Dewey attended I. M. Terrell, where he met Ornette and heard the Jam Jivers, but they never played together. "I was a late bloomer . . . I just played in the church band . . . I didn't go to the Jim Hotel until I was in college," he said, because his mother wouldn't let him.[187] Dewey wanted to take up the trumpet but was discouraged by an uncharitable church bandleader who told him his lips were too big.[188] In truth, the church needed clarinetists and Dewey complied. Later, while attending Prairie View College (majoring in industrial arts with a minor in music), he switched to tenor sax and began working in Fort Worth clubs. After he served two years in the army, and then as a baggage handler at a local airport, his mother found him a job

Ornette with his ten-year-old son Denardo during *The Empty Foxhole*
session, Van Gelder Studio, Englewood Cliffs, NJ, September 9, 1966;
photograph by Francis Wolff.

as band director in a West Texas school. He moved closer to Austin,
where he played on weekends and was told he really belonged in
New York. Dewey decided to earn a master's degree first and moved
to San Francisco, where his father lived.

By the time he arrived on the East Coast, on Ornette's prompting, Dewey had recorded his first album as bandleader (*Look for the
Black Star*, Freedom, 1966) and was soon playing and recording with
Ornette's group. Being "the other saxophonist" in a Coleman ensemble might have placed a lesser artist at a disadvantage, but Dewey was
a gifted, versatile player and composer who saw the opportunity to
advance his creative process:

I consider myself as having gone to the University of Coleman
. . . I learned about space. Phrasing. How not to be caught
up in conventional things but to appreciate them . . . [how]
not to be limited in my scope, or critical of other musicians.
I learned to listen before I critique.[189]

He experimented with voicing, sometimes singing through his sax,
and while retaining its Texan edge his playing held an unmistakable
nobility. "The sound is the most important thing to me [as opposed
to technical prowess]—there's technique in sound," he said.[190] With
Dewey, as with Denardo, Ornette was making music with another
version of himself.

Early in 1967, Ornette became the first of his peers to receive
a Guggenheim Fellowship for composition, a boon previously
awarded solely to academics and/or composers with classical music
backgrounds.[191] That summer, following a police raid on a black after-
hours joint, Detroit erupted in riots, leaving 43 dead and over 1,000
injured, and gutting entire neighborhoods with fire. Ornette began
work on his opus for symphony orchestra and jazz ensemble, *Skies
of America*, a task that would occupy him for several years.[192] Since
his return from Europe, Ornette had been living in hotel rooms or
rented flats, including a Greenwich Village basement. According
to Bobby Bradford, he was a "packrat," storing broken instruments
and sound equipment in "big bags hanging from the walls" and tape
reels "shoved under the beds."[193] In order to write, Ornette needed
a steady base with room for his pre-digital clutter, and in April 1968,
he acquired his first home, on 131 Prince Street in Soho (south of
Greenwich Village). As a shareholder in a co-op that purchased the
old seven-story factory, Ornette was entitled to the street-level and
third floors, each with over 10,000 square feet (900 sq. m) of open
space. "I was just trying to find a place where I could go and make
music at any time," he said, but his loft was soon part of the evolving
scenius.[194]

From the early 1960s until the late 1970s, when Lower Manhattan rents grew prohibitive, lofts served as alternative performance venues where audience members were often artists, "all able to discuss each other's work in a fashion that was not at all academic or historical but real, alive, and very rewarding," recalled composer Philip Glass.[195] Such gatherings were the natural outgrowth of an urban habitat where defunct factories and warehouses with volumes of cheap, luminous space were virtually begging for a new life. Where rows of laborers had once manned their machines, artists struck a congenial bargain between work and play. The plumbing was minimal, the winters cold, but for people with no fixed income, off the clock with time to think and act, the space and its possibilities made a luxury of austerity.

Each with its own character and intention, the lofts were incubators for group projects like FLUXUS, "a fluid association of creative people oriented toward the intermedia rather than any one artistic discipline."[196] Among the FLUXUS composers performing in a building on 112 Chambers Street in the early 1960s was Toshi Ichiyanagi, who produced scores resembling graphs or scattered equations, and his wife, Yoko Ono, who befriended Ornette in Paris and was one of the few women with whom he collaborated and performed.[197] The lofts were organically connected through crossover projects, shared audiences, fliers, posters, word of mouth, and eventually the local press. What they lacked in acoustics, they compensated for in the quality and intimacy of the performances, and Ornette was a frequent audience member.

When Bill Dixon, producer of the 1964 October Revolution (at the Cellar Café), invited Ornette to join a composers' guild with Cecil Taylor, Paul Bley, and Sun Ra, he declined, as he had when Mingus and Max Roach asked him to participate in an artists' collective to produce their own concerts and recordings. Ornette was an initiator, not a joiner. With Artists House, as he later called his Prince Street place, he contributed to the community on his own terms, hosting

Dewey Redman with Ornette (background left), *New York is Now* session, A&R Studios, New York, April 29, 1968; photograph by Francis Wolff.

rehearsals, concerts, recording sessions, dance performances, and art exhibitions.[198] Drummer Rashied Ali (1933–2009), who worked with Paul Bley, recorded with John Coltrane, and later played with pianist Alice Coltrane, described the arrangement:

> Ornette would give out the space to musicians. It wasn't even about renting the space. He would give it to you for almost nothing. We would produce and perform our own concerts there. We were the producer, the performer, did all the leg work, the PR work and everything like that in order to get

people to come. That was a hell of an experience. It taught me a lot. It gave me an incentive to open up a space like that.[199]

The lofts fostered a cooperative form of economics as opposed to the competitive model deployed by the commercial mainstream. No one had everything; every performance was of necessity a group project involving varied resources and talents. Marginality meant freedom, not only in arts production but in the pursuit of a lifestyle where living and working were not separate activities and the individual was beneficially bound to the collective. For a while at least, the fringe was the place to be. The profit was in the process.

Ornette's third-floor living quarters at Prince Street was furnished with "a life raft instead of a couch, and a hammock," recalled Denardo.[200] There was a Chinese folding screen and a pool table that caught the light of one of several large windows, as did the desk where he composed. A kitchen area was installed and eventually a sauna, a concession to luxury in the otherwise unheated space. A big dining table occupied the center and a mynah bird that lived in a cage by the door greeted guests by squawking "good morning."[201] "We all were doing something—*doing*—we were not talking about money, that was the last thing—we share what we have," said Martine Barrat, Parisian dancer and photographer who moved to New York in 1968 to work with Ellen Stewart, director of the La MaMa Experimental Theatre Club on the Lower East Side. Barrat ran video and music workshops for local and Harlem youth, part of which consisted of visiting Ornette on Prince Street. "Ornette was part of all the things going on," said Barrat, "everybody was crazy with music."[202]

Music was an active and salutatory presence in many community projects. Chino Garcia (1946–), cofounder of the Real Great Society, enlisted musicians in an effort to reverse the inertia of addiction and joblessness in Puerto Rican and Latino communities on the Lower East Side and in Harlem. "We knew that through art and music we could gather people together faster than by just putting out a leaflet and telling them to come to our meetings," said Garcia. "We didn't like the idea that there was a whole bunch of social workers and other agencies making millions out of our problems and we felt we could solve [them] ourselves.[203] Tenor saxophonist Jackie McLean was one of several musicians working with addicts in neighborhood rehab programs. CHARAS, as the group was renamed, was originally headquartered on Avenue A and eventually moved to an old school building (El Bohio) covering two residential blocks (between Avenues B and C) where large spaces were devoted to performances or rented out for music, dance, and theater rehearsals at $5 an hour.

When local musicians decided to protest the elitist 1972 "Newport in New York" festival produced by George Wein, they met at Chino's place to mount a simultaneous counter event. Wien's festival used upscale venues such as Carnegie Hall and Lincoln Center that, however prestigious, were removed from the neighborhoods and collectives where music was actually produced. "The entrepreneurs have been able too long to determine what the musicians will play, where they'll play it and when," said Archie Shepp, one of the alternative festival organizers. Artists House was a venue for the July New York Musician's Jazz Festival held in parks, community centers, lofts, and at Slugs, a rough and tumble jazz joint on the edge of the Lower East Side (242 East 3rd Street). It lasted eleven days with over 250 performances, many of them admission-free.[204]

A Harlem branch of Garcia's Real Great Society became the headquarters of an offshoot initiative, the Resurrection Workshop, led by Felipe Floresca (1951–), a half-Russian, half-Filipino eighteen-year-old raised in Spanish Harlem. Floresca had participated in an educational program, Harlem Youth Opportunities Unlimited (HARYOU), founded by civil rights activists and psychologists Kenneth and Mamie Clark. He also worked as an errand boy to Congressman Adam Clayton Powell Jr., who obtained funding for HARYOU after the Harlem riots as part of Lyndon Johnson's 1964 social welfare legislation ("America's war on poverty"). Renamed HARYOU-ACT, the group broadened its reach, sponsoring concerts as part of a jazz appreciation program, and Ornette, whom Powell admired, was one of the performing artists.[205]

The Resurrection Workshop (1968–70) aimed at uniting the Young Lords (a turf gang that grew into an advocacy group for Latino citizens) with their African American counterpart, the Black Panthers, to assist a disadvantaged multiethnic community. Floresca organized free testing for sickle cell anemia and tuberculosis, community breakfasts culled from local merchants' contributions, and poetry sessions featuring, among others, Jayne Cortez and Affendi Shakur (mother of rapper Tupac). While Shakur was a Panther and overtly political, Jayne "never talked political ideology." She did, however, encourage kids to be a part of their community. "Jayne talked about movements, how there should be no divide [between black and brown people] because they faced the same issues," said Floresca. "She was a bridge."[206]

The goal of greater connectedness between individuals and communities pre-dates the Internet and was arguably better achieved in the absence of social media, when everything was geared towards real-life encounters. The closer one was to one's community, the more connected to the world, a sentiment preserved in Ornette's *Friends and Neighbors: Live at Prince Street*, recorded on Valentine's Day 1970. With Dewey blowing a righteous tenor, Blackwell and Haden laying down a heavy groove, and Ornette going interplanetary on violin, the audience sings the chorus of the title track: "Friends and neighbors / That's where it's at / Friends and neighbors / That's a fact / Hand in hand / That's the goal / All the world / Soul, soul, soul."[207]

Ornette's fifth-floor neighbor was Emmanuel Ghent (1925–2003), a French Canadian psychoanalyst and composer who had also been awarded a Guggenheim Fellowship in 1967. Inventor of the "coordinome," which transmitted pulses at different tempos to musicians via earphones so they could play together in separate time signatures, Ghent worked at Bell Laboratories. One of his projects was adapting an electronic speech synthesizer to produce music, a system he developed to incorporate theater lights that brightened and dimmed to the computer-generated sound.[208] Ornette collaborated with Ghent, who contributed electronic effects to a composition entitled "Man on the Moon," a rare jazz single (Impulse!, 1969) recorded in June, prior to the Apollo 11 launch and the first lunar landing (July 20, 1969).[209] Ornette had begun exploring the theme with his 1968 composition "Space Flight" for string quartet that he described as "a sound being made from Speed and Destiny of notes not restricted even though they are written down."[210]

To lend a hand at Artists House, Ornette's cousin James Jordan moved to New York in 1970 from Columbus, Texas, where he'd

Ornette Coleman's *New York Is Now* session, A&R Studios, New York, April 29, 1968; photograph by Francis Wolff.

directed the award-winning marching and concert bands of Riverside High School. Jordan, who later directed the music program of the New York State Council for the Arts, supervised renovations on the ground floor at Prince Street and helped organize and advertise the events held there with increasing frequency.[211] In addition to the performance space, Ornette shared his third-floor home with musicians, some passing through, others trying to make their way in the city. Saxophonist and composer Julius Hemphill (1938–1995), a distant relative of Ornette's and an I. M. Terrell graduate, came from St. Louis, where he worked with the Black Artists Group, a collective of filmmakers, dramatists, visual artists, and musicians. At Prince Street, Hemphill produced the kind of multimedia event for which he is often remembered, incorporating music, video, dance, and the spoken word.

Prince Street was a port of call for violinist Leroy Jenkins and saxophonist Anthony Braxton, members of the Chicago arts and music collective the Association for the Advancement of Creative Musicians (AACM), on their return from a long Paris sojourn. Established in 1965, the AACM embodied the values of the time, fostering the cross-fertilization of the arts while advancing the cause of African American cultural expression in the midst of the civil rights struggle. Managed by artists, independent of industry resources or constraints, AACM fueled the Black Arts movement through concerts, exhibitions, publications, and events. Their motto "Ancient to the future" announced the intention to prioritize historicity and to endure, and so they have, celebrating their first half-century in 2015.[212]

Ornette befriended and maintained lifelong ties with AACM founding members Muhal Richard Abrams (1930–2017) and Henry Threadgill (1944–), both composers and multi-instrumentalists. He was an inspirational reference for the Art Ensemble of Chicago (AEC), started by AACM members Roscoe Mitchell (who composed a song called "Ornette" in 1966) and Joseph Jarman, both multi-instrumentalists and accomplished painters. AEC musicians appeared onstage in costumes and masks or face paint, playing traditional western, African, and other instruments, in addition to installations of sound-makers: gongs, conch shells, bike horns and congas, washboards and whistles, trash cans, and hub caps. "The group demonstrated a readiness to attempt *anything*," including all aspects of jazz, wrote John Rockwell, who called AEC "a kind of a traveling compendium of black musical history.[213] By embracing varied performance possibilities, AEC exemplified the AACM's mission, which, like that of other contemporary collectives, was to unite the arts and change the world—no less. As Anthony Braxton put it, in 1968,

> That the West is in the eleventh hour is now un-debatable.
> We must redefine every aspect of what we now call art . . .
> We must bring spiritual awareness . . . to the center of the
> stage . . . Steps must be taken to show that all art is one.[214]

"Spiritual awareness" meant striving on a personal and group level to achieve a deeper, world-changing humanity through the transformative power of music and the arts, a cause Ornette believed in. In 1971 he helped establish the Woodstock, New York-based Creative Music Studio (CMS, still in operation), "dedicated to the research of the power of music and sound and the elements common to all of the world's music forms."[215]

In 1973, fresh from trips to Nigeria and Morocco, Ornette held a reception for international music journalists at Artists House, which was "a bit like a futuristic school room," wrote Richard Williams for *Melody Maker*.[216] After catching them up on his African adventures, Ornette treated the journalists to a command performance by his South African house guest, Abdullah Ibrahim (formerly Dollar Brand), a "singular and intense experience" that Williams vividly relates:

> He began . . . with a hymn tune direct from the African
> Methodist Episcopal Church in which he worshiped and

sang as a child . . . harmonies that resonated with the richness of entire choirs. Then he changed gear, into a dance tune that moved to a swaying, sinuous beat and gathered momentum until it sounded like a whole township stepping out. Changing up again, his hands began to hammer great tremolos at both ends of the keyboard . . . in a gigantic crescendo . . . Just when it seemed that the intensity might burst the windows, Ibrahim backed off . . . rewound slowly and with infinite care through the dance tune and the hymn, and deposited us back where he had found us, in silence—except that the silence now sounded completely different. As each listener raised his head, he saw something in the others' eyes: an emotion that linked the German, the Brazilian, the Japanese and the Englishman to the most profound recesses of what Hoagy Carmichael called jazz's "deep, dark blue centre." Thanks to a South African pianist in a New York loft, they had touched the core.[217]

One of the last performances at Prince Street (December 1975) was a benefit for Ed Blackwell, who was suffering from kidney failure and staying with Ornette. The neighborhood was changing; new building tenants complained of the noise. Ornette was obliged to relinquish the ground floor in 1974 and would soon be forced out altogether. A number of musicians participated in the benefit concert held on the third floor, including Ornette, Billy Higgins, pianist Randy Weston, and multi-instrumentalist Rahsaan Roland Kirk, who was himself in poor health at the time.[218] The international jazz community mobilized on Blackwell's behalf with *DownBeat* and *Coda* (UK) launching fundraising campaigns and friends organizing benefits in London and in Blackwell's hometown, New Orleans. The donations weren't enough for a transplant, but Blackwell received life-saving treatment he would otherwise have been unable to afford. He lived and performed until 1992, when he became the first of the original Coleman Quartet to pass on.

Ornette left Prince Street in 1976 after a bitter court process, and was without a home of his own until 1982.[219] Loft performances continued as the scenius limped into the 1980s but the network eventually succumbed to the capitalist imperative. When composer Steve Reich recalled "the sense of the creative world as a community rather than, as now, an arena of entrepreneurial gladiators," he was speaking in 1978.[220] Having transformed derelict neighborhoods into thriving urban econiches, underground artists became the victims of their own success, but for nearly thirty years they'd given the status quo a run for its money. That New York still bears the gloss of those decades is proof that a city has no better ally than a self-determined arts community, and cities that leave no place for them have forgotten their purpose. By extending the improvisational group dynamic embodied in the music of Ornette and his peers to encompass the creative process as a way of life, the New York scenius yielded a body of artistically and socially significant work. The international avant-garde was, in many ways, a house built by jazz.

Poster art for Shirley Clarke's *Ornette: Made in America* (1985),
quoting an interview with Ornette from the film. The facade of the
Caravan of Dreams Performing Arts Center appears in the foreground, left.

Part Three: Atmospherics

We must try to construct situations, that is to say collective
ambiances, ensembles of impressions determining the
quality of a moment.

GUY DEBORD

Nowadays it's common for musicians, especially rappers, to be
awarded the key to a city whether or not it's their hometown,
often for some act of philanthropy in addition to musical achievement. The Memphis rap group Three 6 Mafia received one in 2006,
shortly after winning an Oscar for their hit song "It's Hard out Here
for a Pimp." It was somewhat harder out in Memphis for Louis
Armstrong, arrested in 1931 for sitting next to his manager's wife (a
white woman) on the tour bus. After a night behind bars, Armstrong
performed to an audience that included the cops who locked him
up, to whom he dedicated his opening number: "I'll Be Glad When
You're Dead, You Rascal You." Black musicians were more likely to
see jail keys than city keys back then. But in 1965 Armstrong
received the key to his birthplace, New Orleans, where he had been
arrested at age nine for allegedly shooting a gun and was consequently
interned in the city's Colored Waifs' Home. In 1977 Ed Blackwell
also received the key to New Orleans, having left town a decade earlier to escape prosecution for the crime of miscegenation (marrying
a white woman).[1]

Part appeasement ritual, part publicity stunt, the bestowal of city
keys nonetheless signals recognition, the kind Ornette amply deserved
when he became the first African American to be awarded a key to
Fort Worth, in 1983. On a hot late summer afternoon, Ornette and
a group of friends stood at attention while the avuncular mayor Bob

Bolen drawled his presentation speech, noting how Ornette, "born and reared" in Fort Worth, had enriched countless lives, traveled widely, "fashioned for himself an unchallenged right to historical prominence," and "demonstrated that individual initiative and the free enterprise system continue to be the American way of life." The crowd applauded as Bolen declared September 29 "Ornette Coleman Day" and handed Ornette a little box containing a key-shaped tie clip, a replica, Bolen announced, of one that had gone to the moon with Texan astronaut Alan Bean.[2]

Second-hand symbolism aside, the evocation of space exploration was appropriate to the city, now an aerospace engineering hub, and to the man, who had traveled metaphorical light years since leaving Texas. In the interim Ornette had played to enraptured audiences worldwide and his record releases were welcomed by fans and critics with the kind of enthusiastic scrutiny usually reserved for astrophysical events. He'd visited Fort Worth but rarely performed there. In 1966 his sister Trudy organized a concert at the Will Rogers Auditorium with David Izenzon and Charles Moffett.[3] It was the only time his mother Rosa came to hear him play; she'd left unopened the records he sent her over the years. Had Rosa lived until 1978 (she died in 1976), she may have had cause for pride, as Ornette was one of the musicians performing on the South Lawn of the White House that summer.

Organized by George Wien to mark the Newport Jazz festival's 25th anniversary, the event was hosted by Georgian jazz lover President Jimmy Carter and his wife Rosalyn. In his opening remarks President Carter spoke to the role that jazz ("vivid, alive, aggressive, innovative") had played in his life and that of the nation, acknowledging, as no president before him had dared, that its stature had suffered because of racism.[4] The program, broadcast live on National Public Radio, read like a lesson in jazz history, with participants such as 95-year-old ragtime pianist Eubie Blake, Sonny Rollins, Lionel Hampton, and Illinois Jacquet (who reprised his famous solo on

Hamp's "Flying Home"), Max Roach and Dizzy Gillespie (whom President Carter joined to sing the chorus of bebop classic "Salt-peanuts"), next-generation keyboard wizards Chick Corea and Herbie Hancock, and the officiating high priests of free jazz Cecil Taylor and Ornette Coleman, who performed with his son Denardo.

Ornette made another high-profile appearance in 1979, entering millions of American homes via the popular television program *Saturday Night Live* (April 14), a comedy hour led by improvisational actors. He had no home of his own and was touring exhaustively and either staying in the back room of his manager John Snyder's office or cheap hotels. October brought him the shock and grief of David Izenzon's sudden death, at the age of 47.[5] Finally in 1981, after a long stretch of nomadism, Ornette acquired (by auction) a massive five-story building at 203 Rivington Street (Lower East Side), a former schoolhouse where he hoped to expand on his Artists House venture. But he was twice attacked there by marauding junkies who took a hammer to his head on the first occasion and on the second beat him with a crowbar and a wooden plank. When Ornette came to Fort Worth in September 1983, he had just recovered from a punctured lung.

His hometown's star had risen steadily in his absence, parlaying its Second World War aviation boom into a leading position in America's defense industry. In the 1980s locally manufactured Lockheed Martin F-35s, Bell Helicopter Ospreys, and General Dynamic's F-16s whizzed through the skies of the "martial metropolis."[6] The Tandy Corporation (which started out as a shoe leather factory in 1919) was based in Fort Worth, where it established a retail electronics division (RadioShack) and, with Apple and the now defunct Commodore International, launched the personal computer revolution in 1977. Founding father Charles Tandy (1918–1978) was viewed as the visionary successor of oil mogul and Washington insider Amon Carter. Shortly before his death, Tandy started developing eight blocks of downtown Fort Worth real estate, introducing the Tandy Center, an eighteen-story twin-towered combination corporate office, upscale hotel, and shopping mall equipped with an ice skating rink and an underground train to ferry customers from the parking lot.

Every town has its rich people but Fort Worth's were some of the richest in the world, foremost among them the Bass family, heirs to an empire built by rancher and wildcatter Sid Richardson (1891–1959). Born in Athens, Texas, Sid grew up trading land and cattle like his father, but he struck oil in 1919 and was a millionaire at age thirty. Hardworking and unostentatious, he was "known for his ability to condense complicated situations into simple 'horse sense' which endeared him to presidents and business executives."[7] Franklin D. Roosevelt fished at San Jose, Richardson's private island off the west Texas coast, a 21-mile-long (34 km) nature reserve where Richardson bred cattle and saved the longhorn, the state's icon, from extinction. When he died, then senate majority leader Lyndon Johnson attended his funeral and evangelist Billy Graham conducted the services. A bachelor, Richardson left the lion's share of his estimated $800 million fortune to an educational foundation bearing his name, but his sister Anne's son, Perry Bass, who had four sons of his own, was not forgotten. Having steered their inheritance wisely, the family held prominent slots on the *Forbes* list of "America's richest." Of the four brothers who advanced (and dispersed) the Bass fortune, Ed, the second oldest, was by far the most inventive and it was in no small part thanks to him that Ornette returned home to a hero's welcome.

The black sheep of the family, Edward Perry Bass (1945–) grew up in Westover Hills, the Fort Worth neighborhood with "more millionaires per acre than any enclave in Texas." At Phillips Academy Andover in Massachusetts, America's oldest, most exclusive prep school, Ed showed signs of unconventional tastes by starting a jazz club, playing "a lot of Ornette Coleman, because he was the farthest-out thing we could find." Like his father and brothers, Ed graduated from Yale. He later returned for a master's degree in architecture, but dropped out before completing his studies. Instead of joining the family business, he hit the road, selling Navaho carpets and jewelry and settling in Santa Fe, New Mexico, "a mecca for both the jet set and the spiritually inclined."[8] In 1973 he met a group of industrious individuals living on a nearby ranch who were building adobe houses in Santa Fe and hatching plans to build a Chinese junk in San Francisco with a little cash and a lot of ingenuity. They called themselves synergists, referencing Buckminster Fuller's concept of synergetics: that the whole is greater than the sum of its parts.

Everyone on Synergia Ranch, a 160-acre (65 ha) stretch of high desert prairie, worked on both group and individual enterprises, making furniture, tending orchards, conducting hydroponic and organic grow-hole agricultural experiments while reviving the local tradition of adobe architecture; no drugs were allowed. While some synergists held college degrees, projects were advanced by energetic learning on the job. Buckminster Fuller consulted on the ranch's

Edward Perry Bass, Fort Worth Stockyards Parade,
c. 1986; photograph by Juan Gonzales.

geodesic dome, where an in-house troupe staged plays for local audiences, in addition to touring the U.S. and/or Europe annually by bus. On the road, the fourteen-member Theater of All Possibilities used the opportunity to take "eco-tours," like visiting the menhirs of Carnac (Brittany) or studying water use in the industrial cities on the banks of Germany's Ruhr River.

Aside from theater, regarded as "the revelation of the inner life of humans," the group's overriding line of inquiry was the interface between ecology and technology, forces that were increasingly at odds. In 1973 the ranch's founders established the Institute of Ecotechnics (IE) to harmonize these forces by creating economically viable and environmentally beneficial enterprises and projects, like the R/V *Heraclitus*, the Chinese junk made of ferro cement that circled the planet, studying coral reefs, whales, dolphins, and Amazonian flora and fauna.[9] Environmentalism was a nascent and appealing discipline to Ed Bass, who admired his great uncle Sid's conservationist efforts. With his new friends, he participated in a series of apposite joint ventures, including a 1,000-acre (400 ha) sustainable timber plantation in the tropical forest of Puerto Rico, a hotel and cultural center in Kathmandu, a cattle ranch in Australia's savannah grasslands, a conference center/farm in Aix-en-Provence, and a derelict Victorian schoolhouse in London the group renovated as an art gallery and performance space. While Ed helped front the money, the projects were designed to be self-sustaining and developed on a shoestring budget with synergists doing nearly all the work themselves.[10]

Meanwhile, back in Fort Worth, the Bass family fortune was multiplying like the proverbial loaves and fishes. Under the guidance of Lebanese-American financier Richard Rainwater, the eldest brother, Sid (1942–), made a series of stellar investments and acquired a substantial portion of Fort Worth's run-down city center with urban rehabilitation in mind. In 1982, when Bass Enterprises was installed in a 32-story mirror-sheathed tower known locally as "the big black building," downtown Fort Worth consisted of little more than a scattering of defeated storefronts groveling at its feet.[11] When Ed came to town, he stayed at the Blackstone Hotel, where Ornette had once shined shoes, and, surveying the hollow albeit historic urban shell around him, consulted his IE colleagues as to how they might turn things around.

The result was a project for a world-class performing arts facility "designed and managed by and for artists," whose purpose was to revive the city center by providing "a meeting place for the creation of new forms of music, theater, dance, poetry and film."[12] Referencing the last tale of the *1001 Nights*, they named it the Caravan of Dreams.[13] While jazz venues in New York and elsewhere had folded for lack of audiences, the Caravan aimed to revive the live jazz tradition, only Texas-style. No smoked-filled subterranean cranny, this was "a space worthy of the accomplishments of great performers and connoisseurs of jazz, blues and freeform."[14] Ornette Coleman, native son and free jazz maverick, was the perfect choice for the opening act.

Caravan of Dreams Performing Arts Center, 312 Houston Street, 1983, with Tandy Center in the background, prior to its opening.

Designed by Margaret Augustine, CEO of Biospheric Design (formerly Sarbid, Ltd.), a company formed to execute Institute of Ecotechnics projects, the Caravan covered 131,000 square feet (12,200 sq. m) on Houston Street, downtown. Several early nineteenth-century facades were preserved, but the vintage exterior belied an inner structure employing arches, vaults, and clerestories and serving an unusual range of functions. The first floor held a three-hundred-seat nightclub and restaurant, where the Caravan logo, a neon genie smoking a hookah, shimmered softly behind a long and lustrous brass-fitted oak bar. Lushly carpeted, outfitted with oak tables and comfortable chairs, the club was decorated with murals depicting

Portion of the jazz history mural depicting (L–R) the World Wars;
Swing era; New York's Chrysler Building; the Space Age; and experimental
jazz pioneers (far right) Charles Mingus, Ornette Coleman, Thelonious Monk,
John Coltrane, Charlie Parker, and others. Painters: Zara Kriegstein,
Flash Allen, Corinna MacNeice, and Felipe Cebeza de Vaca, 1983,
Caravan of Dreams Performing Arts Center, Fort Worth.

the history of jazz, beginning with the slave ships' arrival through
the first spaceship's departure and ending with a portrait of Ornette.
Plush split-level dressing room and bathroom facilities for the musicians were situated adjacent to the stage. A jewel-like 212-seat theater
with a spacious lobby bar occupied the second floor, along with well-
appointed living quarters and a library for synergists and visiting

artists. There was a karate dojo in the basement, plus storage and administrative areas.

Everything was state-of-the-art, including a sound studio for recording live from the club and theater. On the roof, a 165-foot (50 m) geodesic dome made of plexiglass and studded with neon sculptures housed a collection of cacti from around the world, chosen to represent "'the avant-garde' of nature . . . able to adapt to testing conditions . . . taking advantage of each chance rain."[15] An elevator was purposefully omitted, obliging customers to climb a grand stairway admiring artwork or absorbing information about current performances posted along the way. The *pièce de résistance* was the rooftop Grotto Bar, an open-air lounge with a miniature waterfall issuing from a 15-foot-high (4.5 m) ersatz mountain in the geodesic dome, where a giant Sonoran saguaro and a medusa-like Malagasy succulent stood in defiant juxtaposition to the bland nearby Bass Towers.

The Caravan of Dreams' founders drew inspiration from a collage of sources: the Transcendentalists, Surrealism, the Beat poets, and Tibetan Buddhism; the works of Brecht, Artaud, Jarry, and biogeochemist Vladimir Vernadsky; and friends like Charles Mingus, ethnologist Konrad Lorenz, Timothy Leary, William Burroughs, Brion Gysin, painter Gerald Wilde, and Tamil poet and publisher Tambimuttu. If "Cowtown" seemed an unlikely spot for such a confluence, it was also at the vanguard of another kind of synthesis, the consolidation of corporate culture (as a way of life and political force) and of the "military industrial complex" that President Dwight Eisenhower, in his 1961 farewell speech, had solemnly warned the nation against. The Caravan of Dreams appeared in downtown Fort Worth like an antibody born to neutralize a pathogenic conservatism.

It was *New York Times* music critic John Rockwell who suggested that Ornette open the Caravan of Dreams to Kathelin Hoffman Gray, its artistic director, a former Synergia Rancher and Institute of Ecotechnics cofounder. Raised in Monterey, California, Gray (1949–) befriended Rockwell in 1967 while both were studying with postmodern dance doyenne Anna Halprin in San Francisco. Gray found Ornette in the New York phone book, but his phone was out of order, so she left a note taped to his Rivington Street door. When they finally met in 1982, she described the Fort Worth project and asked if he'd be willing to come to Texas and take part. Ornette readily agreed and asked what exactly she wanted. Gray returned the question and upon reflection Ornette said he wanted to perform with his latest group, Prime Time, an electrified septet with a funky edge, but he also wanted a string quartet, a symphony orchestra, a record, and a film. The 33-year-old Gray, cofounder of the Theater of All Possibilities, unblinkingly said "OK" and set about producing a week-long combination Ornette Coleman homecoming/Caravan of Dreams opening extravaganza.[16]

Ornette Coleman opening the Caravan of Dreams, 1983.

The festivities began on September 29, 1983, when Ornette's monumental *Skies of America* (1972) was performed by the Fort Worth Symphony Orchestra and Prime Time in the Convention Center auditorium. On September 30 and October 1, Prime Time played in the Caravan nightclub, Ornette clad in an iridescent rainbow-hued jacket matching the one he was wearing in the jazz mural. On October 2, Ornette's composition for string quartet and percussion, *Prime Design/Time Design*, dedicated to his "best hero" Buckminster Fuller, premiered on the building's roof in the geodesic dome.[17] From October 3–5, Ornette's Dallas friend James Clay (tenor) and Clint Strong (guitar) celebrated a Texas music tradition embracing blues, R&B, country, and bebop. On October 6–8, percussionist and multi-instrumentalist Jack DeJohnette led his group, Special Edition, on an expedition through dynamic free jazz compositions. On October 7, Ornette's fellow iconoclasts Brion Gysin and William Burroughs inaugurated the Caravan Theater. The performances of Prime Time, the string quartet and Burroughs's reading were recorded and later released on the Caravan of Dreams Productions record label. On October 8, the theater launched its "Planetary Film" series with a retrospective of independent filmmaker Shirley Clarke, who was on hand to shoot the entire week's proceedings as part of the documentary *Ornette: Made in America,* produced by Kathelin Gray and released in 1985.[18]

While announcing the Caravan's intention to advance on several programming fronts, each homecoming event held personal significance for Ornette, beginning with the performance of *Skies of America*. Written with the help of his 1967 Guggenheim grant, an abridged version was recorded in 1972 by the London Philharmonic, replacing the portions designated for jazz quartet with Ornette alone on sax. Released by Columbia's jazz division, the LP was "banded" into separate cuts, ostensibly to get more radio play, but according to Ornette, "[Columbia producers] were trying to keep it from having the image of a symphony . . . it was just another social-racial problem." John Rockwell found the recording's effect "sectional but unified," and praised the composition's

> driving polytonal passages—sometimes on their own some-
> times supporting [Ornette's] soaring solos—alternating with
> slower grander statements that recall the chordal calm of
> American folk Symphonists. There are, certainly, moments
> of naïveté and clumsiness in the conception, arrangement and
> execution of this fresco. But the overall impact is Ivesian in
> scope and in spirit, too. Very few first efforts are so powerful
> as this.[19]

Ornette's symphony was inspired by a visit to the Montana reserva-
tion of the Native American Crow people and the wish "to describe
the beauty [of America], and not have it be racial or [pertaining to]
any territory."[20]

With this expansive work, Ornette situated himself in the tradition of aural Americana essayed by Charles Ives (1874–1954) and
exemplified by Aaron Copland (1900–1990). Copland saw jazz as "a
style of music the whole world recognized as specifically American"
and felt that the same could be done "in the field of serious, concert
music."[21] His *Symphony for Organ and Orchestra* (1924) captured the
angular cacophony of boom-town New York, while subsequent compositions quoted folk and jazz themes; some of the spare passages of
his *Piano Variations* (1930) seemed to mimic the vocalizations called
"scat." Many subsequent American composers of "serious music"
drank at the fount of jazz, but in 1968, appraising the work of Ornette
and fellow Texan Jimmy Giuffre, Copland observed that the "tables
had been turned," with "jazz more influenced by serious music than
the other way around."[22]

For Ornette, it was less a matter of influence or of wishing to emulate modern composers than of furthering his creative process through
music scored for a variety of instruments while exploring—and

Kathelin Gray, Ornette Coleman, and John Giordano looking over
the score for *Skies of America*, 1983; photograph by Brian Blauser.

challenging—different forms. *Skies of America* called for passages of
improvisation on behalf of a 96-piece orchestra and interludes of
Prime Time's free jazz. The alternation between elegiac, admonishing
string movements and the rhythmic fractals of Prime Time, each
playing eight themes, suggested a single world governed by different
logics.[23] While Ornette performed *Skies* for the first time in its entirety
at the Philharmonic Hall for George Wien's New York Jazz Festival
in 1972, he was also hosting the alternative New York Musicians Jazz
Festival at Artists House.[24] His symphony, like his 1962 Town Hall
concert, carried the Whitmanesque message "I am large. I contain
multitudes."

When Ornette requested that *Skies of America* be part of his 1983
homecoming, Kathelin Gray contacted John Giordano (1937–), music
director and conductor for the Fort Worth Symphony Orchestra
(1972–99). Giordano, who coincidentally played saxophone as a teen-
ager with Ornette in southside Fort Worth jam sessions, jumped at
the opportunity, which involved a degree of flexibility on his part
and on that of an often perplexed orchestra:

I got the score and no one knew what to do with it. The notation was not accurate, rhythmically. I was familiar with some of [Ornette's] recordings and having known Ornette I had an idea of what he was doing, and an idea of alleatoric music [indeterminacy]. So what I did was sing the various parts to the orchestra and said, ok when I signal you, you come in, or you, you come in, and then we improvise here—it was kind of concerto grosso style. Prime Time would play, then the orchestra, then Prime Time. I'd have a certain signal for the strings to improvise behind Prime Time . . . and the concert ended up being very successful, which was kind of magic.[25]

After their Fort Worth collaboration, Giordano worked intensively with Ornette to re-orchestrate *Skies* prior to six performances of the symphony with Prime Time in Europe (1987–8). A decade later, the New York Philharmonic performed *Skies of America* at Avery Fisher Hall as part of the Lincoln Center Music festival directed by

John Giordano and Ornette Coleman rehearsing *Skies of America*, 1983.

Ornette Coleman, Prime Time, and the Fort Worth Symphony Orchestra
onstage at the Fort Worth Convention Center, September 29, 1983.

John Rockwell, who attended the Caravan of Dreams opening and
reviewed it for the *New York Times*.[26] There were nine performances
of *Skies* in Ornette's lifetime, his first and last symphony. He was
unable to find funds or a producer for a second major work he planned
to call *The Oldest Language*, envisaged as a two- to three-hour piece
for a 125-member orchestra including two musicians from every state
in the union in addition to one from 22 different world cultures.

The 2,500-seat Fort Worth Convention Center was filled to capacity for *Skies of America*, a turn-out that reflected Ed Bass's and the
Fort Worth Symphony's cachet rather more than Ornette's, whose
existence most locals had previously ignored. The musicians nonetheless received a standing ovation from the audience in evening
dress, some of whom politely repressed their squirms during the
eighty-minute opus. Then came the after-party at the "phantasma-
gorically ambitious" Caravan of Dreams, built at a cost of $5.5
million.[27] A lavish affair with a buffet "piled high with shrimp and
fancy foods" prepared by a Japanese chef, the party attracted a

cross-section of local society, "from cowhands and collegiates [*sic*], to bankers and society matrons, to hipsters."[28] Invitations called for black tie or costume; women draped in gowns and diamonds lined up to congratulate Ornette, calling him "honey"; men came in feathered masks, "oil sheikh" (Gulf Arab) headgear, and the obligatory cowboy boots. Ed Bass wore a white tuxedo, his dimpled face flushed with pleasure and his throat glowing Shiva blue in the light of his neon bowtie.

KATHELIN GRAY MET William Burroughs and Brion Gysin in the mid-1970s, developing a friendship born of shared interests in "biospherics and space age mythology." As "primary inspirations" for the Caravan of Dreams, she invited them to inaugurate the theater and in doing so reunited them with Ornette, whom they'd met a decade earlier under unusual circumstances.[29] On October 7, 1983, Burroughs and Gysin read to a standing-room-only crowd in the Caravan Theater, including a contingent of punks from Dallas, in chains, leather, and not-yet-trendy (in Texas) piercings. As a writer, Burroughs (1914–1997) was the opposite of mainstream but still famous and widely referenced in pop culture.[30] A former junkie who shot his wife in the head at a dinner party and managed to get away with it thanks to his family's money, his dystopian novels were either scorned or lauded by his peers, including Norman Mailer, who in 1962 famously suggested Burroughs was "possessed by genius."

The size and enthusiasm of the Texas turn-out for Burroughs's appearance was somewhat unexpected; then again, his graveyard humor, deadpan dialogues, fondness for guns, and antiheros like his ghoulish Dr. Benway held local appeal. To his fans, Burroughs's dry, saturnine persona was alluring and his every utterance seemed to issue, oracle-like, from an ancient bone. His urbane, charismatic cohort, Brion Gysin (1916–1986), was not as well known, but the unlikely pair made a compelling double act, one that launched a thousand avant-garde ships while they lived and left a growing body of derivative and documentary works in their wake.[31]

When Burroughs and Gysin first met at an exhibition in Tangier in 1954, they disliked one another instantly. At the time, Gysin was operating a restaurant in the casbah called the 1001 Nights, a hotspot for expat glitterati. Gysin told Bowles he wanted nothing to do with junkies, and Burroughs described Gysin as "a paranoid bitch on wheels." But when they met again in Paris in 1958, Burroughs discovered in Gysin "a superb raconteur" whose renditions of "Greek mythology . . . of the magical universe and of Arab culture at its most outré" were appetizers in a decades-long conversational feast the two dished up in novels, essays, painting, sound collage, and performance.[32] Connoisseurs of history and close followers of scientific and technological advances, particularly the prospect of space exploration, Burroughs and Gysin were likewise intrigued by the notion of heightened consciousness, magical powers, and the ideas of synchronicity (meaningful coincidence) and "third mind," an intellectual dimension arising in the course of intensely collaborative projects, that is, the mind of the project itself. In short, they were interested in the tenuous links humans maintain with a broader reality and the possibility of freely accessing it, whether assisted by drugs, sex, art, or what might be called situationality, the ceaseless pursuit of the *rarissime*.

By age 32, Gysin had traveled in the Algerian Sahara, served in the Second World War, written a history of slavery in Canada, and studied Japanese, and was developing a style of painting characterized by grids and incantatory repetitions of an imagined calligraphy. In 1950, invited by author Paul Bowles, he visited Morocco and decided to live there. His sound experiments began in 1960, when he produced "Pistol Poem" for the BBC by firing a studio gun (used for radio plays) at intervals of increasing distance from the microphone and layering the recorded tracks. A similar technique was adopted by composer Steve Reich, who created a tape loop of an evangelical preacher shouting "It's gonna rain!" (1965), playing it back on two

William S. Burroughs and
Brion Gysin in the Caravan of
Dreams geodesic dome, 1983;
photograph by Brian Blauser.

machines at different speeds. Gysin popularized the cut-up method
essayed by Parisian Surrealists to create poems in the 1920s, much
loved by Burroughs, which consisted of randomly connecting fragments of text and/or sound into chance-freshened compositions.

The two began performing together in the early 1960s, notably
at mixed media events with the Domaine Poetique, an offshoot of
Domaine Musical, the collective that introduced electronic music to
Paris in the 1950s. At a 1965 performance at London's Institute of
Contemporary Arts, Gysin "feverishly" painted a gigantic scroll of
paper while Burroughs sat immobile onstage, staring at a "visibly
unnerved" audience while stills from *Towers Open Fire* (an Anthony
Balch film based on a Burroughs text and starring Burroughs) were
projected above his head. A cut-up soundtrack he'd concocted played
at "ear-splitting volume," featuring Moroccan music, radio static, and
himself reading newspaper articles about disasters involving the
number 23.[33]

Burroughs and Gysin's more sedate but nonetheless subversive Texas appearance began with the latter reading from a work in progress about "the richest little boy in all the world," which in a town like Fort Worth seemed appropriate. As did Burroughs's selection, covering topics "from the Old West to the powerful board rooms of corporate America where 'the president of the United States is just an errand boy', to gang war battlegrounds, to ancient Egypt."[34] Frail but formidable (his 33-year-old son had died six months before of liver failure), Burroughs delivered his opening line in a voice like a creaky door: "Immortality to the people. Every man a god."[35] Ornette was in the audience, listening intently. His first meeting with Burroughs and Gysin was in 1973, when he recorded in Morocco with the Master Musicians of Joujouka, an experience that opened the next chapter of his artistic life.

Ornette Coleman, William S. Burroughs, and Brion Gysin on the Caravan of Dreams rooftop, 1983; photograph by Ira Cohen.

African culture was a source of interest and inspiration among artists in the 1960s and '70s, and some of Ornette's closest friends had pilgrimaged there. Don Cherry and Ed Blackwell visited Morocco in the 1960s and no doubt returned with stories about the people and the music. The peripatetic Cherry called his 1964 trip to Morocco his "first big adventure," one of many subsequent "acoustic expeditions" where he explored new instruments "in natural settings like in a catacomb or on a mountaintop or by the side of a lake."[36] Ed Blackwell traveled to Morocco on a State Department-funded tour of Africa in 1967 with pianist and composer Randy Weston. Jayne Cortez and Houston-born sculptor Melvin Edwards, whom she later married, visited Ilé-Ife, Nigeria, in 1970, "the Vatican of Yoruban culture," where Edwards studied metalworking and was inspired by the myth of the blacksmith Ogun, the Nigerian Vulcan. Jayne felt so strong a connection with the country that she requested her ashes be scattered there.[37]

Ornette ventured to Africa in 1972, traveling with his cousin James Jordan and choosing Ibadan, in the Yoruba heartland of southwestern Nigeria, as a destination, likewise attracted by local traditions of music and art. Ornette loved gadgetry and as an early advocate of home videos he traveled with a camera, later screening his clips for visitors to Artists House. In 1973 music writer Richard Williams saw footage of Ornette with Nigerian musicians playing in the street:

> drummers, pipers, and an old man sawing away at a one-string African fiddle. They're all swinging like the clappers. But wait, an alien sound impinges on this musical maelstrom. It's a trumpet-high and piping but unmistakably from the Western World. The camera moves slightly, revealing a black man in a suit blowing the trumpet with an alto sax slung around his neck.[38]

When Robert Palmer interviewed Ornette post-Nigeria, he was wearing a "sparkling green tunic" and showing paintings by Yoruba chieftain Zacheus Olowonubi Oloruntoba in the Artists House storefront.[39] An herbalist and tribal shaman, Oloruntoba (1934–2014) sometimes worked with vegetable dyes made from roots and herbs whose curative properties, he said, were transmitted through his canvases, vivid imaginings of a liminal space occupied by ghosts, mortals, and gods. Oloruntoba believed that "painting, like music, has strong magical powers," a concept congenial to Ornette, who had seen the healing release music provided in the Pentecostal churches of his youth.[40]

Ornette's trip to Morocco came about thanks to Palmer (1945–1997), then contributing editor at *Rolling Stone* magazine. Growing up in segregated Little Rock, Arkansas, Palmer played clarinet and saxophone and was the only white boy in local black bands. In the late 1960s he recorded two albums with a jazzed-up folk octet whose name, Insect Trust, was borrowed from Burroughs's *Naked Lunch*. Palmer loved the Rolling Stones; he jammed and hung out with them, doing a lot more drugs than is good for anyone. When John Rockwell hired him in 1976 to cover rock and jazz for the *New York Times*, he came to work in a "long white sort of Berber robe with a red beard and sandals," which, said Rockwell, "did not fit into the culture of the News Room." Palmer had an addiction problem but he was a brilliant and versatile critic, as interested in avant-garde and minimalist composers as he was in jazz, rock, and blues, and totally enamored of Ornette's music.[41]

Palmer had reviewed Brion Gysin's Morocco-inspired novel *The Process* (1969) for *Rolling Stone*, eliciting an invitation to visit him in Tangier. In 1971 he booked passage on a Yugoslav freighter and traveled with Gysin to the village of Joujouka, a place of "elliptical mountains, rolling fields, valley villages, and enormous trees."[42] Ornette listened to the tapes Palmer made on that journey and surprised him by saying, "let's go." Having secured funding from

Untitled painting by Chief Zacheus Olowonubi Oloruntoba
in Ornette's apartment on 36th Street, New York, made with vegetable
dyes and ink on cloth; photograph by Denardo Coleman.

Columbia Records for the trip and equipment to record on site with
Palmer's assistance, Ornette traveled to Joujouka in January 1973,
accompanied again by his cousin James Jordan.

In the early 1950s Moroccan painter Mohamed Hamri introduced
Brion Gysin to the "fleshpots, magic and misery of the Moors,"
including the village of Joujouka, his mother's birthplace.[43] An otherwise typical farming village two hours south of Tangier, lacking
electricity and sewage, Joujouka was distinguished by the tomb of
Sidi Ahmad Sheikh, a personage locals believed had brought Islam
to the region. Like many Sufi shrines, Sidi Ahmad's attracted pilgrims
seeking cures for infertility and other perceived ailments and was the

centerpiece for a feast, or *moulid*, where music played a cathartic role.[44] The Joujouka musicians primarily played *tbel*, a twin-headed drum; *ghaita* and *lira*, instruments resembling the oboe and flute, respectively; and *kamanja* (violin). Robert Palmer was impressed by the flautists' ability to sustain notes, apparently without using circular breathing. He described the sound as "flutes floating free over a pile-driver 6/8 rhythm straight down from remotest Near Eastern antiquity, and the drummers shouting *aiwa* [Arabic for 'yes']."[45]

Sidi Ahmad's feast featured two personages, Bou Jeloud (translated both as "father of skins" and "father of fear"), a man cloaked in a freshly skinned goat pelt and a floppy straw hat; and Aisha Hamouka ("crazy Aisha"), who lures Bou Jeloud to the village and is "danced by a crowd of little boys dressed as women."[46] Bou Jeloud carries a branch he uses to swat women gathered around the ceremonial bonfire to enhance their fecundity. To Gysin, the feast was reminiscent of both the Lupercalia, a Roman festival where straps of skin from

Brion Gysin,
c. 1980; photograph
by Ira Cohen.

sacrificial animals were used like Bou Jeloud's branch, and the Greek Rites of Pan, the goat-legged piper, god of shepherds and the mountain wilds. Such associations proved irresistible to the cognoscenti, and the modest village of Joujouka was soon host to friends of Gysin such as counterculture psychiatrist R. D. Laing, Rolling Stones guitarist Brian Jones, and Harvard professor Timothy Leary, who described Gysin as "one of the great hedonic mystic teachers."[47] The Joujouka musicians belonged to an extended family named Attar, Arabic for herbalist or perfumer, leading Gysin to remark that during particularly inspired performances, "instead of hearing [the music] you smell this divine perfume."[48] Burroughs, who said the Joujouka musicians looked like "a bowling team from Newark" when he first saw them, later noted that he'd smelled the divine perfume twice.[49]

The village was located an hour off-track at the end of a muddy trail that reminded Burroughs of "Missouri country roads in the 1920s."[50] However minimal the amenities, wrote Burroughs, Joujouka was "a place of casual miracles . . . food for 50 people produced on a charcoal fire in a tent no bigger than a bed-sitter kitchen." According to Burroughs, Ornette imparted "an impression of quiet strength and competence," and his first jam with the villagers was "a meeting of professionals" that lasted three hours:

> Ornette started slowly at first, feeling his way. He is clearly an expert in this musical splicing—"musical surgery" he calls it—and the music that emerged as the session developed was a palpable force felt by everyone present. Magnetic spirals spun through the room like clusters of electronic bees that meet and explode in air.[51]

While playing, Ornette quickly understood that the drummers cued the other musicians on shifts in rhythm and tonality. They were likewise checking out Ornette. Palmer and Gysin were startled when the eldest ghaita player, Djenuin, walked over to Ornette and "played certain tones at or *into* [him], like he was bouncing sonar signals off his insides, doing some kind of psychometry reading using sound."⁵²

The next night Ornette and Palmer recorded with fifteen flautists and as many drummers for an audience of tribesmen and women numbering in the hundreds. "The fires were burning," recalled James Jordan, "the musicians standing in line on the hilltop." Ornette, wearing a *djellaba* with the hood up, "looked . . . and he *sounded* like he was at home, and the feeling of what he was playing was the blues." With Jordan, Ornette visited the Cave of Bou Jeloud near Joujouka where muscians practiced, no doubt because it was cool and commanded a fine view, though local legend, probably Gysin-inspired, associated it with Pan. Later that day Ornette wrote "Music from the Cave" to record with the Joujouka musicians, selecting three pipers, three drummers, three *gimri* (a three-stringed instrument) players, a *kamanja* player, and Palmer on clarinet. Ornette played trumpet and conducted. "He found a theme, a kind of riff," said Palmer, "that was the perfect bridge from his idiom to theirs."⁵³

Ornette was struck by the musicians' stamina; although many were in their sixties and seventies, they played for hours with "more energy than any young person I've ever seen," he said. He asked the eldest, purportedly aged 110, about what music was like when he was a boy and how it had changed in his lifetime, perhaps with his own trajectory in mind. The man told Ornette, "he doesn't think about anything like that. He said if he had a young woman he could live another fifteen years." Living conditions in Joujouka were even more spartan than those of Ornette's Fort Worth childhood, and he commended his hosts' austerity, noting the musicians had nothing to live on but music and that music was considered enough. But what "really fascinated" Ornette about Joujouka was "the atmosphere of how people get along":

> I didn't see anyone getting uptight about not relating to some-
> body. That was really beautiful to see that a person could

Brion Gysin, *Black Dancers*, 1968, ink and paint on card.

maintain his own identity without trying to get you to like
him and getting along with you.[54]

Freedom and acceptance were likewise embodied in the music played
exclusively on untempered instruments that, unlike Western ones,
were not tuned to a particular note or bound to the fixed intervals
of the tempered scale. Ornette liked playing a little sharp or a little
flat, bending the intervals, and was often accused of being off-key as
if he didn't know what he was doing. With the Joujouka musicians
key was not an issue, only attunement. Natural pitch did not prevent
them from achieving unison, a musical concept Ornette understood
as an innate, essential agreement. On the contrary, with Joujouka,
the voices of the individual and the collective were so closely bound
they could scarcely be told apart.

Joujouka reminded Ornette of when he played in a "sanctified
church" where an out-of-tune piano still restored the congregation.
Having determined that church music functioned on an emotional
level, he believed the music of Joujouka operated on a higher, creative one, and concluded that "every human being has a non-tempered
psyche."[55] He had heard that someone dying of cancer was cured in

Joujouka; "I believe it," he said, "there is a music that has the quality to preserve life."[56] Musical healing was a recurring theme with Ornette post-Morocco; "I don't try to please when I play. I try to cure," he later said.[57] The Joujouka musicians marked Ornette, not because he'd discovered something new and esoteric but because their existence validated ideas he'd held since youth. If Ornette had previously been upset by spurious critiques of his sound and direction, "Joujouka got him past all that," wrote Robert Palmer, "[it] gave him back his own soul, and gave it back to him whole."[58]

It was following his return from Joujouka, between concerts in Europe with either a trio or quartet, that Ornette began assembling Prime Time, his first non-acoustic band. The personnel would shift over the course of twenty-plus years, but the configuration generally included a pair of electric guitarists, electric bassists, and drummers; in a later edition of the group, Ornette added keyboards. The band's music was sometimes described as a funkified version of "fusion," a blend of jazz and rock that emerged in the 1970s, as jazz record sales declined and musicians sought their footing on the industry's slippery slope. Miles Davis's *In a Silent Way* (Columbia, 1969) and *Bitches Brew* (Columbia, 1970) jumpstarted the fusion era (1970s–80s); his band featured younger virtuosos such as electric keyboardists Chick Corea and Herbie Hancock, guitarist John McLaughlin, and saxophonist Wayne Shorter, all of whom subsequently launched innovative, influential, and commercially successful bands. Imbued with jazz wisdom and rock logic, fusion incorporated synthesizers, whose use in composition and performance demanded a new kind of technical prowess. To a generation of listeners old enough to know jazz but young enough to be looking forward, the studio-enhanced, weirdly exhalant sounds of bands like Weather Report, Return to Forever, and the Mahavishnu Orchestra seemed to transmit a sense of knowing optimism in a high-powered, tech-intoned future.

Ornette was heading in that direction with *Science Fiction* (Columbia, 1972), an eclectic compilation of original compositions that spoke to the 1960s' enthrallment with space as well as the darker imaginings of humanity overcome by its inventions. The instruments were all acoustic but the effect was manic, martial, electrified: what space would sound like if it wasn't silent. The title track, a jittery galactic assault, is overlaid with the heavily reverbed reading of "Rock the Clock" by the poem's author, David Henderson, whose literally spaced-out words are punctuated with an infant's outraged squalls. Indian singer and later disco diva Asha Puthli adds silken, feline vocals to the R&B-inflected "All My Life" and "What Reason Could I Give," an aural odalisque reclining on a bed of crisp and complex rhythms.[59] Portions of the 1971 *Science Fiction* sessions were later released by Columbia under the title *Broken Shadows* (Columbia, 1982), including tracks featuring Dallas pianist and bandleader Cedar Walton and Fort Worth vocalist Webster Armstrong.[60] Armstrong sings on the jazzed-up "Good Girl Blues" and croons a straight-up ballad, "Is It Forever," with Ornette providing a tenderly melodious accompaniment. Both compositions sounded a note of nostalgia and perhaps for this reason were dropped from *Science Fiction*.

Ornette added electric guitarist James Blood Ulmer to his sextet in 1973, touring Europe with him in 1974. Raised in South Carolina, Ulmer (1940–) started young in his father's gospel quartet, later playing R&B and eventually moving to New York, where he worked with Ornette's friends Paul Bley and Rashied Ali. Ulmer's sound, tinged with the blues but refracted through a free jazz prism, placed him in perfect synch with Ornette. Ulmer's first album, *Tales of Captain Black*, recorded in 1978 on the Artists House label and produced by John Snyder, featured Ornette in a rare appearance as sideman, with Ulmer's vocals and guitar as full of swaggering verve as a swordfight on a ship's deck. "The [electric] guitar is to pop music what the violin is to symphonic music," said Ornette, who nurtured hopes of appealing to a wider audience and had recognized a shift in the collective ear.[61]

"Our acoustic environment has changed immensely," Bertolt Brecht wrote in 1939. Referencing a 1930s film where Fred Astaire incorporates the syncopated noise of factory machinery into a tap-dance routine, Brecht remarked on "the astonishingly close relationship between the new noises and the percussive rhythms of jazz."[62] Likewise, from the sci-fi films of the 1950s when flying saucers and aliens were accompanied by uncanny buzzes and drones, to the encyclopedic sounds reproduced in the cockpit-like complexity of synthesizer consoles, the soundtrack of the future was electronic.[63] Space was the natural destination for free jazz, and in that context,

James "Blood" Ulmer, in New York, 1993; photograph by Jimmy Katz.

pianist, composer, and bandleader Sun Ra was the first to experiment with electronic keyboards (early 1960s) and a prototype of the Minimoog synthesizer (1970).

In 1961 Herman Poole Blount (Alabama, 1914–1993) re-named himself Sun Ra (after Egyptian solar deity Amun-Ra) and with his Arkestra performed in quasi-Pharaonic costumes of shimmery synthetic fibers and headgear rigged with battery-operated flashing lights. Sun Ra, who liked to say he came from Saturn, possessed an otherworldly genius for melding the earthy and ethereal in music grounded in the jazz heartland but reaching for the stars. In 1957 he issued his "instructions to the peoples of Earth," announcing the intention "to co-ordinate the minds of peoples into a intelligent approach to the living future."[64] His oeuvre influenced the afro-futurist aesthetic emerging from the Chicago music and art collectives (AACM and AfriCOBRA), marrying the empowerment of a historic past to the possibilities of an allegorical space representing "release, fate and aspiration."[65] "When the black man rule this land / pharaoh was sitting on his throne," runs a lyric from Sun Ra's *Space Is the Place* (ABC Records, 1973), which opens with an apocalyptic maelstrom of trumpet, percussion, and synthesizer.[66]

While Ornette eschewed synthesizers per se, he'd experimented with computer-generated sound in the 1960s and reached places with his saxophone no synthesizer could be programmed to go. With Prime Time he entered new territory in terms of instrumentation, but Ornette was more down to earth, so to speak, about the sound of the future. Rather than introducing technology for its own sake, the challenge was integration, to bring all his acquired knowledge into play under changing circumstances. Guitarist Pat Metheny, who performed and recorded with Prime Time, said the band represented Ornette's effort "to transcend the wires and knobs and buttons and ascend to true soul music."[67]

The crew Ornette assembled for Prime Time included guitarist Bern Nix (1947–2017), a Berklee School of Music graduate who met

Ornette at Artists House in 1975. To Nix's more traditional jazz guitar, Charles Ellerbe added a synthesizer-rock dimension using distortion pedals attached to his amplifier.[68] Ornette knew powerhouse percussionist Ronald Shannon Jackson (1940–2013), another I. M. Terrell alumnus, from Texas and from his work in New York with Charles Mingus, Albert Ayler, Kenny Dorham, McCoy Tyner, and Jackie McLean.[69] While talent-scouting at New York's High School of Music and Art, Ornette heard Albert MacDowell (1958–) playing electric bass like a solo guitar and invited him along. Likewise, electric bassist Jamaaladeen Tacuma (1961–) was eighteen years old when he joined Prime Time, "in a raw stage" that suited Ornette's goal of constant rejuvenation.[70]

When he started rehearsing the band, Ornette insisted everyone listen to the music he had recorded in Joujouka. His experience there had helped him consolidate a "unified field theory" of music he called "harmolodics," whereby the harmony, melody, and movement (the rhythmic aspects) of a composition are assigned equal value as the

Sun Ra (left) and his Arkestra (Marshall Allen, sax, right) at the "Nuits de la Fondation Maeght," Saint-Paul-de-Vence, France, in 1970.

Ronald Shannon Jackson (left) with members of his band,
the Decoding Society, saxophonists Zane Massey (center) and bassist
Melvin Gibbs (right), at the Caravan of Dreams Performing Arts Center
in Fort Worth (Jackson's home town), March 15, 1984.

basis for improvisation.[71] In Joujouka Ornette found affirmation of
the same *e pluribus unum* concept that had driven his double-quartet
album *Free Jazz* (1961). He also found a music that defied categorization along standard market lines, since being classified as "world
music" is not to be classified at all. "Any person in today's music
scene knows that rock, classical, folk and jazz are all yesterday's titles,"
Ornette wrote in 1977. "I feel that the music world is getting closer
to being a singular expression, one with endless musical stories of
mankind."[72]

Prime Time's first appearance was at the Newport Jazz in New
York Festival in 1977, followed by a Carnegie Hall concert in 1978.
Some critics said that the compelling bass lines and rhythm guitar
that drove some compositions made Prime Time danceable and
signaled Ornette's return to the physicality of rhythm and blues.
But the band's tempos were typically either too fast or too slow to

actually dance to, and while they may have found their groove in the rhythm, concert-goers only rarely got up and busted a move. Keyboardist Dave Bryant, a member of Prime Time's later edition (post-1988), found Ornette's relationship with funk rhythms the same as his relationship with jazz rhythms:

> He wanted the energy and support of the rhythm section, but, having famously dispensed with traditional song forms and chord changes as cyclical bases for improvisation, he wanted total freedom for his improvised phrase lengths . . . All of his rhythm sections have had the job of accommodating his irregular and unpredictable phrasing, while making it sound like nothing untoward is going on—smoothing it over, metrically rounding it up to an even number, if you will.[73]

Bryant describes a Prime Time rehearsal with drummer Calvin Weston putting the idea into action:

> He kept straight (funky) time with his feet, but he followed Ornette's phrasing with his hands, playing the snare drum. It was uncanny, and it really helped solidify for me what was going on—he wasn't just splitting the difference, but really attending to both halves of what was metrically happening.[74]

More than body music, Prime Time was the sprightly, enigmatic sound of third mind. When Ornette began work on Prime Time's first album, aptly titled *Dancing in Your Head* (A&M, 1977, recorded in 1975), he was unable to use the tapes recorded with the Joujouka musicians as he'd intended, since Columbia Records had abruptly ended his contract, along with those of Charles Mingus and other formerly courted jazz names, to cut costs. Another visitor had recorded the sessions and although the sound quality is poor, the track entitled "Midnight Sunrise" is the only bit of sonic memory we have of that

Prime Time opening the Caravan of Dreams, (L–R) Jamaaladeen Tacuma, Denardo Coleman, Al MacDowell, Ornette Coleman, Bern Nix, Charles Ellerbe, and Sabir Kamal, Fort Worth, September 30, 1983; photograph by Brian Blauser.

1973 Moroccan moment. Several scraps of video from Joujouka and Nigeria were, however, excavated by Kathelin Gray from Ornette's Rivington Street schoolhouse, where he kept a morass of unmarked film cans and video boxes beneath his bed. They appear in *Ornette: Made in America*, along with cameos of Gysin and Burroughs at the opening of the Caravan of Dreams.

A "PALACE OF the avant-garde" to some and a scandalous waste of good oil money to others, the Caravan of Dreams Performing Arts Center drew mixed reactions.[75] A prominent local businessman told the *Washington Post*:

> I think the word folly applies to this project. It is a very unusual fruitcake of ideas . . . and it's going to hit an insular town like a bolt out of the blue, sort of like rolling an FI6 into the middle of an aboriginal village.[76]

Caravan's managers had high hopes that Texans, proud of their rugged individualism, would embrace the endeavor. "Avant-garde is a French word that means the scouts," Gray explained to a local paper; "in Southwestern terms it means the pioneers."[77] Gray's long-time colleague Oklahoman John Allen, a graduate of the Colorado School of Mines and Harvard Business School and motivating force behind the Institute of Ecotechnics, expressed a similarly left-footed enthusiasm: "Fort Worth is full of vulgarity in the old root sense of the word," he said, "meaning people vitality. There's no phoniness here." Allen was right: the public's mistrust was genuine.[78]

The first month's programming included the Mingus Dynasty and Art Ensemble of Chicago, in addition to pianist McCoy Tyner and Texan tenor David "Fathead" Newman. Ornette, who had forged a close friendship with Gray and Allen in the year prior to the opening, feared the line-up was too highbrow, not to mention too black, telling them, "you don't know [Fort Worth]. You don't really know. You should have followed me with a white man; two or three white men."[79] Allen and Gray had considered the risks, financial and otherwise, a venue like the Caravan would face in Fort Worth, as opposed to a city like San Francisco or Berlin. Ed Bass acknowledged that "it wouldn't be an interesting entrepreneurial venture, if there wasn't a risk involved."[80] On a practical level, Caravan was banking on the support of the large African American community in the Dallas-Fort Worth area (also known as "the metroplex").

On an ideological level, the prospect of establishing an inclusive, progressive cultural center in Fort Worth, a defense industry stronghold where desegregation had yet to take full legal effect, was irresistible.[81] One of John Allen's "great political teachers" was W.E.B. Du Bois, civil rights activist and founder of the National Association for the Advancement of Colored People (NAACP). Allen met Du Bois while working as a labor organizer in Chicago (1950–52), where the meatpackers' slogan was "black and white, unite to fight."[82] The Caravan immediately attracted black audiences downtown, while Sid

Caravan of Dreams
Performing Arts
Center, Downtown
Fort Worth, *c.* 1986;
photograph by
Juan Gonzales.

Bass's adjacent re-development project, a series of shops, office space, and restaurants dubbed Sundance Square, had an almost exclusively white clientele.[83] For the opening, local authorities insisted that riot police be stationed at the club to discourage racial clashes and finally agreed to post plainclothesmen instead, but there were no problems, that night or any other. Although it may have percolated privately, the race issue, à la "there goes the neighborhood," was never officially raised, but another kind of prejudice was soon apparent.

"This is an extremely conservative, commercially oriented town when it comes to theater," said Jerry Russell, director of Stage West, a local repertory group; town residents were unlikely to purchase tickets for anything "more adventuresome than *The Importance of Being*

Earnest.[84] The Caravan of Dreams' first theater production (October 1983), *Kabuki Blues*, was consequently problematic:

> A parable about a group of actors and dancers, forced to abandon New York by the evil money-makers of Western Civilization, [who] travel to Mars where they peer through a telescope and watch a nuclear holocaust consume Earth.[85]

The scathing reviews that followed might have been predictable. Gray and Allen had been warned by an important ally, Edmund Pennington ("Ted") Pillsbury Jr., who as director of the American Center in Paris had booked the Theater of All Possibilities to perform a Burroughs-inspired play entitled *Deconstruction of the Countdown* (1979). Pillsbury was what Americans call "old money"; his father's family were some of the world's largest grain producers and his mother's started the farm equipment giant John Deere. In 1980 Pillsbury was placed in charge of the Kimbell Art Museum, designed by Louis Kahn and endowed by Fort Worth industrialist Kay Kimbell to house and expand his art collection. "Never use the word avant-garde," Pillsbury advised his friends; "the west side of Fort Worth [that is, the ruling families] will get you for it . . . the word avant-garde means a threat."[86]

The Caravan's in-house managers (who doubled as members of the theater troupe), some of whom were European and had worked on Institute of Ecotechnics projects abroad, were accused of cultural snobbery. The press called attention to their colorful (for Texas) clothing and the nicknames some adopted, which, while reminiscent of jazz musician "handles," smacked of a hippiedom that in Texas signified an unsavory combination of promiscuity and communism. Some locally hired waitresses and bartenders referred to "the more exotic [in-house staff] as 'the stinkies.'"[87] Nor was the service in the club very good in the early days, wrote one reviewer; "there were nights when it was easier to find someone to recite Rimbaud than it was to get a

Caravan of Dreams nightclub, *c.* 1983.

beer from the bar."[88] Within months of the opening rumors began to fly, intimating that Caravan was "a solipsistic, closed circle of true believers, completely out of touch with its audience." Such critiques elicited a response from Decision Team Limited (DTL), a company formed by Ed Bass with members of the Institute of Ecotechnics:

> Any corporation would be sensitive to the question that it was influenced by any cult, party line, ideology or any other blinkering of reality. DTL is sometimes asked if it is CIA-influenced by some in India or by profit value maximizers by some in France, by the [Communist] party by some right wing [Americans], and by Gurdjieff, or Sufi, or Lamaism or Cabala by some American occultists. DTL makes its judgments on the basis of ecology and economics—profitable, interesting, and life-enhancing are its criteria for projects, period.[89]

George Gurdjieff (and his student P. D. Ouspensky), in addition to Sufism and all manner of Eastern and Western philosophies, were in fact represented in the splendid synergists' library and topics of group discussion, as were world history, planetary science, classical literature, the culture of cities, and the Soviet and American space programs. The word "synergist," however, was not bandied about publicly, only the term "in-house managers." While Texans participated in theater productions and were invited to meals in the living quarters where Ed, a member of the theater troupe, also stayed, the group was perceived as an unknown and therefore suspect quantity. Guy Debord described the social dynamic in the *Situationist Manifesto* (1960):

> Under the existing dominant society, which produces the miserable pseudo-games of non-participation, a true artistic activity is necessarily classed as criminality. It is semi-clandestine. It appears in the form of scandal.[90]

The scandal broke on March 30, 1985, with the *Dallas Morning News* headline "Edward Bass Funds 'Intellectual Cult,'" followed by similar articles in the *Fort Worth Star-telegram* and the *Washington Post*.

The controversy was ignited by Fort Worth-based Carol Kaminski (also known as Carol Line), who worked as Gray's assistant. Charged in December 1984 with stealing from her employers, Kaminski subsequently signed a confession and a promissory note to repay the pilfered funds, an arrangement that evidently rankled. In March 1985 she approached both the press and the eldest Bass brother, Sid, saying that Ed was being controlled and/or abused in a cult led by John Allen, citing acting classes where Allen roughed up and yelled at Ed. Ex-CIA agent Joel Glenn, chief of the private Bass security force, was present at the meeting and, according to Kaminski, planned to hire a "deprogrammer" to rescue him from Allen's clutches. Ed Bass flatly denied Kaminski's allegations and his family issued supportive statements. Kaminski later apologized and retracted her story, as did some of the print outlets that had covered it. Rehired by the Caravan, Kaminski paid off an agreed-upon portion of her debt. In reference to the Kaminski kerfuffle, Gray said, "We're into culture, not cults," while Ornette, when later asked if he thought Caravan had a secret agenda, said only that he liked "that Sufi stuff."[91]

Despite the spate of bad PR, the Caravan was catching on, thanks to both the quality of the music on offer and firmer management, with Greg "Chutney" Dugan, who had recently captained the R/V *Heraclitus* from Penang to Crete via the Suez Canal, at the helm. A square-jawed, straight-talking Coloradan, Dugan inspired confidence: "You have to earn your spurs before they'll accept you here," he said soberly; "we're doing that."[92] In 1984 an appearance by Living Theater founders Judith Malina and Julian Beck was grudgingly hailed as an event that could only have happened in Fort Worth thanks to the networking of Caravan's "colony of international and not always talented bohemians."[93] Six months after the scandal, the conservative *Fort Worth Star-telegram* was paraphrasing Buckminster Fuller and congratulating the Caravan on bookings that appealed to a wide public.[94]

Prior to 1983, Fort Worth's most famous music venue was Billy Bob's, "the world's largest honky-tonk," a massive entertainment complex in the old stockyards catering to a country and western audience that embodied the retro cowpoke image hanging like a millstone around the city's neck. Even the prestigious Van Cliburn (classical) Piano Competition was burdened with bovine connotations: for the 1985 edition, the finalists were photographed in the stockyards with a Steinway grand surrounded by longhorn bulls. With repackaging in mind, someone hired a PR firm that asked a hundred residents to describe the city as if it were a person. Only three said it was a woman. The rest saw it as a 38- to 40-year-old male, "old enough to know better, but young enough to be aggressive."[95] The city's power brokers, a band of Ivy League golfers (and seasonal quail hunters) and high-stakes players in Washington and on Wall Street, were aiming for something a tad more refined. Fort Worth could legitimately promote itself as a town at the frontiers of not just the West but technology (with the aerodynamics industry and a new robotics research center as touchstones) and art, thanks to the Kimbell and Amon Carter Museums. As for the Caravan, it brought life to a desultory downtown, attracting audiences from neighboring cities and states, and went a long way towards cinching Texas's claim to its desired "third coast" status, as a cultural hub to rival the urban East and West. Before long, the Caravan was celebrated as part of the city's remaking and Ornette's participation was frequently cited in connection with it, as code for "serious art."

In 1985 Ornette and Prime Time played for the New Year's Eve bash held annually in the Caravan nightclub, featuring guest guitarist Pat Metheny, with whom Ornette had recently recorded *Song X* (Geffen, 1986). Metheny (1954–) had studied Ornette's early albums well before he began performing in Kansas City at age fifteen. A musician's musician, he noticed "the way Ornette and bassist Charlie Haden could listen to each other and create these vast webs of implied harmony." Metheny worked with some of Ornette's closest band-mates, recording *80/81* (ECM, 1980) with a quintet that featured Haden and Dewey Redman, in addition to Jack DeJohnette, a frequent Metheny sideman, and tenor saxophonist Michael Brecker. Metheny finally met Ornette around 1981 while playing at the Village Vanguard with Billy Higgins and Charlie Haden, who introduced them and suggested they collaborate. He and Ornette practiced for several weeks, ten hours a day, before starting rehearsals for *Song X* with Denardo, DeJohnette, and Haden. Coauthor of several of the tracks, Metheny called the work "a high point in my life as a musician."[96] Among Ornette's most memorable ballads, "Kathelin Gray" first appeared on *Song X*, one of the few compositions he named for a woman and the only one explicitly so aside from "Jayne" (1958).[97]

In the course of his long career, Ornette collaborated with a handful of women who remained good friends, including pianist and educator Geri Allen (1957–2018), with whom he recorded several albums, Kathelin Gray, Shirley Clarke, and Yoko Ono (1933–). Ono had a New York loft in 1960, but Ornette met her in Paris in 1967 at a cabaret on Place de la Contrescarpe where she performed her "black-bag piece" from inside a cloth sack. According to Ono's friend Jean-Jacque Lebel (1936–), art critic, poet, and instigator of Paris happenings, he and Ornette "took turns inside the sack with Yoko."[98] Also in 1967, Ono's offer to screen her film *Bottoms* (consisting of 365 close-ups of naked backsides walking away from the camera) was declined by Royal Albert Hall officials "concerned with the [venue's] protection."[99] Ornette's proposal that Ono accompany his quartet for a concert in early 1968 at that same venue must have afforded her some satisfaction. On February 29, Ornette performed his composition "Emotion Modulation" with David Izenzon, Charlie Haden, and Ed Blackwell. Writing for the *Jazz Journal*, Barry McCrae described Ono's "brief contribution" as "shattering . . . it was, in fact, the sound of a woman making sexual love . . . moaning with an

(L–R) Pat Metheny, Ornette Coleman, Denardo Coleman, and Charlie Haden, Caravan of Dreams, New Year's Eve 1985.

ecstasy that was frightening in its realism."[100] In 1968 Ornette played trumpet on the only live recorded track on Ono's debut studio album, *Yoko Ono/Plastic Ono Band* (Apple, 1970).

It was Yoko Ono who introduced Shirley Clarke to Ornette in Paris in 1968. A dancer and choreographer, Clarke (1919–1997) entered New York's experimental film scene in the late 1950s, working with Robert Frank, Nicholas Ray, and other members of the New York scenius. *The Connection* (released in Cannes in 1961), her film adaptation of a Jack Gelber play, staged by Living Theater and directed by Judith Malina, was about a group of addicts waiting for Cowboy (their dealer) to deliver their horse (heroin), and was banned in New York for obscenity. In 1963 Clarke won an Oscar for *Robert Frost: A Lover's Quarrel with the World* (1963) as best documentary feature. In 1964 she released *Cool World*, based on a novel about Harlem street gangs, and in 1967 a feature-length interview with a gay black hustler entitled *Portrait of Jason*, shot at Clarke's home in the storied Chelsea Hotel.[101] Shortly after meeting Ornette, Clarke conceived a project for a film about jazz focused on him and Denardo. She shot historic footage of father and son performing at the 1968 Poor People's March in Washington, DC, and elsewhere, but the project was derailed for lack of funds. When Ornette and Gray decided to build a film around his Fort Worth homecoming, he resurrected Clarke's reels from beneath his Rivington street bed, and Gray contacted her, offering her the possibility of bringing the film to completion.

Ornette: Made in America (1985) embeds information and insight regarding Ornette's life and times in an audio-visual ode that doubles as a documentary. In composing the film, Clarke and Gray followed their subject's harmolodic lead, improvising imagery using the latest formats and effects to provide a vivid, non-linear portrait of the artist, his work, and his worldview. "The first thing I laid down was the sound," Clarke noted, drawing from the Fort Worth performance of *Skies of America* and Prime Time inaugurating the Caravan of

Dreams. "I edited to the music . . . the film looks like how Ornette sounds and has the same basic thinking." In Gray's words, "the music became the 'plot' . . . to test just completed rough edits, we would sometimes stand and move to the shape and tempo of the images."[102] Portions were shot in New York, where Ornette (at the World Trade Center) and Denardo (in Harlem) performed electronically together but physically apart for "The Link," a then cutting-edge video simulcast designed by Shirley's daughter Wendy Clarke.[103] In Fort Worth Ornette reminisces with old friends, recalling how tenor saxophonist and fellow I. M. Terrell alumnus King Curtis (1934–1971) picked him up at the train station when he first arrived in New York, driving a Rolls-Royce. Curtis was playing R&B and making "heavy money," said Ornette, while he was making "peanuts."

Edited at the Chelsea, where Clarke lived, the film struck a note of symmetry between its subject and its makers. According to Gray, who worked closely with Clarke throughout the project,

> *Made in America* pulled the various strands of [Clarke's] creative life together, the avant-garde, classical music, race and gender issues, film, video, radical and precise intellect, generational transmission, sexuality, heightened consciousness, dance as inspiration . . .[104]

The same connective threads ran through Gray's life and that of Ornette, who participated both on and behind the camera, particularly in the editing process. "Ornette loved that the image flow was styled like his music," Gray said.[105]

While producing the film, Gray worked with Ornette on *Celestial Navigation*, a play for the Caravan troupe that she coauthored with Johnny Dolphin (John Allen's nom de plume). Ornette had contributed music to at least one other theater production, *Zeki Is Coming* (1971), performed by the Rites and Reasons Theater and directed by the troupe's founder George Bass (1938–1990), professor of theater

Shirley Clarke (R) and Ornette Coleman (L) during the filming
of *Ornette: Made in America* (1986), Fort Worth, 1983.

arts and Afro-American studies at Brown University, Rhode Island.
Rites and Reason's repertoire aimed to elucidate theatrical forms
rooted in African cultures, involving artists, scholars, and researchers
in the process. *Zeki Is Coming* "evoked the spirit of Langston Hughes
and the Harlem Renaissance," according to Felipe Floresca, who
attended the opening at Harlem's National Black Theater, where
Ornette provided live accompaniment.[106]

For *Celestial Navigation* Ornette wrote the score and played
onstage with Prime Time during its several Fort Worth and New
York performances. The plot kicks off with a producer asking a director to stage a play about the origins of drama. Ornette liked the
premise and was cast as Orpheus, the archetypal musician-poet, son
of a muse and a god. Ornette and Prime Time rehearsed with the
troupe and opened in Fort Worth (November 29, 1984) before heading to New York's Tower Gallery. Gray, who often wrote or performed
music for the Theater of All Possibilities (renamed the Caravan of
Dreams Theater), helped Ornette develop the score while staying at

Rivington Street. Sometimes he asked her to sing a melody or add lyrics to a song or else to go downstairs and play the piano. "Then I would realize he was listening to me," wrote Gray, "and he would come and make his comments."[107] According to a *New York Times* reviewer, *Celestial Navigation*'s music "stabilized the mood for the actors' histrionics":

> Jubilantly sprawling, bluesy march-like pieces . . . improvisations that writhed and tangled like Medusa's snaky hairdo . . . [and] atmospheric passages . . . with Mr. Coleman delivering eerie, vibrato-free violin slides as Bern Nix and Charles Ellerbe played skulking guitar lines.[108]

In the role of Perseus (who slays the Gorgon Medusa), Greg Dugan recalled that for the last act, Ornette/Orpheus soloed in the spotlight center stage: "very cool, intensity engaged, in the present moment, alert to both given circumstances and the history of the drama, sweat rolling down his face, giving it up."[109] The Fort Worth press was more appreciative than the *New York Times*, which called the production "amateurish," but Ornette enjoyed the experience; he was always "rarin' to go," said Dugan, and in New York took cast members to his favorite clubs and restaurants, places like Jezebel's that served posh soul food which he invariably paired, said Gray, with "a well-chilled bottle of *Pouilly-Fuissé*."[110]

In Kathelin Gray, Ornette found an exacting intellect balanced with a finely calibrated emotional sensibility and musicality. Her childhood in Monterey, California, was shaped by nonconformist parents with an interest in mysticism (both later practiced the Reiki healing method, developed by a Japanese Buddhist monk) and charismatic friends like Jack Kerouac, labor union organizer and longshoreman Harry Bridges (1901–1990), and Manly Palmer Hall (1901–1990), Canadian-born scholar of metaphysics. Gray's uncle Eli Brandi, a Second World War refugee from Berlin and economist at the Stanford

Research Institute, introduced her to the novels of Thomas Mann and the sheet music for Bela Bartok's piano compositions "For Children." Around age twelve, Gray discovered Cecil Taylor and a taste for the atonal, and was enamored of John Cage, composer Arnold Schoenberg (1874–1951), and his student Alban Berg's operas, *Wozzeck* (1925)and *Lulu* (1937).

Working as a nude model for art classes in her later teens, Gray met Stewart Brand (1938–), publisher of the *Whole Earth Catalogue* (1968) whose cover art, NASA's first color photograph of the planet, alerted a generation to the beauty and vulnerability of our world. Ken Kesey (1935–1991), author of *One Flew Over the Cuckoo's Nest* (1962), was another member of Gray's cultural milieu. Kesey toured America in a school bus named "Further" with the Merry Pranksters, a band of 1960s bon vivants promoting the joys of LSD. At seventeen, after a Charles Lloyd Quintet concert at the Fillmore, Gray met Jack DeJohnette and pianist Keith Jarrett, who became close friends along with other musicians and artists circulating the 1960s San Francisco free zone.[111]

As director of Caravan of Dreams Productions, Gray produced a series of recordings in a harmolodic vein that were acclaimed in the international music press and stand today as artifacts of an avant-garde Alamo, when big record distributors had the market cornered and independents held just 10 percent.[112] Most of the label's artists had played in the Caravan nightclub, where some were recorded live, beginning with Ornette and Prime Time (*Opening the Caravan of Dreams*, 1985) followed by James Ulmer, *Live at the Caravan of Dreams* (recorded 1985), and Ronald Shannon Jackson with his group the Decoding Society and with Yoruban bandleader and artist Chief Twins Seven Seven.[113] Caravan's landmark release was *Ornette: In All Languages* (recorded in New York, February–March 1987), a two-album set featuring Ornette with Prime Time on one LP and with Higgins, Haden, and Cherry on the other.[114] Their reunion for *In All Languages* marked the thirtieth anniversary of the original Coleman

Quartet, prompting Robert Palmer to compare the late 1980s jazz scene to when they first stormed New York:

> Yesterday's modernism becomes today's cool, graceful classicism. Meanwhile a new brand of modernism appears. The music needs both for its continued vitality, and this is something Mr. Coleman has cannily understood. The quartet takes care of the classicism; Prime Time offers the equally essential shock of the new . . . this process, always cycling through fresh resolutions toward new beginnings, is the essence of jazz.[115]

Approaching his sixtieth birthday, Ornette was himself a classic yet hungry for new projects and encounters. To nourish his mind and music he looked to friends, people who kept pace with his oblique turns of thought, adding new inflections to his ideas and helping him zero in on his heart's desire; he did the same for them. This was the sort of friendship Ornette shared with Kathelin Gray and John Allen.

BORN "SLAP IN the prairie" of Oklahoma, John Polk Allen (1929–) related to Ornette as a fellow survivor of the Great Depression, when Midwesterners watched drought winds raise walls of dust that blotted out the sun.[116] Brought up on a ranch by frontiersmen and women, at age fourteen Allen lit out to greener pastures, hoboing and picking fruit further west. A machinist and sharpshooter in the army, he became a student of Gustav Mueller ("the last Hegelian"), an admirer of Marx, Spengler, and Machiavelli, a labor agitator, and the defiant subject of a thick FBI file. For a while, Allen mined coal and uranium for the U.S. Atomic Energy Commission until he grasped the implications of his work for the planet while under the influence of peyote. He dropped out, hitchhiked across Africa, trekked through Nepal, Tibet, Burma, and Thailand, apprenticed with an Indian guru, toured South Vietnam on a wartime press pass, visited a kibbutz, wrote poetry and frequented Slugs' in New York. He meanwhile hatched plans for an enlightened comeback centered on his belief that conscious, collective effort was required for humanity to survive its destructive childhood into a wiser maturity.[117]

Allen met Kathelin Gray at a bus stop in San Francisco in 1967, the "summer of love," when tens of thousands of rebel youth spontaneously assembled in Haight-Ashbury, their Dionysian motto coined by Timothy Leary: turn on, tune in, drop out. In the course of Allen's conversation with Gray, an oddly prescient almost-eighteen-year-old, Allen asked what she intended to do with her life. Gray handed him the book she carried around like a talisman, *Mount Analogue* (1952), René Daumal's unfinished masterpiece about a ship named *Impossible* whose crew of artists, scientists, and explorers set out to know the world and its place in the universe.[118] Daumal's narrative contributed subtext to the lifetime endeavor Gray and Allen would share with a group of friends, practiced in theater and actualized through Institute of Ecotechnics projects.

In 1982 Gray and Allen invited Ornette to attend the Institute's annual conference in Aix-en-Provence, where Buckminster Fuller was scheduled to make a presentation. Held at Les Marronniers, a comfortably worn, wisteria-draped eighteenth-century manor framed by ancient chestnuts and figs, the three-day event was casual, leaving plenty of time for around thirty guests and their synergist hosts to mingle with the dozen or so speakers, sipping wine while seated on the mottled stone ledge of a koi-full basin. Talks were held in an old pottery studio converted to an annex known as "the theater," where meals were served by synergists (who prepared them in the main house) and the guests entertained with music, songs, and a short theater piece after the last evening's talk. The conferences in France began in 1977 with "Man, Oceans and Opportunities," proceeding through Earth's biomes (rainforest, desert, and so on) to "Planet Earth" (1980), the "Solar System" (1981), and beyond. An educational exercise designed to benefit ongoing IE projects, the gatherings kept synergists and their guests apprised of developments in myriad fields: evolutionary biology, astrophysics, genetic engineering, planetary geology, renewable energy, nanotechnology, and neurophysiology, to name a signature few, while allowing the speakers a chance to exchange ideas.[119] Artists, inventors, and explorers contributed perspectives, among them Thor Heyerdahl (who crossed the Pacific in a raft to test ancient navigation techniques); Apollo 9 astronaut Rusty Schweickart; Chris McKay, planetary scientist in NASA's Mars exploration program; and Albert Hoffman, discoverer of LSD.

When Ornette was 24, he heard Buckminster Fuller speak at Los Angeles's Hollywood High School and was thoroughly, if bewilderedly, inspired. Meeting Fuller in 1982 helped clarify his affinity for the architect/inventor. During his talk ("The Galaxy: A Comprehensive Anticipatory Design Challenge"), Fuller expounded

John Polk Allen, 1944.

Ornette Coleman and Eden Harding at Les Marroniers, Aix-en-Provence,
September 1982 photograph by Marie Harding.

on the structure of the universe using a wood-stick model of the geodesic polyhedron (made from triangles that approximate a sphere).
"He turned [the model] inside out, made it dance," recalled Ornette.
"I said to myself, that's just like my music."[120] Afterwards, Fuller took
everyone outside and laid his wooden polyhedrons on the ground to
show there are no straight lines in nature and to warn against preconceptions as a substitute for thinking and seeing for oneself. Fuller
liked to remind his audiences that the sun neither rises nor sets; it is
we who are circling it as we hurtle through space. In Ornette's words,

> Fuller said that there is no such thing as up and down. There
> is only *out*. That was the first time I was ever touched aesthet-
> ically by a scientist . . . When Fuller illustrated his geodesic
> dome concept, I saw that we were brothers.[121]

After the talk, Ornette composed *Prime Design/Time Design*, his
interpretation of Fuller's vision of the birth of the universe, the fusion
of chaos and harmony. Fuller died several months before Ornette's

tribute premiered at the opening of the Caravan of Dreams (October 2, 1983). The performance with three violinists, a cellist, and a percussionist was fittingly recorded live in the geodesic dome on the Caravan rooftop.[122]

In 1983 Ornette said he'd received "a questionnaire from NASA" asking if he'd be interested in "working in space." He answered in the affirmative and listed several friends he'd like to take along. Whether or not there was follow-up, a saxophone coincidentally became the first instrument played outside Earth's atmosphere, by African American astronaut Dr. Ron E. McNair.[123] Commissioned by Joseph Celli, Ornette later wrote "In Praise of NASA" and "Planetary Soloists"(1986). Although he expressed a willingness to go there, Ornette viewed space metaphorically, equating it with answers to questions regarding life and death. "In a sense, heaven is a form of space," he said, but "if space is only [there] to communicate to us if there is a being or a theme," he felt he had it covered. "Whatever

Buckminster Fuller and his geodesic polyhedron, with Mark Nelson, chairman of the Institute of Ecotechnics and biospherian, at the lower right; Galactic Conference, Aix-en-Provence, September 1982; photograph by Marie Harding.

is out in space I have met and whatever is not out in space I have met," Ornette said. He agreed with Bucky Fuller that as passengers of Spaceship Earth, humanity is already "out there" and that whatever the planet's destiny, Ornette was confident that "the human form will never cease to exist."[124] His optimism echoed that of his friends from the Institute of Ecotechnics, who were about to break ground on their most ambitious project, a miniature Earth under glass in the high desert near Oracle, Arizona.

The culmination of several decades' work, Biosphere 2 was designed as a laboratory for the study of global ecology, comprising a miniature ocean and coral reef, rainforest, desert, savanna grassland, mangrove marsh, agricultural area, tech zone, and human habitat enclosed in a 3-acre (1.2 ha) space age cathedral of glass and steel.[125] In addition to a world's worth of flora and fauna, eight people lived inside for two years, determining how much air, soil, and water they needed to live, while envisaging how, if humanity is to sojourn in space, it might create an economically sound and psychologically satisfying environment. The building (1985–91) and operation of Biosphere 2 involved a pooling of knowledge resources from around the planet unique in the history of science and engineering. Institutions and individuals at the forefront of their disciplines (including, thanks to glasnost, the Soviet experts in closed ecological systems) united beneath the banner of a holistic understanding of Earth's regulatory functions and an interplanetary future for its life forms. Marking the convergence of science and technology with art and nature, they called Biosphere 2 "the human experiment," one whose outcomes have only begun to be properly assessed.[126]

Inside Biosphere 2, the crew spent their days monitoring its functions, caring for its plant life (their "main allies" in combating the rise of carbon dioxide) and working in the half-acre (0.2 ha) Intensive Agriculture Biome that provided them nourishment; after their evening meal, they performed theater and played music.[127] Perhaps their most significant act was to establish an intimacy with their

Biosphere 2, Oracle, Arizona, 1992.

environment reflective of their utter reliance on its health for their water, food, and breath. Creating a quantifiable experiential model of this neglected reality was one of the project's prime objectives. "Without the feeling of personal connection with the cosmos, the work and consequences of hypothetical scientific effort disappear into a lumpen intellectual professionalism," wrote John Allen.[128] Ornette felt precisely that way about musical effort; it had to be real, in his own ever-deepening terms, to be of any use.

In the course of their early conversations, Ornette gave John Allen a saxophone and told him to play. After hours of puffing and blowing, Allen finally made a sound. "Now that's an authentic note," Ornette said. He paid his friend an even greater compliment with *The Sacred Mind of Johnny Dolphin* (1984), a composition for trumpet, eight strings, percussion, and timpani.[129] Tracks entitled "Space Church" and "Biosphere" appeared on *In All Languages* (1987), and Ornette's association with Gray and Allen was likewise reflected in his wish to develop the Rivington Street schoolhouse as "a multiple expression center which involves space, artists, dramatics and science."[130] The project never materialized; Ornette decided to sell the cavernous building where he'd been nearly beaten to death twice, which ironically turned out to be the most lucrative business transaction of his life.[131]

Aside from financial relief, the 1980s brought renewed recognition. An arts center (Real Art Ways) in Hartford, Connecticut, mounted a week-long "Ornette Coleman Festival" in 1985, and Ornette received the key to another city. His music was part of a soundtrack for Jean-Luc Godard's *Détective* (1985) that included works by Wagner, Chopin, and Liszt. *Ornette: Made in America* premiered at the New York Film Festival, eliciting praise for his music and the sweep of his career. If iteration is a form of flattery, a band comprised of "Coleman University" alumni (Cherry, Haden, Blackwell, and Redman) called Old and New Dreams had been performing and recording his vintage compositions for nearly a decade, expanding the music's possibilities while displaying the creative mastery these musicians had achieved through interacting with one another. "The whole tradition of jazz flowed through their playing," wrote critic Stanley Crouch, just as it flowed through Ornette's.[132]

In 1986, backstage at Town Hall while ironing his suit for a concert with Pat Metheny, Ornette was interviewed by *People Magazine*, the pride of every middle-American waiting room.[133] In 1987 composer, conductor, and multi-instrumentalist Joseph Celli presented Ornette's works for chamber ensembles at the Weill Recital Hall (formerly Carnegie Recital Hall) and the First International Conference of Jazz Studies, held at the University of Bologna, focused on his life and music. With Prime Time and John Giordano, Ornette brought the re-orchestrated version of *Skies of America* to Europe for multiple concerts. A sought-after composer, he was commissioned for music to celebrate the bicentennial of the French Revolution and approached by Milan's La Scala to create an opera.[134] A member of the *DownBeat* Hall of Fame since 1969, Ornette was voted "musician of the year" in 1987, following the release of *In All Languages*, his last recording on the Caravan label.

Roy Hargrove,
Caravan of Dreams,
May 1987;
photograph
by Juan Gonzales.

The Caravan of Dreams was likewise enjoying a heyday, draw-ing crowds from throughout the Southwest with the help of a new computerized sales system called Rainbow Ticketmaster. Musicians loved the nightclub, a large yet intimate space with great acoustics, a knowledgeable staff, and a responsive crowd. Big names such as Dizzy Gillespie, Herbie Hancock, and trumpeter, bandleader, and composer Wynton Marsalis settled in for four- or five-night runs, using the nightclub as a daytime rehearsal/recording space.[135] Local musicians sometimes sat in, and a star was occasionally born, such as trumpeter Roy Hargrove (1969–2018), who debuted with Marsalis at the Caravan in 1987. A staunch advocate of high school bands and jazz education, Marsalis (who established a jazz program at Lincoln

Center that year) visited local schools while touring. At Dallas's Booker T. Washington School for the Visual and Performing Arts, he heard the Waco-born Hargrove and was so impressed that he invited him to sit in. The crowd that night (May 31) was indulgent, like parents at a talent show, when Wynton asked the timid-looking eighteen-year-old in his tweed topcoat and porkpie hat onstage.[136] Before long they were cheering with astonishment that one so young could play so hot. Performances like these were broadcast live from the club weekly on KERA (the station carrying National Public Radio programming), promoting the musicians and the club while enriching the regional soundscape.

Upstairs in the theater the in-house troupe (under Gray's direction) staged a series of classics (Aeschylus' *Oresteia*, Noh drama, Calderon's *Life is a Dream*, and Sanskrit love saga *Shakuntala*), in addition to events like a tribute to Martin Luther King, narrated by Eartha Kitt and performed by a hundred-voice gospel choir.[137] In February 1987 Timothy Leary (then president of software design company Futique) came to the theater, predicting that while computer technology might improve human intelligence, it was "more addictive than heroin."[138] A two-night June happening had cyberpunk authors William Gibson (*Neuromancer*, 1984) and Texan Bruce Sterling (*The Artificial Kid*, 1980) enthusing about virtual reality in the theater while downstairs in the club, Sun Ra and his Arkestra in full Pharaonic gear chanted their mantra, "space is the place" (June 1987). "My hat is off to you pioneers of the creative human spirit," Herbie Hancock wrote in the Caravan guestbook; Dizzy Gillespie told everyone it was his favorite club. To musicians and other artists, the Caravan was not just a place you showed up and played, it was a jazz-fueled gesamtkunstwerk.

"The people at the Caravan, they're all artists in their own way," Ornette said, "the kind that are pure in their mind . . . they respect what I do and what I've gone through to get where I am." But Ornette wanted more, wistfully telling Howard Mandel in 1987 that there had been no "major campaign to bring me to millions of people, like if I was Bruce Springsteen."[139] The Grateful Dead concert Ornette attended that autumn whet his growing appetite for a mass audience. Accompanied by Cecil Taylor, the outing was a revelation, and both men marveled at the enraptured crowd of over 20,000 Deadheads packing Madison Square Garden.[140] With their 1970 hit "Truckin'" the Grateful Dead established their feel-good folksy rock persona, but lead guitarist Jerry Garcia (1942–1995) occasionally took the music in "psychedelic" (improvisational) directions. Both Garcia and bassist Phil Lesh admired Ornette, and the Dead's configuration (with two drummers and two electric guitarists) resembled Prime Time's. But what impressed Ornette most was that "[The Grateful Dead] could have done anything up there and those people would have screamed. If these people [are] into this, they could dig what we're doing." Ornette featured his new friend Jerry Garcia on his next album with Prime Time, the first on a new label, *Virgin Beauty* (CBS Portrait, 1988) and his biggest commercial success.[141]

"In music, the only requirement is for it to be heard," wrote Ornette, and on February 23, 1993, he performed with the Grateful Dead at California's Oakland-Alameda County Coliseum for an audience of over 60,000. Teaming up with a band so out of his world in terms of background and experience was another way of challenging what Ornette perceived as the tyranny of categories. "It is the category concept of all subjects that keeps ties with the past," he wrote, preventing freedom of movement. In June 1994, at the Musik Triennale, Cologne, Ornette premiered *Architecture in Motion*, a composition/performance commissioned by the Cologne Philharmonic for eight dancers, electric and acoustic instruments (including his new quartet), and chamber orchestra. The composition's title, he explained in the program, represents "being or existence and the art of movements as one."[142] Ornette chose dancers from seven traditions (Middle Eastern, Chinese, Indian, Flamenco, ballet, breakdancing, and tap dance) to illustrate his "harmolodic-democratic" principle that whatever its origins, music has a potentially positive effect on the listener. "We [the harmolodic "we"] will not allow any prejudice to be in the way of the energy of the expression that can be shared, which we call removing the caste system from sound."[143]

Ornette wished to define the qualities of the "energy of the expression," to arrive, as it were, at the organic truth of sound. A mid-1980s recording of a Sabbath service by a Jewish cantor, Josef Rosenblatt, moved him to tears. "[Rosenblatt] was crying, singing and praying all in the same breath," said Ornette, "you can't find those notes. They don't exist," and yet he searched for them.[144] Guitarist Kenny Wessel, who performed with Prime Time from 1988 to 2000, recalled visiting Ornette in Harlem, where he lived after selling the Rivington Street schoolhouse. Wessel found him engrossed in a video portraying an Indian fakir hanging by the skin of his chest from a meat hook. Wessel was "horrified," but then Ornette turned to him and said, "Man, if I could only find those notes."[145]

Soon afterwards Ornette presented a multimedia event at the San Francisco Jazz Festival in the Masonic Auditorium on Nob Hill (November 1994). The show incorporated Ornette's acoustic quartet with Geri Allen, the first pianist he'd played and recorded with since the 1950s. There was a poetry reading by Vincent Harding (friend and chronicler of Martin Luther King), video projections, and, most controversially, a demonstration led by Fakir Musafar of several individuals who impassively skewered their faces and bodies with metal rods while dancing to Badal Roy's tabla.[146] Half the audience fled in horror, half remained transfixed. Some reviewers felt that Ornette wished to shock the audience out of its complacency that they might better experience the music. Others said he was pointing to the possibilities of higher levels of consciousness. But Ornette was still looking for those notes, the ones that feel no pain. His sister Trudy had died a month before, the person who knew him from the start of his life's adventure, sister, friend, and champion, a stabbing loss like the rending of flesh.

Around that time, Ornette received the MacArthur Foundation award, the so-called "genius grant" in recognition of "exceptional creativity," several hundred thousand dollars, no strings attached. With Denardo, his manager since the early 1980s, he launched Harmolodics, "a record label for the equal access to information expression."[147] Coinciding with the rise of the Internet as a public utility, the label's first release with Prime Time, *Tone Dialing* (1995), included "Search for Life," Ornette's foray into rap ("there's an art form there," he said). When Ornette remarked that "communication is a form of energy that allows everyone to have the same equal time or position," he might have been describing the Internet, except that the relay of data doesn't always qualify as communication, in the same way that a letter, an online chat, or video may approximate but never render the sensory, situational, and intuitively grasped information available in a real-time conversation or performance.[148]

Within weeks of *Tone Dialing*'s release, Don Cherry died (October 19, 1995) aged 58. Ornette's personal and musical connection to Cherry ran deep. According to Cherry's step-daughter and award-winning singer-songwriter Neneh, who knew Ornette from childhood, "they were two souls looking for each other . . . for the music to happen the way it did, it needed both of them."[149] Cherry's death was followed by that of lifelong friend Charles Moffett, on Valentine's Day 1997. Moffett had devoted his later years to teaching and performing with his family. "After playing with Ornette," he said, "it was hard to find people to equal his soul, equal his tension. The closest I could come to it was playing with my children."[150] Moffett's son Charnett (named after his father and Ornette) was playing bass with Ornette's acoustic quartet at the time. In November that same year, Robert Palmer died of liver failure, age 52.

Ornette had reached that stage of life when one can't help wondering who's next, but he rarely lingered on the topic of death. "I'm not interested in what's going to happen to me after I pass," he said, only "in what I can experience while I'm alive."[151] In July 1997, under the direction of John Rockwell, the annual Lincoln Center Festival built the music portion of its multi-genre program (entitled "? Civilization") around Ornette. There were two performances of *Skies of America* with the New York Philharmonic (conducted by Kurt Masur), in addition to appearances by the quartet and Prime Time concerts featuring dancers, rappers, and video artists, with Lou Reed and Laurie Anderson as special guests. "We hope," Rockwell wrote in the program, "that we can do our part in establishing [Ornette Coleman's] artistry in the mainstream of American music."[152] But Ornette's place was history, not the mainstream. A self-appointed sound-keeper in the Library of Babel, his mission, like that of all master musicians, was to compile volumes of aural emotions, thoughts, and situations from the fund of human experience, that we might one day borrow them back.

Part Four: Transmission

I'm trying to express a concept according to which you can
translate one thing into another.

ORNETTE COLEMAN, 1997 INTERVIEW
WITH JACQUES DERRIDA

Ornette must have been sitting in or near the front row at New
York's Radio City Music Hall sometime around 1960 because
his description of the acrobat on stage was precise and full of wonder:

> A Hawaiian was balancing four cocktail glasses on a six-by-
> four [inches, 15 × 10 cm] piece of wood. The board was on
> the knob of a two-foot [0.6-m] sword. The Hawaiian put
> a dagger in his mouth and balanced the dagger—point to
> point—against the sword, climbed fifteen feet [4.5-m] up
> a ladder, spread his hands [that is, opened his arms], and
> not a drop spilled. It was the most beautiful piece of art I'd
> ever seen. I said to myself, where am I at, if this guy can do
> something so unbelievable?[1]

Aside from appreciating a balanced performance, Ornette was fascinated by the gestalt of many things happening at once, relating it to
the aural density he craved. As he explained to Prime Time guitarist
Kenny Wessel,

> When you're in the city and walking down the street, you
> could see a couple walking along holding hands, and then
> you hear a taxi honking its horn, then you see an argument
> between two people in front of a store, and all these things

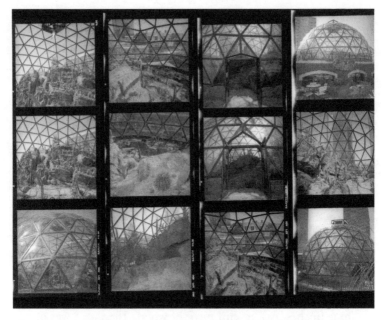

Geodesic dome with cactus garden, Caravan of Dreams Performing Arts Center, Fort Worth, 1983; photograph by Brian Blauser.

are happening in your scope of view—so why can't music be like that?[2]

In 1987 Ornette described what he was after with Prime Time as "multiple unison":

> Which means that you can see, smell, talk, move and run all at the same time . . . you can do all those things right now . . . that's what I try to get every person who plays with me to do. To think of himself as being a multiple person.[3]

As bandleader, Ornette gave his utmost and demanded the same of the ensemble, practicing relentlessly prior to recording dates and gigs, yet he seldom gave direct instructions. "Rehearsals always begin with a 'lead sheet,'" wrote John Snyder, who studied trumpet with

Ornette and produced several of his albums; "this was usually a line
... written out using the typical notation of notes on a staff." Chord
changes were rarely provided but if so, "[they served] the same purpose as the notes, [as] signposts not directives engraved in stone."[4]
According to Bobby Bradford, Ornette said, "I want us to play tighter
but I don't want you to play what I'm playing—I want you to sur-
prise me," an approach, Bradford noted, that in the 1950s "was so
revolutionary, a lot of people said it was bullshit."[5] Thirty years later
Ornette felt the same way: "I don't want [band-members] to follow
me," he said, "I want them to follow themselves but to be with me."[6]
Musicians who brought their best chops to rehearsals were discouraged; Ornette could spot a preconceived riff a mile off. "You're playing
roadmaps," he told Kenny Wessel at the outset of their collaboration
in 1988. "I don't want you to play what you know, I want you to play
what you don't know."

Ethnomusicologist and saxophonist Daniel Paul Schnee, who
met Ornette in 1997 and subsequently became his student, relates
how "un-naming pitches" was an essential part of the learning process. "'C' is just a name," Ornette told him, "and the sound is the
reality of the note. You could call it 'Tokyo' or 'wisdom' or 'sandwich'
but that doesn't signify the sound." Schnee discovered that

> thinking "notes" led me to be concerned with modality [key]
> and intervallic relationships—playing C led to automatically
> thinking about the idea of something "being" C and thus
> leading to D—which unconsciously establishes habitual/
> theoretical thinking . . . [Ornette described] the melodies he
> wrote as "territories": a kind of sound landscape in which
> many things were possible.[7]

Drummer Shelly Manne, who recorded on *Tomorrow Is the Question*
(1959), remarked how "[Ornette] makes you hear [his compositions]
eighteen million different ways."[8] Decades later, Kenny Wessel noted

that "Ornette was consistent about trying to generate as much information as possible from a single piece of music."[9] Ornette's twin releases, *Sound Museum: Three Women* and *Sound Museum: Hidden Man* (Harmolodics, 1996), featuring different renditions of the same compositions (except for one), did just that.

Robert Palmer related Ornette's interest in visual art to his approach to music:

> One gets the impression that he is "seeing" melody or sound. [Ornette's] penchant for developing musical ideas doesn't always work in sequences of theme-and-variation. Sometimes it's more like he is visualizing a note or phrase as a three-dimensional construct, to be studied at close range and arm's length . . . examined from a variety of angles.[10]

Ornette maintained a lifelong rapport with the visual arts, through his own canvases and acquisitions (often the works of African and African American artists), the considerable time he spent in galleries and museums in America and in Europe while touring, and the friendships he cultivated with artists and gallery owners. In 1989 he curated an exhibition entitled "Don't You Know By Now," for the opening of Philippe Briet's gallery in Soho, New York. Briet (1959–1997) had run a contemporary art program in Caen (Normandy) and toured an exhibition of French contemporary art in Africa before moving to New York in late 1985. In 1986 he returned to Africa to mount a show by his friend Jean-Michel Basquiat at Abidjan's Centre Culturel Français. For Briet's opening, Ornette chose paintings from his personal collection, including some by his own hand and others by friends like Z. K. Oloruntoba, Bob Thompson, African American Abstract Expressionist Edward Clark, and Beauford Delaney (1901–1979), an African American Modernist whose work Briet tirelessly championed.[11]

In 1992 Ornette curated the inaugural group exhibition of Nigerian artists for the Skoto Gallery (25 Prince Street), owned by

Ornette Coleman, Fort Worth, Texas, 1983; photograph by Ira Cohen.

Skoto Aghahowa and his French wife Alix du Serech; the exhibition was among the city's first to focus on African art. Ornette suspended one of the paintings from the ceiling and placed several sculptures together in the center of the small space, as if to encourage their conversation. With everything arranged to his liking, Ornette asked Skoto and Alix to turn off the lights, so they could have a closer look. "We saw black squares at different levels," said du Serech, "and it allowed us to get the rhythm of the hanging. Usually we squint to see if the levels work but turning off the lights was very effective." In presenting art, Ornette told them, "don't fall into the trap of other people's expectations."[12] Similarly, Ornette's advice to listeners—that they follow the idea not the sound—can "[shift] how artists think about producing art," said visual artist David Hammons (1945–), who adopted this approach in his own work, calling it "a logic that moves in the realm of poetry as opposed to the actuality that people are used to or expect."[13]

(L–R) Ornette Coleman, the painter Beauford Delaney, and two attendees at Delaney's exhibition at Galerie Darthea Speyer, Paris, 1973.

Ornette Coleman at the opening of Skoto Gallery, 25 Prince Street, New York, February 7, 1992.

In 1997 Ornette collaborated with Todd Siler (1953–), the first visual artist to earn a doctorate from the Massachusetts Institute of Technology, composing and performing music for the opening of Siler's installation "Changing Minds" at the Ronald Feldman Gallery (31 Mercer Street). Siler's work, exploring the neuroscience of the aesthetic experience, intrigued Ornette, as did the topic of the installation, designed to examine "the nature of mind, creativity, and our uniquely personal ways of making sense of physical reality." On opening night, Ornette performed "Ode to Art" with a group called Harmolodics (four female vocalists, keyboards, and percussion) against the backdrop of a large canvas Siler called "a wailing wall of mind icons." According to Siler, "the enlightening-speed of intuition" was one of Ornette's favorite topics, and he shared the belief that the science of art and art of science are equally worthy of study.[14]

Denardo described rehearsals with his father as "laboratory sessions where we test and get ideas."[15] In the cover notes for *Skies of America* (Columbia, 1972), Ornette announced the idea that would dominate his musical discourse for decades to come, writing that his symphonic composition was "based on a theory book called the Harmolodic Theory which uses melody, harmony and the instrumentation of movement of forms." The book never surfaced but when asked in 1978, Ornette offered a brief explanation:

> What some people call improvising, which I now call the harmolodic theory and method, which has to do with using the melody, the harmony and the rhythm all equal—I find that it's much easier when a person can take a melody, do what they want to do with the melody, then bring his expression to yours, then combine that for a greater expression. The people I have worked with they know how to do that.[16]

Ornette spoke about his theory often and many musicians have grappled with it.[17] Don Cherry called harmolodics "a profound system based on developing your ear along with your technical proficiency on your instrument" and offered an example:

> If I play a C and have it my mind as the tonic [tonal center], that's what it will become. If I want it to be a minor third or a major seventh that had a tendency to resolve upward [mount the scale] then the quality of the note will change.[18]

However pragmatically intended, explanations often took an esoteric turn. "Technically speaking," said Charlie Haden:

> [Harmolodics] was a constant modulation [changing keys] in the improvising that was taken from the direction of the composition, and from the direction inside the musician and from listening to each other.[19]

James Blood Ulmer remarked that "if it's free music, coming from the soul, playing any kind of changes and any number of bars, going somewhere else on a moment's notice, that kind of blues is really ground zero for harmolodics." Guitarist Vernon Reid, alumnus of Ronald Shannon Jackson's Decoding Society and founder of the black rock band Living Color, agreed that "the blues influence is very central to harmolodic expression."[20] When asked about the nature of harmolodics, Ornette's band mate Dewey Redman deflected: "[Ornette] told me that I had it," he said, "but . . . I think you have to ask him."[21]

Writing for *DownBeat* (1983) Ornette elaborated on his theory, as exemplified by Prime Time:

> Harmolodics is the use of the physical and mental of one's own logic made into an expression of sound to bring about the musical sensation of unison executed by a single person or with a group. Harmony, melody, speed, rhythm, time and phrases all have equal position in the results that come from the placing and spacing of ideas. This is the motive and action of harmolodics.[22]

Ornette presented unison (which came with its own set of definitions) alternately as an aspect of harmolodics and an interchangeable term for it. In *DownBeat*, Ornette called unison "the sound of one's own voice." Later, in 1987, he stressed that "melody is only unison, it's not melody . . . But there are as many unisons as there are stars in the sky."[23] For John Snyder, unison was

> The oneness of sound occasionally achieved by a group of listening and forward moving musicians. And when it was achieved, they knew it and everyone else knew it. The best way I can describe it is that it's a ringing sound that doesn't last very long.[24]

While touring *Skies of America* in Europe, John Giordano asked Ornette to explain harmolodics:

Ornette said "well, one of the things it's like, is if everyone in the world were to sing and all of those voices got together in a unison." Then, years later at a football game, with 60,000 people yelling together, it hit me all of a sudden—I realized that they would start all over the place and eventually those voices blended in a big unison in the same note—and it was an A-flat—and that was the most bizarre thing. I went to games for years and never heard this settling into the same pitch. Now I'm just wondering if that was harmolodics.[25]

As theories go, Ornette's was flexible and to many who tried to divine its meaning, "singularly opaque."[26]

In his *DownBeat* article, Ornette offered a hint to his thinking, citing *On the Sensations of Tone* (1885), a treatise on the properties of sound by physician and physicist Hermann von Helmholtz (released as a Dover paperback in 1954), a seminal work in acoustics studies. Born in Potsdam, Helmholtz belonged to a German upper class that aspired to social ideals emphasizing education across the humanities and science, and the importance of interactions with both artists and scientists. "The horizons of physics, philosophy and art have of late been too widely separated," wrote Helmholtz in his introduction, describing his intent to close the gap as relates to music. Helmholtz played piano and reportedly could "pick out melodies and chords amidst the splashing and noise of [a] fountain."[27] Trained in physiology, he experimented with optics and colors before approaching sound, examining the path between stimulus and receptor. To explain the sensation of sound (vibrations, sympathetic resonances, combinational tones, and beats) Helmholtz used mathematical models, ingenious experiments involving purpose-built gadgets, anatomical studies of the inner ear, and discussions of the tonal systems of different cultures and of the "presumed characters" of major and minor keys.[28] Calling music "the most immaterial, evanescent and tender creator of incalculable and indescribable states of consciousness,"

Helmholz demonstrated how science, particularly mathematics, was "pre-eminently fertile" in understanding its "action on the mind."[29]

To Ornette, who wished to use music the way a physicist uses math, to map complex relations, Helmholz's approach must have seemed a vindication. A scientist at heart, it bothered him that artistic experimentation was dismissed as whimsy, rather than recognized as a valid means of advancing knowledge:

> Only the scientists, technicians and doctors can actually use the whole world as a guinea pig. But artists, we can't do that. If you decide tomorrow that something is outdated, that you can make new music, that people would enjoy, someone would say "this is way before its time." They don't say that about television. They don't say that about penicillin.[30]

Among the arts, Helmholz argued in his introduction, music had the most "immediate connection with pure sensation" and his comparisons to visual art surely resonated for Ornette. In painting, said Helmholtz, only the element of color "is directly appreciated by sensation, without any intervening act of intellect." The beauty of a marble statue "does not depend on the white light it reflects into the eye" but on the form it represents. In music, however, "the sensations of tone are the material of the art [itself]." There need be no additional reference, nor does the aesthetic effect depend on any conception of the instrument, only the sound it makes. "Tones and sensations exist for themselves alone, and produce their effects independently of anything behind them," wrote Helmholtz.[31] Taking these ideas into account, Ornette wrote: "In my musical concept [of harmolodics], not only the sensation of tone to the nerves is released, but the very reason for the use of the tone . . ."[32] Similarly, describing harmolodics in 1987, he said, "What I want to do is to make the *coloring* of the melodies. Not to *color* the melody, but make the melody the actual statement [of color] itself."[33]

Having compiled reams of experience-based data, Ornette's ability to distill it in composition and performance became second nature and he essentially backed into harmolodics as a means of explaining his creative process, its possibilities and results. He wanted it to be everything at once: the sum of his knowledge, a hypothesis defining the parameters and methodologies of his experiments, and a theory, proof of an underlying truth he called unison. It was Ornette's way of saying all this at once that made his formulations difficult to parse.

Ornette was not the only composer to devise an "idiosyncratic theory" whose purpose, as John Rockwell pointed out, was "as much to clarify instinctually arrived-at practices as to lay guidelines for other composers."[34] The proof of harmolodics was in the praxis, a method calling for acute listening, attunement with self and other, and the capacity to both follow and set melodic, harmonic, and rhythmic courses, only to leave such distinctions behind. The harmolodic ensemble sails with the prevailing winds, riding out storms and doldrums, hauling in the canvas, letting it out again, sparing no effort not to arrive at a particular destination but to come to know the sea. According to Kenny Wessel, "[Ornette] would always say, 'Yeah, we're getting there guys'—it was never, 'We did it.'"[35] As an approach to making music, harmolodics was less a theory than a conative act situated between volition and affect, a striving for experience and knowledge whose usefulness, Ornette believed, extended beyond music:

> Harmolodics can be used in almost any kind of expression. You can think harmolodically, you can write fiction and poetry in harmolodic. Harmolodics allows a person to use a multiplicity of elements to express in more than one direction.[36]

Over time, Ornette refined his navigational skills; "Improvising is an outdated word," he said in 1986. "I try to play a musical idea that is not being influenced by any previous thing I have played before."[37] Improvisation, however integral, was just the starting point.

When you consider the music, Ornette made a decidedly Bergsonian sense, whether or not he was familiar with the French philosopher. "The immediate data of consciousness are a multiplicity," said Henri Bergson (1859–1941), calling the temporal nature of the data "the duration." Roughly speaking, whereas a quantitative multiplicity orders things or states of consciousness by separating them, a qualitative multiplicity expresses difference without juxtaposition. The duration is a qualitative multiplicity where "conscious states are organized into a whole, permeate one another, [and] gradually gain a richer content," rather like music as Ornette intended it.

To illustrate life's duration, Bergson used the image of tape spools; as one increases (the past), the other (the future) grows smaller. Memory, like the larger tape spool, conserves the past but doesn't make it static. On the contrary, each passing moment augments and alters it, so that what is recalled today differs from yesterday's recollection. Ornette could plausibly play what he'd never played before; technically (in Bergsonian terms) everyone always does, but Ornette was paying attention. His views on intellect and emotion are also reminiscent of Bergson's, who distinguished between analytical (quantitative) and intuitive (qualitative) intelligence. The former involves circling an idea, the latter full immersion; with music, Ornette did both.[38]

In a 1997 interview with Jacques Derrida, Ornette said, "[the music] I call harmolodic is like we're fabricating our own words, with a precise idea of what we want those words to mean to people." He believed that sound "has a much more democratic relationship to information [than language] because you don't need the alphabet to understand music" and often said, "You don't have to learn to spell to talk."[39] But for someone who felt music should be self-explanatory, Ornette did a lot of explaining, and verbal precision, in the conventional sense, was not his forte. Credited with inventing his own musical language, he spoke as he played, thinking on his feet, veering off topic in seeming non sequiturs. Ornette didn't write much: some liner and program notes, a few articles, some poems that appeared with his records. He cared about words but used them in writing and speech as a kind of shorthand, the same way he used musical notation, "as signposts, not directives."

Gnomic, querulous, "[Ornette] spoke as someone asking questions of himself, not answering someone else's," wrote Howard Mandel; "each idea comprised common, simple words conjoined in newly-minted syntax."[40] Conversing with Ornette, recalled producer Michael Cuscuna, was "like somebody reading you *Finnegans Wake* aloud; you're trying to follow along but you're hanging on by a bare thread."[41] Music writer J. B. Figi struggled while transcribing an Ornette interview in 1973:

> [His] speaking does not translate easily into print. His sentences are free form, his grammar sometimes country. The meanings ordinarily assigned to words are not always the meanings he means. But underneath there's an amazingly unified vision of the world, the relationships which exist.[42]

Daniel Paul Schnee noted that Ornette used "multiple metaphors at once [in a] very pleasant Zen-like manner . . . much like a *koan*."[43] But if Ornette sometimes sounded guru-esque, he was as often pithy and occasionally crass. For instance, on the topic of showbiz, he said:

> In a society where what you do becomes known and you become known as a celebrity, the male has two choices: to be a celebrity or to afford being with celebrities. The people in between only read a lot.[44]

As for the financial rewards he deemed incommensurate to his achievements, Ornette remarked, "It costs a lot of money to be free."[45] On industry folk who basked in the reflected light of recording artists, Ornette said, "some people think talent is like fleas; if you stand around it enough, you'll get some."[46] When Stanley Crouch asked how he found his way through the thicket of sound he and his bandmates created, he quipped, "every golfer needs a hole."[47] "Sound," he once said, "is as free as the gas that passes through your butt."[48]

WITH AGE, ORNETTE achieved a kind of beatitude, though in his earlier life, however mild-mannered he might appear, he could be ornery and defensive, even paranoid about being exploited; people's misbehavior in a business context or their failure to appreciate him darkened his mood and sharpened his tongue. Yet in all his utterances, from the most down home to the farthest out—indeed, throughout his life and despite many disappointments—Ornette displayed an unwavering *amour propre.* John Snyder relates how when preparing for an imminent European tour, Ornette discovered that he had lost his passport and their plans were about to be derailed. "Call the White House," Ornette said, having played there some weeks before. Snyder reluctantly made the call without expecting results, but the passport was miraculously expedited. When he reported that help was on the way, Ornette looked at him "with those slightly condescending, twinkling eyes of his and said . . . 'I know.'"

Snyder further recounts how Ornette confidently presented him with a composition called "Ball Song," insisting it should be played in stadiums, à la the national anthem, no matter what the sport. On another occasion Ornette instructed Snyder to contact industry A-listers Barbra Streisand, Tony Bennett, Lena Horne, and Mariah Carey about a song called "A Girl Named Rainbow," convinced that if they all recorded it they'd have the first ever cross-genre simultaneous smash hit.[49] In the wake of the success of *Virgin Beauty* (Portrait, 1988, with Jerry Garcia), Ornette said, "I always told people I was commercial [marketable], because I was the only person doing what I was doing. Nobody did it but me. There's not two Coca-Colas; there's only one Coca-Cola."[50]

Ornette in his 36th Street, New York, apartment in 2005;
photograph by Jimmy Katz.

However opposed to branding in music and the arts, Ornette
didn't mind a little packaging. Since adolescence he'd used clothes
to express his individuality and the large closets in his last home
(coincidentally in New York's Garment District) were neatly filled
with a museum-worthy collection. In the early days he purchased his
band-members' suits, three tuxedos (red, white, and black), according to Charles Moffett, who had two of each so he could change

his sweat-drenched outfits between sets.[51] When Ornette no longer played clubs, he had a suit made for every concert, often in resplendent colors or shimmery fabrics; John Snyder recalled one that looked like a "TV test pattern."[52] For the 1985 New Year's Eve gala at the Caravan of Dreams, Ornette chose royal purple. For his 1997 performance at Lincoln Center, it was a checkerboard print, topped with a black leather cap. He eschewed berets, but wore fedoras, homburgs, trilbys, flat-tops, bowlers, and the occasional Stetson. He once had a floor-length mink coat and was fond of silk, which he felt "has something to do with light," expressing dismay that "in the Western world [silk] has been related to pimps and preachers."[53]

Ornette was not your average dandy. Growing up, he noticed that people dressed smartly for church but otherwise lived in the threadbare work clothes he associated with poverty and discrimination. A black man in a suit was less likely to be sent to the back door. His appearance also reflected his attitude towards performing, representing a *mise en valeur* of the music and a gesture of respect to his audience: "Who wants to see a guy standing in front, looking like a bum, doing something that bums don't do? I like to have an appearance first that is harmless and secondly, that is interesting."[54] While rock stars, punks, and other musicians adopted a certain aesthetic "so they don't have to tell you what you're listening at," Ornette liked to keep folks guessing with his genteel eccentric style:

> I don't dress to represent wealth, music, race or nothing. It's more like a religion really . . . clothes make the performer stronger before he even gets on the stage. The clothes enlighten [him] to feel good, and the playing and the music they both have a positive effect on the people.[55]

Ornette enjoyed gifting feel-good outfits to women he liked; when one of his students asked for advice after quarrelling with his girlfriend, he told him to buy her a dress.

When it came to the opposite sex, Ornette was old-school gallant but wary. While his profession offered ample opportunity, he was not a womanizer. On the contrary, from the time he started playing publicly, he was uncomfortable with the fact that being a musician gave him traction. This was partly because he wanted to be accepted as a person who happened to be a musician. But he also looked down on those who used music "to stimulate their sex organs" and feared sex might interfere with his creative development.[56] Nor was he convinced that sleeping with someone necessarily enhanced intimacy; "the most emotional separation is done by the mating of the genders," he said.[57] After Denardo's birth, Ornette had entertained the idea of castration to "[eliminate] any sexual feeling I could have in my body," but on a doctor's advice settled on circumcision, which predictably did not solve "that problem."[58] Ornette came to the conclusion that he'd "rather be a man than a male."[59] He wanted to separate genuine affinity from basic drives, a fine art, seldom mastered. When asked the difference between love and sex, he said "Well, you're not always sure you're in love. But when you're having sex, there's really no mistaking it."[60]

In a long conversation on the subject, Ornette told Kathelin Gray:

I don't know how to speak to women. I'm not a bad, what is it called, companion for women, but I don't know how to flirt with them and do all that stuff that people do . . . I don't know how to free the relationship that men and women have with each other.

Whatever concerns he may have had about relationships, Ornette regarded women with a certain reverence. "[They] can save everything," he said, "don't you know that women are the most advanced creatures in the world? Aren't they the only ones that can have babies?"[61]

Entering his seventies, Ornette was well situated in life and love. In 1995 he'd acquired a flat on 36th Street, a large open space for his art collection, and a soundproof room for work. Shortly afterwards he met a woman with whom he remained close until the end. A living legend to an eclectic global tribe of listeners, his name was synonymous with artistic integrity. Substantive international accolades placed him in the limelight even while some of his closest partners in making music history were taking their final bow. In 1997 he was elected a member of the American Academy of Arts and Letters, as Igor Stravinsky, Aaron Copland, and former mentor Gunther Schuller had been before him, and the French Order of Arts and Letters granted him the title of *chevalier*. In 2001 Ornette received the Japan Art Association's *Praemium Imperiale* award ($140,000), the same year that Billy Higgins, with whom he'd begun his adventure in Los Angeles, died aged 65.

During the cherry blossom season of 2002 Ornette travelled to Japan on the invitation of the Minister of Culture and was "treated like a god," his every lisp-anointed remark treated as if "straight from Mount Sinai."[62] In 2004, "for ushering in a new era for jazz," Ornette was awarded the Dorothy and Lillian Gish Prize ($250,000), whose recipients include Bob Dylan and Arthur Miller. In 2006 he lost Dewey Redman, a musician possessed of a creativity that Ornette called "one of the highest forms of spirituality [he'd] ever experienced."[63] That year, the Smithsonian acquired a painting of Ornette by his friend from the Artists House days, Frederick J. Brown (1945–2012), for the National Portrait Gallery, placing Ornette alongside other "[Americans] of remarkable character and achievement." Also in 2006, his first album in nearly a decade, *Sound Grammar* (Sound Grammar, 2006), was nominated for a Grammy Award for best jazz instrumental performance. Reviewing it for *Slate*, Fred Kaplan offered an apt assessment of Ornette at this stage of his life:

> [He] is at the center of things, guiding it all. There's always been a conciseness to his music. The two other colossal saxophonists of his era, John Coltrane and Sonny Rollins, were

probing improvisers (Rollins very much still is), prone to take a passage or verse through endless perturbations, searching for the right note or interval that would open the portal to the rhythm of the universe. It's this boundless restlessness that makes their music so thrilling. Coleman's improvisations are no less intricate, but he heads straight for the prize. He seems to have figured out the various mazes of jazz from the get-go, as if he'd designed them all himself.[64]

Frederick J. Brown, *Ornette Coleman*, 1992, oil and charcoal on linen.

Recorded live in Ludwigshafen, Germany, in 2005 by Ornette's longtime sound engineer, Chris Agovino, and featuring an acoustic quartet (with Denardo and bassists Tony Falanga, who mostly bowed his instrument, and Greg Cohen, who plucked), *Sound Grammar* is as polished and seamless as any studio session. Ornette's lyricism, the quartet's cohesion, and the background presence of an attentive and appreciative audience make this recording one of exceptional grace. Released on Ornette's eponymous new label, and incorporating some old but mostly new compositions, *Sound Grammar* was proof that the muse never deserts those who serve her best. Ornette's last self-produced recording, *Sound Grammar* epitomized both past achievements and the allure he continued to hold for young artists, providing "as thrilling and timeless an entry into his music as the most revered of his old classics," wrote Gary Giddins, who had followed him closely for decades.[65]

In June 2006 Ornette played Carnegie Hall with the musicians who recorded *Sound Grammar* plus Prime Time electric bassist Al MacDowell. "With that much activity on the sonic bottom," wrote musician and author Taylor Ho Bynum (1975–), an Ornette admirer since youth, "the music was a marvelously oblique rumble, a tangle of thick roots over which Coleman's alto blossomed . . . his sound, his whole concept, sounded impossibly fresh yet familiar . . . the music was deceptively simple and implacably radical."[66] Backstage after the concert Ornette befriended photographer and jazz aficionado John Rogers (1978–), a fan since his teens in Nashville. Ornette invited Rogers to his home the next day, the first of many visits that moved him to have a portrait of Ornette tattooed on his leg. When Rogers was ill, Ornette brought him "sorbet, soup and magazines." For his part, Rogers delivered Ornette a bouquet of musicians, instigating impromptu jams, conversations, and pool games. Seasoned players and rising stars (including guitarist Bill Frisell, drummer Joey Baron, bassist Ugonna Okegwo, pianist Jason Moran, bassist Shayna Dulberger, and guitarist Mary Halvorson) came with energy and admiration and invariably left feeling somehow blessed. Jamming in his loft, said Joey Baron, was "a complete affirmation of how great it is to make music in this world."[67]

By all accounts, Ornette was as unfailingly generous with his time as he was with his possessions, hosting a steady stream of musicians, students, friends, and the occasional stranger he spontaneously brought home. Tenor saxophonist Ras Moshe (1968–) was fifteen when he looked Ornette up in the phone book. "He talked to me like he knew me all his life," Moshe said.[68] According to bass clarinetist and trumpeter Matt Lavelle (1970–), who studied with Ornette from 2005 until 2006, he made no fixed appointments. "The policy was you can come by anytime, but you have to *feel* that it's time to go see him and then you go and if he's there and not busy it's the right time." If several musicians showed up, "he'd turn it into a session, regardless of the combination [of instruments, or degrees of skill]." One day, Lavelle found Ornette giving a sax lesson to a waitress he'd met earlier that day at a diner, telling her "music is for everybody."[69] Once he started playing (music and/or pool) he'd go for hours, sometimes without food, feasting on the music and the company.

Ornette Coleman and Michaela Deiss, *Sound Grammar* executive producer, attending the 2007 Grammy Awards ceremony, New York; photograph by Kathelin Gray.

Ornette nonetheless liked to think of himself as a loner who spent all his time composing. "That's how come I don't have no furniture," he told Kathelin Gray, "[people would] stay if they could sit down." He had a hard time refusing company and was accustomed to feeding the energy of interactions into his work, but as he grew older, striking the balance between give and take became more demanding. Ornette admired Gray's ability to impose distance when necessary. "You know when you can turn on the alarm," he commented, "now I don't know how to do that; I'm always on the surface of miracles, and I see people . . ." Gray recounts how his voice trailed off as he went to a window to look down on the street, and she asked if it was cold, if people were wearing coats. "Everyone looks stark naked to me," he said, "Everybody's naked—underneath."[70]

In February 2007 Ornette received a Grammy for lifetime achievement at an un-televised ceremony where Charlie Haden, the last of his closest and oldest collaborators, was on hand to introduce him.[71] In March Ornette was in Washington, DC, for a Kennedy Center awards ceremony honoring jazz royalty including Dave Brubeck, whose commercial success had once irked Ornette; Benny Golson of the Jazztet, who opened for him at the Five Spot in 1959; and his old friend composer George Russell.[72] At the same time, Ornette's home state rallied, with the Texas Cultural Trust Council naming him one of several recipients of their medal of arts.[73] The *pièce de résistance* of a halcyon year came when *Sound Grammar* won the Pulitzer Prize for "distinguished musical composition by an American." John Rockwell, who sat on the Pulitzer music vetting committee, nominated Ornette and was certain he would win "because they wanted someone hip and he was the most unusual and brilliant of the candidates." Ornette was only the second jazz musician to receive a Pulitzer in its then eighty-year history. Had Duke Ellington won following his 1965 nomination, one of the indisputably greatest musician and composers of the twentieth century would have been the first. That honor went to Wynton Marsalis 32 years later, reflecting the belated status accorded jazz and its makers.

Despite the awards and the standing ovations that greeted him wherever he went, Ornette underplayed his achievements. More than praise, he wanted audience and was responsive to requests of collaboration from musicians of every persuasion. Vocalist and composer Joe Henry (who later produced several Grammy Award-winning albums for other blues and folk artists) convinced him to record a composition inspired by African American comedian Richard Pryor on his album *Scar* (Mammouth Records, 2001). Lou Reed, who had attended every 1960s New York Coleman club performance he could find, considered it a high point of his career when Ornette agreed to play on *The Raven* (Sire Records, 2003), a tribute to Edgar Allan Poe.[74] In 2007 Ornette shared a bill that included his old friend James Blood Ulmer; the recently reunited Police; Australian hard rockers Wolfmother; and Ziggy Marley, son of Bob, at the Bonnaroo Music and Arts festival, a four-day event in Tennessee that attracts a crowd of about 80,000. In an interview for Bonnaroo, Ornette said:

> Making music is like a form of religion for me, because it soothes the heart and it increases the pleasure of the brain . . . my real concern for the things that I would like to perfect in music is to heal the suffering, the pain . . . music seems to be a very good dose of light that can cause people to feel much better.[75]

It was a muggy June day when he took the stage, and after a set the *New York Times* called "superb," Ornette collapsed from heat stroke.[76] Undaunted, he flew to London for a concert at the Royal Festival Hall a few weeks later (July 9, 2007).

In 2008, having toured Canada, Croatia, Spain, Hong Kong, New Zealand, and Australia (where he performed in Sydney's Opera House), Ornette returned to New York's Town Hall, where he'd staked his claim on a larger-than-jazz territory a half-century before. Approaching eighty, he had scarcely slowed down, though the dementia that would mark his final years was creeping up on him. Bobby Bradford, who was teaching at Pomona College in California at the time, played New York's Jazz Standard in October 2009 as part of the Festival of New Trumpet Music. It made for a joyful reunion with Ornette, who came with Michaela Deiss and James Jordan, with whom Bradford had maintained close ties since their Texas days. After that last meeting, Bradford kept in touch with Ornette by phone and said regretfully that in conversation he could hear "things were beginning to come loose."[77]

A proud autodidact, Ornette received honorary doctorates from the University of Pennsylvania (1988), the California Institute of the Arts (1990), the New England Conservatory (1992), Bard College (1999), Berklee College of Music (2006), the City University of New York (2008), and the University of Michigan (2010), with President Barack Obama in attendance to deliver a commencement speech. Aside from the odd lecture or seminar, Ornette never taught formally, like many of his friends (including Bobby Bradford, Charles Moffett, John Carter, Dewey Redman) who spent years in classrooms. But he willingly took students regardless of their instrument or level of previous instruction. He gave sax lessons to his grandson Ornette Ali, and praised the seven-year-old for playing his own version of what he'd heard, not replicating what Ornette had shown him. "He got way ahead of me," Ornette said.[78]

If someone approached him for lessons, Ornette asked, "what do you want to know, philosophically?" and as a teacher he was patient and penetrating.[79] The first thing a student did was play for or often with him, an act that revealed skill and technique alongside character and temperament. Musicians often speak of Ornette's ability to grasp the matters closest to their hearts, counting such sessions among their most memorable musical experiences. Ornette likewise reveled in their interactions. Students could double as confidantes, collaborators, or protégés. Among the latter, Japan-born vocalist Mari Okubo was studying *bel canto* in Italy when she met Ornette, who encouraged her to move to New York and study harmolodics. Her otherworldly voice inspired *Cosmic Life* (2004), an album Ornette produced with Okubo performing his compositions including "Space Woman," where he quite exceptionally plays synthesizer.[80]

Ornette's discussions with his student Matt Lavelle touched on astrology, metaphysics, and "the dynamics between male and female." Ornette told Lavelle that there was too much male energy in music, as in life. ("Jazz is like the penis," he later said.)[81] To redress the imbalance he suggested that Lavelle start a band with as many women as men, and he did. Ornette's advice was sometimes hard to take. On one occasion, Lavelle was playing what he considered an impressive riff, "a long vocal swell, like singing but almost like a siren" that he'd modeled on a device of altoist Johnny Hodges. Ornette stopped the music, annoyed. "You can't just say play a bunch of things if you're not going to put it together coherently," he said, "if you don't resolve your ideas, you're not really saying anything."[82]

Ornette's advice to musicians was to dig deeper, to speak in their own voice. He believed that everyone, musician or not, has a sound that is their most intrinsic quality. "Your voice means more to anyone than how you look tomorrow," he said.[83] His own was obviously distinctive. "Within the space of a few notes—a crying glissando, say, or a chortling squeak—[it] is as unmistakable as the voice of a loved one," wrote Gary Giddins.[84] But as Dewey Redman pointed out, "Music is in the ear of the behearer," and what one listener found sublime, another likened to "the penetrating wail of a man who's stubbed his toe on the bathroom door." Reviewing Ornette's duet with pianist Geri Allen (*Eyes in the Back of Your Head*, 1997), *DownBeat* critic John McDonough fumed that "nothing here or anywhere . . . justifies the rather ludicrous heights of absurdity to which Coleman worship has risen over the years."[85] Yet clearly something did, and it wasn't just the music.

"Ornette's thing transcends what he actually plays," wrote guitarist Pat Metheny, referring to his character and ideas.[86] Ornette's life was an extension of his music and vice versa, reflecting a continuity of purpose few individuals strive for, fewer achieve, and many can't help but admire. And however elliptically set forth, his discourse had a through-line, a worldview articulated in his dual role of artist-emissary that boils down to "be yourself but be together." Far from self-indulgence, he considered self-expression a civic duty. "There are no second players, everyone is in the lead," he often said, and with leadership comes responsibility. According to Todd Siler, Ornette was fond of Buckminster Fuller's "trim tab" metaphor describing how the actions of an individual can move the collective. A small attachment to the tail-end of a ship's rudder, the trim tab enables even the most ponderous vessel to fluidly shift direction.[87]

Those who enjoy Ornette's music often find in it a call to action, an impetus for their own creative thinking and work. Music writer Howard Mandel remarked that "[Ornette's] sounds gave rise to notions I came up with [at] no other time, listening to no other source."[88] Nor is Mandel alone in experiencing what may be called the "Ornette effect," which presents itself as encouragement to attempt the new or difficult and to trust, like a funambulist setting foot on the wire, that the exhilaration of reaching the other side is worth the risk. Writing about the first Ornette concert he attended in his hometown of Syracuse, New York (1986), Brooklyn-based pianist James Carney (1964–) recalled that hearing the song "Kathelin Gray," "I felt an incredible wave of emotion, and it seemed as if a bunch of auditory nerves collectively merged inside my body for the first time." The next month Carney left for California to study with Charlie Haden at CalArts. "When you heard [Ornette] play or speak," said pianist and composer Jesse Stacken (1978–), "he made you realize how self-limiting your own thinking is." His "harmolodic approach" to life, wrote Daniel Schnee, was a matter of "[seeing] the world fresh, to see it unnamed, to stop pre-conceiving the world before it had spoken."[89]

Describing a late 1990s performance with Pat Metheny and Prime Time at Boston's Berklee Performance Center, trombonist Josh Roseman (1967–) wrote:

At the end of "Kathelin Gray," over a soft, shifting panoply of arco, cymbals, rumbling analog drumpads and perhaps a high-res, low-octave chamber string pad Pat had conjured— one gorgeous, sweet, willowing note escaped into the ceiling from Ornette's bell—his exact intonation sounded like every Christmas mouse, like a tendril from a pipe, so fun, tender, and everyone said "awww!" all together, every last person in the entire auditorium. I grew up [in Boston], and I'm sure that I fell deeply in love with my city that day for loving Ornette back, for getting it and for exhaling together.[90]

Unlike other artist celebrities, Ornette never advocated a particular cause; he didn't have to, his music was his model, a universal fix. His ideal, of "everyone making their contribution in perfect unison," may seem sentimental, but were it realized it would amount to that most revolutionary of creative acts, the recognition of our shared destiny.[91] Among humanity's shortcomings, Ornette counted racism the most insidious and returned to it often in conversation. Observing the suffering it caused, not just the bloodshed but the unconscionable waste of creative potential, racism seemed to sadden him even more in his later years than it had in his earlier life. In some ineffable yet direct way, music had taught him that humanity is at its best when it mirrors nature by nurturing and reveling in diversity.

Fort Worther, artist, and ceramicist Letitia Eldredge related Ornette's thoughts on creativity, as he explained them to her one day in his Rivington Street schoolhouse:

Creativity is an element, Ornette said, like mercury and iron and there's only a limited quantity of this substance, and people are endowed with it and when they pass on, if they have activated their creativity, that active substance will pass to someone else who is active, and empower them. And that theory was unique and not unreasonable the way he stated it . . . he said, think of Picasso, who had taken what creativity he had and by the use of it and continued attention to it, he had magnified the power in it so that when he passed away, that power was available to others that were already in a position with their own seeds to receive and act upon it.[92]

Ornette's store of creativity would travel far and wide. Perhaps the best, if counterintuitive proof is that while other legendary saxophonists have generated talented and deliberate imitators, few try to emulate Ornette's sound. "He had no disciples as a player," said music producer and writer Michael Cuscuna, "but as a musical architect he created schools."[93]

Pianist and Harvard music professor Vijay Iyer (1971–), a luminary of today's jazz scene and 2013 recipient of the MacArthur fellowship, shares Ornette's perspective that music operates on multiple levels, from the physiological to the metaphysical. Iyer, who majored in math and physics at Yale, describes his improvisational work as both historical and contemporary in addressing what "people have been dealing with for centuries: the mystical and transcendent powers of music."[94] His doctoral dissertation (University of Berkeley) was in the emerging field of embodied cognition, involving the study of music's quantifiable effects on organisms. Iyer's essay "Are Cities Music?" echoes Ornette's observation that the multiplicities of urban sound and activity are analogous to music:

The capacities to coordinate and synchronize our actions, to incorporate each other's rhythms, to make choices together in real time – to groove and to improvise – these are human skills, not merely musical skills . . . we evolved to like the stuff that music is made of. We selected for it [because] knowing how to listen is a skill worth having.[95]

Vijay Iyer, Half Moon Bay, California, April 29, 2018;
photograph by Brian McMillen.

Ornette, who held similar ideas, felt that his intellect was discounted, while Iyer, raised in a middle-class family of Indian origin in upstate New York, regretted that, in being perceived as Asian, "I was seen as having only my intellect to use."[96]

Like Ornette, Iyer did not formally study his instrument (though he did take violin lessons), disapproves of labels like "jazz" (preferring "creative music"), is dismissive of "the athletic rigor" of virtuosity, rehearses his compositions exhaustively with likeminded bandmates, and was distressed by reviews early in his career. "Critical writing used to attempt to place me by othering me, by putting me outside the history of jazz. Everything I did was seen as different and not as the continuity of a tradition," he says. Similarly accused of a precipitous break with the past, Ornette had in fact subsumed and advanced the music. Likewise, Iyer represents a natural extension of the trajectory

Ornette helped launch. The qualities he commends in Ornette's work ("the conceptual innovation, rigorous detail and profound emotional resonance") are present in his own ensembles.[97] "To me, the best way to pay tribute to Mr. Coleman is to follow his lead—i.e., to be radically, audaciously yourself," Iyer says, which is what he and collaborators like drummer Tyshawn Sorey (1980–), pianist Jason Moran (1975–), and trumpeter Ambrose Akinmusire (1982–), to name a representative few, have done.[98] And there could be no fitter tribute. Making music was never enough for Ornette; it had to make things happen.

CLAIRE O'NEAL, WHO writes children's books about science and nature, penned a biography of Ornette for readers aged nine to twelve that begins like a fairy tale: "One November night in 1959, a screeching, pleading sax solo sliced through the broken shadows of the cold New York City air."[99] While not quite the stuff of bedtime stories, Ornette's life has sometimes been likened to that of the characters in Horatio Alger's formulaic novels about poor young men who live the doctrinal American dream, progressing from "rags to riches" or in Ornette's case, from obscurity and ridicule to widespread appreciation and respect. Ornette would have objected to such comparisons; despite voluminous compositional output and countless performances, he was never really rich or as famous as he might have been. In his liner notes for *This Is Our Music* (Atlantic, 1961), he dispelled the notion that he was special at all, writing that anything worth knowing about him was present in the music. "The other autobiography of my life is like everyone else's. Born, work, sad and happy and etc." Nor did he romanticize being stubborn enough to have succeeded in holding his individualist course. "I don't think I've been lucky," Ornette told Howard Mandel in 1978, twenty-plus years into his career; "it's been a disaster," he said, complaining that "one of the [bad] things is that no one believes you."[100]

Time and a growing number of believers absolved the bitterness but inured as he was to struggle, Ornette never rested on his laurels nor could he begin to calculate the protean influence of his life's work. A paper appearing in the *Journal of Management Inquiry*, for instance, references Ornette's music:

> to explore the possibility of responding to issues within organ-
> izations in more participative and improvisational ways,
> without losing an appreciation of the inherent impossibility
> (perhaps even absurdity) of the managerial condition.[101]

Michael Selekman, author of *Pathways to Change: Brief Therapy with Difficult Adolescents* (2005), urges therapists to note how listening to Ornette "[propels] us into novel and creative musical realities," suggesting it may help "to liberate therapists from the shackles of complacency and the fear of taking risks."[102] In the expanding field of music therapy, Ariel Weissberger, founder of Berko Therapy, which addresses the problems of ageing, writes that "the expansive ways in which Ornette thought about music" are instructive in "the process of exploring our authentic musical self."[103] Theoretical physicist and sax-ophonist Stephon Alexander studied with Ornette, and his book *The Jazz of Physics* (2016), partly inspired by their conversations, under-scores the roles of intuition and improvisation in scientific discovery.[104]

As patron saint of all things dissonant and defiant, Ornette's musical appeal extended through his own to subsequent generations. Epoch-shaping 1960s bands who acknowledged his transmissions include the Velvet Underground, Soft Machine, and Cream ("secretly an Ornette Coleman band with Eric [Clapton] not knowing he was Ornette," said bassist Jack Bruce). Filtered through their unique beings, a tincture of Ornette emerged in the work of Frank Zappa (1940–1993), Brian Eno (1948–), and Captain Beefheart (Don Van Vliet, 1941–), whose music has been described as "Delta blues run through Coleman's 'harmolodic' blender."[105] In the music Ornette

recorded in the 1970s, including early Prime Time, at least one practiced listener found the "future raiments of disco *in excelsis* . . . with
1972's masterpiece, *Science Fiction*, as the fulcrum, an afro-futurist
scrying mirror, or more properly, a disco ball, that would cast black
futures from black pasts."[106] Along with Ronald Shannon Jackson,
Ornette begat what has been referred to as "black rock," exemplified
by Vernon Reid's group Living Color. "Without [them]," said Reid,
"I would never have started [the band]. Even though the music was
different the impulse was the same."[107]

Vocalist Neneh Cherry (1964–) compared the music her father
Don played with Ornette to punk, calling it "total confrontation."[108]
It's too bad punk icon Patti Smith (1946–) didn't get Ornette to play
on *Radio Ethiopia* (Arista, 1976), dedicated to Rimbaud and Brancusi,
as she'd wished. Smith met Ornette in 2006 at a pizzeria in Italy,
and he invited her onstage at the Bologna Communal Theater to
improvise a poem. "As you enter his world," she said, "you feel his
confidence, enthusiasm and sense of wonder." Smith is one of many
influential artists to acknowledge Ornette's far-ranging attraction.
"Part of his appeal to the people of rock and punk is that he doesn't
require you to be a complex musician," she said, "he just requires that
you listen, communicate and play with feeling."[109]

Composer and saxophonist John Zorn (1953–) was an early and
prolific passenger on the Ornette train. His album *Spy vs. Spy: The
Music of Ornette Coleman* (1989, Electra) presented Ornette's compositions pulverized into brief, high-speed doses of what has
sometimes been described as noise-core (descendant of hardcore
punk, grindcore, and thrashcore). Reviewing Zorn's frenetic extracts
delivered in concert at earsplitting volume, Francis Davis remarked,
"Who would have thought that a quintet without a single electric
instrument could inflict such pain?" Zorn maintained that "visceral,
physical" volume was essential in "bringing [Ornette's music] up to
date."[110] His album *Naked City* (Nonesuch, 1990), with a band of the
same name, arguably did a better job, though it features but a single

John Zorn, *c.* 2007;
photograph
by Scott Irvine.

Coleman piece, "Lonely Woman" (1959), one of Ornette's most
beguiling melodies, which Zorn turns into a soundtrack for a filmic
SWAT raid on a bank heist when the safe's about to blow.

Zorn's earlier album, *The Big Gundown* (Nonesuch, 1986), covered
the film scores Ennio Morricone (1928–) composed for Sergio Leone's
westerns, where Clint Eastwood snarls and rolls a toothpick around
his mouth. Naked City's second album, *Grand Guignol* (Avant, 1992),
recapitulated the compositions of Debussy, Scriabin, and Messiaen.
Thrashing and grinding aside, Zorn's work with diverse musics and
musicians (including the string ensemble Kronos Quartet that had
to growl and bark as per his score) helped restyle perceptions of the
avant-garde as a musical stance, rather than the cutting edge of any
genre. Zorn, who credits Ornette with "completely changing the
way [he] thought about music," started The Stone (2005), a non-
profit experimental music performance space in the East Village ("a
place for exploration and discovery"), and is also a director of the

non-profit National Sawdust (2015), an artist-managed venue where "multicultural artists tell their stories through their music," with Ornette's compositions often figuring in their plots.

The Bad Plus, a New York-based trio that has paid the complement of reinterpretation to everyone from the Bee Gees and Yes to Stravinsky and Babbitt, tackled Ornette's *Science Fiction* (1972), an album that acoustic bassist Reid Anderson (1970–) said corresponds to the band's "DNA."[111] While the original recording did not include keyboards, in Bad Plus's version of *Science Fiction* (first performed in 2014), pianist and composer Ethan Iverson (who has written authoritatively about Ornette's technics and context) plays, as it were, past his instrument. Anderson and drummer Dave King assembled an electronic collage echoing the space-placed tracks of the original recording and guests Tim Berne (alto sax), Ron Miles (cornet), and Sam Newsome (soprano) filled the reed roles of Ornette, Dewey Redman, Don Cherry, and Bobby Bradford. Ornette, who heard one of the band's early iterations of his work, paid Bad Plus the ultimate compliment: "They all sound like individuals," he said.[112]

The list of musicians who shared the stage with Ornette during his last years reflects the breadth of his reach. Appointed curator for the 2009 London Meltdown, a ten-day annual arts festival held in the Southbank Centre, Ornette (the first black musician chosen for the job) assembled a line-up of old friends and new. For opening night, he selected The Roots, a Philadelphia hip-hop band featuring MC Black Thought (Tariq Luqmaan Trotter), multi-instrumentalist and producer Questlove (Ahmir Khalib Thompson), and guitarist Vernon Reid. The dancing began "in the first minute," remarked a reviewer who had "never seen so many black faces in a Royal Festival Hall crowd."[113] Ornette sat in that night along with saxophonist friends David Murray and then 91-year-old Andy Hamilton, who arrived in the UK in 1949 from Jamaica as a stowaway on a banana boat.

Along with the consecrating presence of the Master Musicians of Joujouka, who played admission-free concerts each afternoon,

Ornette's Meltdown presented Yoko Ono and the Plastic Ono band with Sean Lennon and members of Japanese experimental pop band Cornelius; Senegalese vocalist and bandleader Baaba Maal; electronic musician Moby (Richard Melville Hall); the electronics-tinged jazz hybrid of Kieran Hebden (also known as Four Tet) and drummer Steve Reid (who played with Miles Davis, James Brown and Fela Kuti); improvisational vocalist Bobby McFerrin; and harmolodic veterans James Blood Ulmer, Jamaaladeen Tacuma, and Charlie Haden's Liberation Orchestra with pianist Carla Bley. Ornette's sessions with Denardo, Al MacDowell, and Tony Falanga were interspersed with cameo appearances by festival guests, including Naked City guitarist Bill Frisell, Red Hot Chili Peppers bassist Flea (Michael Peter Balzary), and Patti Smith.

On September 7, 2010, when Sonny Rollins celebrated his eightieth birthday at New York's sold-out Beacon Theater (2,894 seats), he and Ornette traded riffs as they had by the Pacific a half-century before. With two artists representing the heroic essence of American musical culture onstage, according to an audience member, "the place went . . . batshit crazy."[114] Later that month, New York's Jazz Gallery ("where the future is present") honored Ornette with a three-day event showcasing the shape of the jazz that came in his wake.[115] He was in Japan in October, and Brazil in November, where the São Paolo venue experienced a power cut, and the band played in the dark while "the audience roared."[116] Ornette's last official concert was at the London Jazz Festival in November 2011, but he wasn't through just yet.

Every year on March 9, Ornette invited friends to his birthday party, usually in his home. Denardo threw a big one in 2012 with at least a hundred guests, including James Jordan; Jayne Cortez and her husband Melvin Edwards; Charles Moffett's son Charnett; Dewey Redman's widow, Lidija Pedevska-Redman; Muhal Richard Abrams; Karl Berger and Ingrid Sertso (cofounders with Ornette of Woodstock's Creative Music Studio); *Blues People* author Amiri Baraka and music writer Stanley Crouch (with whom Ornette spent

Sonny Rollins on West 26th Street, New York, 1998; photograph by Jimmy Katz.

hours on the phone); gallery owners Skoto and his wife Alix; vocalist Mari Okubo; Brent Hayes Edwards from Columbia University's Center for Jazz Studies (who helped resurrect interest in Artists House and New York's loft era); and DJ Phil Schapp, who had been broadcasting 24-hour birthday marathons of Ornette's music on WKCR (Columbia's radio station) for over forty years.

The pool table was covered in case of spillage and copious amounts of soul food were served: spicy turkey meatballs, deviled eggs and hushpuppies, rice and beans, clam and chicken stew, and red velvet cupcakes. With this many musicians in the house, including James Blood Ulmer, Vernon Reid, former Prime Time members Chris

Rosenberg, Kenny Wessel, Albert MacDowell, Tony Falanga, and Greg Cohen, Iranian saxophonist SoSaLa (Sohrab Saadat Ladjevardi), and country rocker Steve Earle, a jam was bound to break out. Bern Nix called the party a meeting of "harmolodics anonymous."[117]

However auspiciously it began, 2012 ended sorrowfully for Ornette and his son when Jayne Cortez passed away on December 28. In mid-April 2013, with Melvin Edwards, Denardo travelled to Nigeria to scatter Jayne's ashes in Benin City, at a ritual conducted by Oba (king) Eriadiuwa. Shortly after Jayne's death, Ornette fell and broke his hip; between personal loss and physical strain, it was a hit from which he would never fully recover. In 2014 he nonetheless hosted another birthday party and, later that year, looked out from the bandstand on a large, enthusiastic crowd one last time. The June 12 tribute concert held at Prospect Park as part of the annual Celebrate Brooklyn Festival was an appropriately free event (no tickets required). Eric Adams, African American president of the Brooklyn Borough, introduced the honoree, frail but resplendent in a purple pinstripe suit, assisted onstage by his grandson, Ali.

At the beginning of the concert, featuring Denardo's band Vibe, Ornette sat cradling his white plastic sax in his lap. When he finally picked it up, the blues issued forth and his shallow breath grew stronger as the band joined in on one of his early compositions, "Ramblin'" (1960), a "prairie theme," wrote T. E. Martin, "[that] seems to create the sense of western emptiness across which men move with their mixture of bravado and loneliness."[118] Tap dancer Savion Glover mounted the stage to add a kinetic thrill, perhaps reminding Ornette of the nights he danced on the tabletops of Fort Worth clubs. Laurie Anderson (who on first hearing Ornette play violin said "I want to talk like that") played electric violin over feedback loops created by her recently deceased husband, Lou Reed, accompanied by John Zorn and bassist Bill Laswell. Patti Smith chanted a poem about Ornette's odyssean life. Wilco guitarist Nels Cline and Sonic Youth guitarist Thurston Moore improvised an Ornette-flavored duet and the Master Musicians of Joujouka piped a whiff of the Rif Mountains over Brooklyn. Towards the end of the three-hour concert, the sultry June night relented with a fine cooling rain. When he wasn't playing, Ornette just sat there and smiled.[119]

The extent of Ornette's influence is impossible to track fully because it's ongoing, but also because it did not come solely from Ornette. The force he so skillfully channeled is a human constant, the need to communicate experience. He and artists like him awaken something in others that is present but seldom attended to, an ember that grows hotter when fanned. Ronald Shannon Jackson referred to Ornette and fellow trailblazer Cecil Taylor as suns: "not planets, but light for other planets."[120] Cecil Taylor, coincidentally, did not perform at Ornette's tribute, but he attended his old friend's 85th birthday party, a three-day-long celebration replete with music and feasting. And three months later, he played at Ornette's funeral.

(L–R) Al MacDowell, Patti Smith, Tony Falanga, and Ornette Coleman at Ornette's 80th birthday party, March 9, 2010, New York; photograph by Jimmy Katz.

WHEN A YOUNG niece died in 1997, Ornette attended her wake and was puzzled by the way her body was presented. He wanted to name a composition after it—"She Was Sleeping, Dead, and Wearing Glasses in her Coffin"—but on second thought, he changed the title to "Blind Date," which is a pretty accurate description of how death is met, regardless of what one is wearing.[121] Ornette didn't discuss his own mortality often; when he did, he used the euphemism "when I close my eyes."[122] But during his acceptance speech for the Lifetime Achievement Grammy award, Ornette ruminated on the topic at harmolodic length, marveling at how death and life could coexist and how death, which kills all, apparently cannot itself be killed. Being born human in a world so full of living things, he pointed out, is something to be grateful for, as is the birth of generation after generation, since it improves our collective chance of understanding life, which we partake of but is independent of us.[123]

The closing of Ornette's eyes, shortly past midnight on June 11, 2015, made headlines in newspapers coast to coast and beyond, from *The Guardian* and *Irish Times*, to the *Indian Express* (Uttar Pradesh) and Japan's *Yomiuri Shimbun*. In France, both the conservative *Monde* and leftist *Libération* lamented his passage, as did Sweden's *Svenska Dagbladet*. In Italy, a country Ornette loved and had toured extensively, *La Repubblica* covered his passing, as did *Corriere della sera*, under the title "Addio al padre del free." Homages were posted to scores of websites and articles published in music magazines and literary journals, elegant, broad-stroke biographies that reflected on the man, the music, and the era. Many lingered over his New York debut, when the Coleman Quartet "didn't just take the roof off the Five Spot; they took the roof off the idea of the roof and left jazz exposed to the elements."[124]

Since 1959, reviewers have done their poetic best to describe Ornette's sound; "a wail of self-possessed originality . . . a knowing but Edenic worldview," wrote Peter Watrous in the *Village Voice*. For anyone familiar with the South, Stanley Crouch's phrase, "the blues seep through it, like rain through a window screen," reached to the music's heart. Writing for *The Wire*, Brian Morton was, as Texans say, "sharp as a twig" in calling Ornette's work "a series of small autotelic gestures, with each song a sufficiency of content and information" that taken together "resemble a prolonged and orderly Tractatus."[125] It's all true, but what is striking is how words, however artfully deployed, fall short when it comes to music. While visiting a 2006 exhibition of Jackson Pollock paintings, Ornette defined abstract art as "something that causes you to see more than what you're looking at." Likewise, his is a music that makes you hear more than you think, or can ever really say. The caption beneath a Pollock canvas that Ornette admired that day read, "Untitled." "Ah," he said, turning it over in his mind, "that's a good title."[126]

The funeral was held at the interdenominational Riverside Church in Upper Manhattan, coincidentally established the year Ornette was born and the subsequent scene of some exceptional gatherings. Martin Luther King Jr. spoke out against the Vietnam War there in 1967; César Chavez, Desmond Tutu, Fidel Castro, and Nelson Mandela had all stood at the lectern. But on June 27, 2015, Riverside earned a place in music history as the venue for a send-off that began with the green-robed Joujouka masters leading Ornette's casket cacophonously to the altar. For several hours, the Neo-Gothic nave reverberated with the sounds of artists practiced in the art of striving and of sharing their attainment, beginning with Pharaoh Sanders and Cecil Taylor. Sonny Rollins didn't play but his presence was strongly felt. Just as Ornette had offered a musical prayer at John Coltrane's funeral, so Coltrane's son Ravi played at his. An assembly of former Prime Time members chose a composition from the group's vintage first album, *Dancing in Your Head* (1977).

Duets pairing Henry Threadgill with Jason Moran and Jack DeJohnette with tap-dancer Savion Glover signaled Ornette's trans-generational impact and a passing of the baton. Music journalists who covered Ornette throughout his career gave stirring orations, as did Melvin Edwards, who situated Ornette's work in the context of the twentieth-century avant-garde alongside Picasso and composer Edward Varese. Yoko Ono said a few words and left a white scarf she'd knitted by her old friend's bier. Steve Dalachinsky recited a poem comprised of Coleman song titles and got a laugh with his story about meeting Ornette and giving him a copy of one of his poetry books. Ornette signed it, and gave it back.

Dressed in a lustrous silk suit, Ornette's remains were interred at Woodlawn Cemetery, an unexpected stretch of parkland in the Bronx with moss-mottled mausoleums evoking ancient Egypt and Greece. Around him lay some of the musicians whose names and sounds every schoolchild should know: Edward Kennedy "Duke" Ellington (1899–1974), Coleman Hawkins (1904–1969), Lionel Hampton (1908–2002), Illinois Jacquet (1922–2004), Maxwell "Max" Roach (1924–2007), and Miles Dewey Davis (1926–1991). When Phil Schaap, who officiated at the funeral, remarked he had

Ornette Coleman with the Master Musicians of Jajouka
at his Meltdown in London, June 2009.

"the feeling of the conclusion of the age of the prophets," he wasn't being nostalgic. Maybe another cohort of geniuses will surface against stacked and somber odds to birth an incandescent art, a form of communication so compelling it brings ideas to the dance floor, fuels collectives, illumines cities, and lends resolve to those who would rally against injustice in such great and persistent numbers that the powers-that-be grow afraid and back off. Sure, it could happen again, theoretically. But it may take a while.

SHORTLY AFTER ORNETTE died, a small arts cinema in Brooklyn (Spectacle) mounted a film series in his honor. Shirley Clarke's documentary was screened, as was Conrad Rooks's *Chappaqua* (1967), with a soundtrack remix by musician and filmmaker Chifu Spencer Yeh replacing the score Ornette had recorded and Rooks had removed. In 2016, a half-century after Ornette recorded the music for *Who's Crazy* (dir. Thomas White, 1965), the film finally debuted in New York at the Anthology Film Archives (March 25, 2016), thanks to then 35-year-old documentary filmmaker Vanessa McDonnell, who resurrected and restored a copy. Acts of remembrance like these, performed by artists who find consonance in Ornette's work, help keep it alive, and Denardo Coleman has already begun an effort to preserve and present his parents' legacies that could easily occupy the rest of his life.[127] Not all artists are fortunate enough to have a family member so implicated, knowledgeable, and willing to devote his time, nor are all musicians created equal when it comes to attracting scholarly and institutional attention; however remarkable their stories and output, many will vanish without a trace.

Universities and institutions scattered throughout America house fragments of jazz history: scores, recordings, photographs, film and video footage, correspondence, and memorabilia. The Library of Congress (LOC) has a holding so large it's like an archeological site whose deep strata await excavation. In 2005, during work on another collection held there (the radio broadcast Voice of America), tapes were unearthed of a 1957 Thelonious Monk-John Coltrane concert at Carnegie Hall, the jazz equivalent of Tutankhamen's tomb.[128] The LOC houses archival collections of musicians such as Charles Mingus, Shelly Manne, Dexter Gordon, and Ella Fitzgerald, the "first lady of song," whose effects are spread over several institutions, including the Ella Fitzgerald Charitable Foundation and the National Museum of American History, another Smithsonian unit, where Duke Ellington's oeuvre is also preserved. But while "superstars" are likely to find a home for their archives, those of lesser-known musicians, says music educator and author Gary Giddins, often "don't go anywhere."

In 1986 Giddins approached music industry mogul Ahmet Ertegun (Atlantic Records), who was unsympathetic to the notion of funding efforts to find and acquire such materials before it was too late. "He spent twenty minutes telling me I was wasting my time, jazz wasn't the future and he was putting all his money into rock and roll," Giddins said.[129] Rock history found a patron in Microsoft billionaire Paul Allen, and a home in the palatial building he commissioned from Frank Gehry. Opened in 2000 as the Experience Music Project, the more accurately re-dubbed Museum of Pop (MoPop) is a Seattle landmark attracting over 700,000 visitors annually. Similarly intended as a destination for music tourism and education, the National Museum of African American Music in downtown Nashville, Tennessee (under construction at this writing, 2019), is a 54,000-square-foot (5,000-sq.-m) facility that plans to present "fifty musical genres" from "slave music to hip-hop," including jazz.[130]

Among the institutions more focused on preserving historical documentation is Rutgers University's Institute of Jazz Studies (IJS), a suite of rooms on the fourth floor of the New Jersey campus library. It offers scholars and students of the university's graduate and postgraduate jazz studies programs a multilingual range of pre-Internet music magazines and journals, oral history recordings, records, photographs, and memorabilia, including the archive of New Jersey-born

Count Basie, everything from press clippings to pianos. The National Jazz Museum in Harlem, a Smithsonian affiliate supported by state and private sponsors, is a 129th Street storefront preserving collections of recordings, including talks given by author Ralph Ellison, who was himself a living archive of jazz history, in addition to presenting performances, exhibitions, educational programs, and symposiums uniting musicians, scholars, and aficionados.

Neither the IJS nor the Harlem museum is equipped to meet the challenge of collecting and preserving a body of work as sprawling as that pertaining to jazz. The opening of the Smithsonian's National Museum of African American History and Culture (2016) offers hope in that regard, and the Smithsonian's declaration of 2019 as the "year of music" came with the promise to "highlight and share with the public [the institution's] vast musical holdings."[131] An essay describing "Musical Crossroads," an exhibition at the National Museum of African American History and Culture, acknowledged that "African-American influences are so fundamental to American music that there would be no American music without them," while referring to the task of adequately describing that influence as "intimidating—if not impossible." The exhibition presents an array of artifacts: a wooden drum, carved by South Carolina slaves in the 1800s; a neon sign from Minton's; a tambourine from Prince's 1990 Nude Tour; and a "custom Mapex black panther snare drum" used by Living Color percussionist Will Calhoun. While jazz falls within the museum's daunting purview, a search of its digital archives in 2019 returned one entry for Ornette (a 1972 photo with Dewey Redman onstage in Florida). Cecil Taylor yielded no results; Duke Ellington, twenty; Coltrane, two.[132]

Documentation for many of Ornette's contemporaries, like the pioneering Texan musicians mentioned in Part One of this book, is thin on the ground. While institutions may be willing to receive documents relating to lesser-known yet significant contributors to jazz history, rarely are efforts made to purposefully acquire them.

Occasionally, a dedicated scholar comes across some unsung artist's archive and is able to help salvage it, adding greatly to the record. Michael C. Heller's *Loft Jazz: Improvising New York in the 1970s* (2017), detailing a landmark decade, would not have been possible without percussionist Juma Sultan (1942–), who shared his richly documented life story.[133] It's disheartening to think that Donald J. Trump's presidential tweets will be more comprehensively and accessibly preserved than the stories and sounds of the musicians who actually did "make America great."

While researching this book, hints of hidden treasure turned up, like the tapes of Ornette's 1960s sessions with John Coltrane and with Albert Ayler, never heard; and of the 1962 Town Hall Concert, never released in its entirety; or the 1990s "promo video" Ornette apparently made called "What is Harmolodic?" featuring Lou Reed, Thurston Moore, and others, seldom, if ever, seen. John Snyder mentioned recorded conversations and sessions with Ornette ("Mozart speaks") that will hopefully one day be transcribed.[134] A glimpse of available materials and an intimation of all that awaits discovery was provided by Ken Burns's nineteen-hour documentary *Jazz: The Story of America's Music* (2001), incorporating over 2,000 archival film clips, 2,400 stills, and five hundred pieces of music and accompanied by a 552-page eponymous publication.[135] Reviewers' complaints that the six-year effort focused too heavily on early jazz history to the detriment of blues and the experiments of Ornette's era miss the point that jazz is a moving target, and however one tells the story, there will always be another angle, more characters and events to sweeten the plot. Music makes history when it embodies and outlasts the context of its origins, but unlike other art forms it is animate, unconstrained by time or space. Whoever experiences a piece of music adds to its life. "Music never stops," said Don Cherry. "It's you who is stopping. It's you who is ending."[136]

Epilogue: Last Night

The year Louis Armstrong died (1973), a New Orleans park, located in what was once Place des Nègres, the area assigned to slaves for Sunday gatherings, was named in his honor. Kansas City paid tribute to Charlie Parker in 1999 with a 10-foot-high (3 m) bronze cast of his head mounted on a pedestal that reads "BIRD LIVES". A slightly larger than life-size bronze of John Coltrane was dedicated beside the city hall of High Point, North Carolina, in 2006, when he would have been eighty years old. In 2005 the Fort Worth municipality approached the matter of recognizing hometown heroes more expediently. Evans Plaza, on Evans Street in the Southside, dispensed with over a century's worth of African American musicians, educators, Pullman Porters, publishers, entrepreneurs, and Second World War vets in one fell swoop.

Situated off a highway on the edge of the historic neighborhood and covering about 1,000 square feet (90 sq. m), the plaza (completed in 2008) features commemorative portrait plaques positioned along a low semi-circular wall, or in the red-brick pavement beneath the visitors' feet. Ornette's face is there on the ground, along with, among others, that of Raymond "Pie" Melton (1909–1991), who founded the *Fort Worth Mind*; William "Gooseneck" McDonald (1866–1950), who opened the first Texan bank for African Americans; and Roger Hughes (1890–1975), community leader and proprietor of Ornette's favorite barbecue joint. Ornette was alive when his plaque was placed, as was Dewey Redman. Charles Moffett, John Carter, Prince Lasha, and Ronald Shannon Jackson were among the overlooked, but other I. M. Terrell alumni were remembered, including "King" Curtis Ousley (who was born in 1934, not 1935 as his plaque states) and Julius Hemphill (1938–1995).

Returning to Texas after more than twenty years, I spent time visiting places that were no longer there: Ornette's childhood homes, the Jim Hotel, the Rocket Club, and the Zanzibar. Ornette's nephew, Truvenza's son Sean, had died, and his mother's old house was being prepared for new tenants by a man who answered the door with a gun tucked in his belt. The Morning Chapel Church where Ornette was baptized was still standing, as was the Allen Chapel and I. M. Terrell High School, then undergoing an expansion and recently reopened as the I. M. Terrell Academy for Science, Technology, Engineering, Math, and the Performing and Visual Arts. Ornette's photo appears on the academy's website, but talk of naming the auditorium after him hasn't yet panned out.

The Fort Worth soundtrack was Lockheed jets and the whoosh of cars over sun-softened asphalt. Texans don't walk, but I don't drive and in my perambulations was often mistaken for a hooker. Pedestrians were more common downtown, which, despite its recognizable contours, had profoundly changed. When efforts to revive the city center began in the 1980s, the Caravan of Dreams Performing Arts Center, with its copper awning and geodesic dome, was the main attraction, bringing crowds to a part of town they would otherwise never frequent after dark. Back then, new office spaces had begun to be rented, and the area known as Sundance Square comprised a couple of pleasant outdoor restaurants, a Whataburger, Pier 1 Imports (founded in Fort Worth), the Tandy Center, Worthington Hotel, Billy Miner's Saloon, and, adjacent to the Caravan, the Red Goose Shoe store (est. 1903) run by Ira Solomon, who refused to sell out to the Bass brothers, no matter what. When my friend Marie Antoinette, daughter of a well-known Baptist minister and doyen of

The author beside Ornette Coleman's hometown tribute in Evans Plaza,
Fort Worth, October 29, 2016; photograph by Butch Clemons.

the Black Chamber of Commerce, opened a perfumery, it seemed
downtown was getting interesting, that is, if you ignored the Bass's
private security force (headed by a former CIA agent) cruising around
their properties in golf carts.

Walking downtown nowadays is like being in a computer-
generated model: everything seems to exist at a remove, the carefully
selected retail outlets tastefully presented and purposefully themed
to underscore a church-going pioneer/cowboy identity: shops selling westernalia, National Football League souvenirs and high-end
camping kits, and eateries for ribs, Tex-Mex, and pizza. The palatial
Bass Performance Hall, home to the Fort Worth Symphony Orchestra,
opera, and ballet companies, hosts wholesome entertainments like
Broadway magic shows and Rogers and Hammerstein's *Cinderella*.
Replacing a large ugly parking lot is an elegant town square, where a

stage was set up for a western swing band. The musicians and the people sipping supersized soft drinks at a few of the scattered tables were all white. The Basses decreed, "Let there be Fort Worth!" And behold, wonders were wrought. But a city's character is not bestowed by fiat, nor is its history served by a makeover reducing it to marketable clichés. There is perhaps no plainer proof of such misconjecture than the erstwhile Caravan of Dreams, once the harbinger of an open-ended, arts-driven urban future, now a "ranch-themed" steakhouse.

While working at the Caravan (1985–92) I was marked by the musicians' ability to enthrall a crowd, but only now do I appreciate their modesty despite all they'd seen and done. Dizzy Gillespie, who performed with us frequently, first came to Fort Worth in 1946, yet he never hearkened to his epic past or behaved as if he had one except when he blew his horn. The Atlas of drummers, Elvin Jones, so shy of manner, rumbled like a gentle earthquake when he played. McCoy Tyner, the picture of affability, his hands in mine like sacred artifacts. "Oh . . . Egypt," Sun Ra said when I reminded him we'd met there, removing one of his self-produced records from its psychedelic slipcover to sign as a gift. Every musician had his or her way of commanding the audience's attention: Cecil Taylor attacked the Bösendorfer with an assassin's stealth; Shirley Horn, seated at the piano in a cocktail dress and pearls, removed her gloves, signaling the crowd to hush; Carmen McRae, part Delphic oracle, part lady bus driver, mounted a center-stage bar stool and stared the crowd down before delivering her wisdom of tough love.

The place was packed with around three hundred people on weekends, the largely black crowd dressed to the nines: women in sequined gowns, capes and boas, men in suits of metallic fiber, fedoras, and bling. Solos and improvisational crescendos were met with hoots and hollers: "Yes, Lord!"; "I know that's right!" Sometimes women doffed their heels, stood on chairs, and waved napkins or Kleenex like pennants welcoming long-lost heroes home. It was an appreciative, raucous crowd that freely expressed its feelings. When the South African a cappella group Ladysmith Black Mambazo appeared within days of Nelson Mandela's release from prison in 1991, the entire audience—black, white, and brown—remembered segregation and many of us wept. For years I stood at the door, welcoming strangers, tearing tickets, greeting and seating. However amorphous the crowd when the night began, by its end we'd cohered, made friends, the music forging for us a subtle bond.

I lived above the stage in the apartment reserved for in-house managers, also known as synergists. Ed Bass had a room there, as did Kathelin Gray, John Allen and a half-dozen others. People travelled a lot in those years when Biosphere 2 was being built in Arizona and the *Heraclitus* sailing the Caribbean to gather specimens for the ocean biome. In the midst of it, a hurricane sank the ship at harbor in Mexico, but it was resurrected by the crew, who installed under-water balloons they inflated to float it back up. Aside from visitors from other Institute of Ecotechnics projects, Texan friends and the occasional Rinpoche, Andrei Voznesenski, Yevgeny Yevtushenko, Timothy Leary, Trilok Gurtu, and of course Ornette were among those who dined at a long oak table. Our several weekly shared meals were taken in silence, except if we had guests or on Sundays when there was wine and toasts, and everyone gave a short speech.

Synergists were responsible for different aspects of the business, but everyone cared for the cactus collection in the dome, which was arranged by desert. I was in charge of the Malagasy; someone else Namibian, Sonoran and so on. The cacti, we observed, were like artists: able to flourish in harsh environments, never consuming more than they required, blossoming infrequently but emphatically, and sporting thorns sharp enough to draw blood. We all belonged to the in-house theater troupe (along with a handful of locals) under Kathelin Gray's direction, which brought the mordant likes of *Ubu Roi*, *The Good Person of Szechuan* and Aeschylus' *Oresteia* to the Fort Worth stage. We meanwhile managed the day-to-day operations of the nightclub, theater, record label, and a food and beverage operation serving as many as several thousand people weekly with the help of around fifty Texan staff. On a given night I would banish the Furies as Athena in the theater and be downstairs in the club in time to clear the house between sets.

In its incarnation as a steakhouse, the wall to the right when you entered the Caravan, once filled with a painting of dancers from world cultures, now bears the portrait of a giant cowboy. The night-club has been subsumed by a dining hall with private side rooms for business lunches, all polished leather and dark wood. It was early when I visited, the place was empty, but I was seeing ghosts. Lynn the oil heiress, sailing into the club in a full-length mink trailing frozen peas like gazelle droppings from the pack she'd strapped to her back to ease her disks. Morris, another regular, in his three-piece suit and gel curls, arriving late after his shift as "maître d'" of the Swiss House Restaurant, bearing brown paper bags full of snacks for the staff. Conan, who manned the soundboard, introducing the acts in his velvety baritone and ever equipped with a fanny pack full of esoteric repair items—a drum key, a guitar string, a set of reeds. Cheri, recep-tionist and ticketing computer whiz, a pencil tucked behind her ear. Troy, the bouncer, built like a samurai, gentle as a lamb.

The history of jazz mural that once made the space glow was gone, the main decorative element now consisting of large animal head trophies, all impressively horned and embalmed. The brass banister of the lobby stairs was exchanged for a more rustic wrought-iron one, but there's an elevator now and hardly anyone walks. Those who do are treated to a series of photographs of dead Republicans—mayors, oilmen, corporate kingpins—hanging along the stairwell. On the second floor, the door that once led to the synergists' quarters beside the theater had disappeared without a trace. The tall, oak-framed glass arches, beyond which the theater lobby bar was once visible and inviting, were converted into showcase cabinets for saddlery and lassos. The roof, praise Jesus, retained its magic thanks to the faux rock waterfalls and the Grotto Bar sprouting wildflowers and tall, spikey grass. The geodesic dome, alas, had lost its mountain and all else. It's a dining room now, with a chandelier.

After I left Caravan, a new general manager was hired who took the booking in a different direction and the old staff (including the in-house management) was phased out. By the later 1990s, the club was open only 150 nights a year and no longer a reliable feature of the downtown scene. It closed altogether on September 29, 2001, the same day it opened in 1983 and coincidentally Ornette Coleman Day, which had long since gone uncelebrated. That a polka band was chosen for the closing night was an additional poke in history's eye. But the Caravan had served its purpose in real estate terms, kick-starting interest in the surrounding property and lending downtown a bit of sparkle. The facility's extensive archive (photos, videos, newsletters, posters, and so on) was either destroyed or consigned to an undisclosed Bass-owned location, and the once exciting idea that Fort Worth might add a vibrant performing arts scene to its anodyne cultural menu was entirely forgotten. Heraclitus (the philosopher) was right when he said everything turns into its opposite, but how much so depends on what it was before. The Caravan's success in bringing progressive art to a welcoming, multiracial audience may thus be judged by its deface-ment and the erasure of its history, an act that itself was but a small measure of the city's hard swing to the Christian right.

A few months before his 2016 election, candidate Trump was invited to Fort Worth by the exclusive City Club in the Bass Tower. For his last act as Exxon CEO prior to becoming Trump's secretary of state, Rex Tillerson had purchased the Bass's oil and gas interests in the West Texas Permian Basin to the tune of around $6 billion. The Basses employed Steve Bannon (later Trump's chief strategist) osten-sibly to manage downtown properties. But it is worth mentioning that when Ed Bass wearied of his affiliation with the Institute of Eco-technics in 1994 and decided to shut down operations at Biosphere 2, it was Bannon and a bevy of armed Federal Marshals who ousted the Arizona facility's occupants.

In his brief essay "Theater and Science" Antonin Artaud spared a few choice words for the machinations of what Texans call "the good old boys," which, in any discussion of the arts and free expression, bear repeating:

> And no political or moral revolution will be possible so long as man continues to be magnetically held down—even in his most elementary and simple organic and nervous reactions—by the sordid influence of all the questionable centers of the Initiates, who, sitting tight in the warmth of the electric blankets of their duality schism laugh at revolutions as well as wars, certain that the anatomic order on which the existence as well as the duration of actual society is based *will no longer know how to be changed.*[1]

The assumption that people are easily fooled has a basis in fact, but as is often overlooked by the rich and hurried, so does Newton's third law of motion, that for every action there's an equal and opposite reaction.

The muscular arm of elitist influence does not reach into Fort Worth's black neighborhoods, where the sheen of wealth is as absent now as it was when Ornette was a boy. The flimsy houses lining pitted streets are smothered in vegetation bursting from sidewalk cracks and in every available space. Signs warning citizens to beware of mosquito-carried West Nile Virus are posted at intervals, a reminder of the perils of the Trinity River lowlands. Religiosity comes naturally in such settings, where everything is temporary, as likely as not to be swept away by flood, tornado, shooter, or cop. Sunday church gatherings typically revolve around acceptance of a Jobian lot and relief that it won't last forever. Church was important to Ornette, and attending a service in the (Baptist) Inspiring Temple of Praise Church brought me closer to him.

The emotional crescendo built by the band, the preacher, and the congregation was like a plane clearing turbulent clouds into the light. At the end we shook hands or embraced, feeling clearer of mind. The purpose of such music-driven group ritual is to rise above a baser nature; not carnality, as some (mostly white) Christians would have it, but the redness of tooth and claw that lurks beneath the veneer of society, business, and politics. At an early age, Ornette understood that music was power of another order, the kind that opened minds and options, beginning with his own. A territory beyond the reach of the mundane, music was a space filled with sound and meaning, a vantage point. In a world where achievement is measured by having, Ornette opted for being.

I didn't know Ornette well; we spent some hours together during one of his return engagements to Caravan in the late 1980s; he was kind, and pretended not to notice that his hometown audience that weekend was very thin. We went for lunch to Roger Hughes' Barbeque, a clapboard shack with a parking lot. "You ever been here?" he asked. I confessed I had not. "You just wait," he said. The man behind the counter was the smoker, someone who spends the night feeding mesquite chips to a barbecue grill made from a discarded oil barrel. He prepared our sandwiches on Wonder Bread that dissolved on contact with the thick sauced-up slabs of beef; on Ornette's recommendation, we washed it down with strawberry soda. I wasn't Ornette's biggest fan in those days; I found the music difficult and was preoccupied with ticket sales. But while they did not always draw the largest crowds, Ornette and others like him formed the substance of our mission, to apply the transformative balm of music to America's rawhide heart. Listening again after thirty years, Ornette's is the only sound I know that captures the texture and complexity of that time.

The music business has certainly changed since then. It's harder than ever to earn a living as a musician in New York, America's jazz HQ, where the "important" live venues are few, the competition fierce, and a degree from a noted conservatory is not only expected to advance a career, it's expected, period. As for listeners, we're more likely to discover a piece of music via an algorithm nowadays than through a serendipitous encounter at a record store, in a club, or on the radio, as once upon a time. The stadium-sized audiences Ornette desired are nothing compared to the exposure offered on social media platforms, where tens of millions of YouTube hits and Facebook "likes" are bestowed upon pop stars and citizen performers alike. The world Ornette hoped for, where everyone has a chance to sound their voice, is here and now.

Writing for the *Village Voice* in 1985, Peter Watrous described how reading press coverage of Ornette's Five Spot debut reminded him of the days when "paradigms came one at a time, where the newness of Ornette was possible." Musicians of his stature were less likely to emerge, Watrous wrote, "in a world where all styles and genres coexist, where there isn't one target, one style's back to break," an observation that might be all the truer now. But perhaps amidst the staggering profusion of musics past and present available literally at one's fingertips, the concept of new versus old has at last been rendered meaningless. If so, Ornette would call that progress.

Ornette at home in New York in front of a painting by Ed Clark, 2005;
photograph by Jimmy Katz.

References

Part One: Coming Up

1 John Rockwell, *All American Music* (New York, 1983), p. 190.
2 Richard Selcer, *A History of Fort Worth in Black and White: 165 Years of African American Life* (Denton, TX, 2015), pp. 25, 33.
3 Tina Nicole Cannon, "Cowtown and the Color Line, Desegregating Fort Worth's Public Schools," doctoral dissertation, Texas Christian University, Fort Worth, TX (2009), p. 6. Research conducted by the Equal Justice Initiative in Montgomery, Alabama, indicates that 335 lynchings occurred in Texas between 1877 and 1950. "Lynching in America" (2017), available online at eji.org. The total number across the twelve states studied was 4,000.
4 Sara Valdez, "American Abject," *Art in America* (October 2000), pp. 88–9, a review of the exhibition "Without Sanctuary: Lynching Photography in America," New York Historical Society, March 14– August 13 and September 13–October 1, 2000.
5 "Texas Centennial," Texas State Historical Association, *Handbook of Texas Online*, www.tshaonline.org, accessed December 29, 2016. The Centennial's first Negro Day attracted 67,000 African Americans from all over Texas, and two more Negro Days were subsequently planned in the course of the six-month event. See Selcer, *A History of Fort Worth in Black and White*, p. 342.
6 Kenneth N. Hopkins, "The Early Development of the Hispanic Community in Fort Worth and Tarrant County, Texas, 1949–1949," *East Texas Historical Journal*, XXXVIII/2 (2000), p. 63, http://scholarworks.sfasu.edu.
7 Selcer, *A History of Fort Worth*, p. 79; Cannon, *Cowtown and the Color Line*, p. 54. Organizations that relied on the church included the Willing Workers, the Youth Society, the Wide-Awake Society,

and the Fort Worth branch of the National Association for the
Advancement of Colored People (NAACP), established in 1918.

8 John Litweiler, *Ornette Coleman: A Harmolodic Life* (New York,
1992), p. 24. According to the Fort Worth City Directory, Ornette's
parents lived at 301 E. 1st Street in 1930 and at 807 E. 2nd Street
in 1936. The 1940 U.S. Federal Census shows the family residing
close by, at 309 Elm Street. Ornette was baptized in the Colored
Methodist Episcopal (CME) Morning Chapel, known as the "rock
church" for its rusticated limestone exterior (est. 1885) at 901 E. 3rd
Street. Mount Gilead, Fort Worth's first black Baptist church (est.
1875), is nearby at 600 Grove Street, as is St. James Baptist (est.
1895) at 210 Harding Street; Allen Chapel, an African Methodist
Episcopalian church built in 1914 by architect William Sidney
Pitman, son-in-law of educator and author Booker T. Washington,
is located on 1st and Elm Street.

9 Raleigh Kenneth Dailey, "Folklore, Composition and Free Jazz: The
Life and Music of John Carter," doctoral dissertation University of
Kentucky, School of Music, Lexington, KY (2007), p. 25. Avant-garde
composer, recording artist, and music educator John Carter played
clarinet, saxophone, and flute.

10 Ibid., p. 24.

11 Alan Govenar, *Texas Blues: The Rise of a Contemporary Sound*
(College Station, TX, 2008), p. 177. The "honeypot" was emptied by
a "honeyman" who came through the neighborhood on horsecart to
collect the waste. The father of Dewey Redman was a Pullman porter
living on the Southside.

12 Ibid., p. 8. Playing simultaneously guitar and "quills," a kind of
panpipe made of sugar cane, Thomas imitated train sounds on
"Railroadin' Some"; see Dave Oliphant, *Texan Jazz* (Austin, TX,
1996), pp. 38–42. He was probably called "Ragtime" because he
favored up-tempo beats for his songs, some of which were revived
in the 1960s by Bob Dylan, Canned Heat, and the Lovin' Spoonful.

13 Albert Murray, "Improvisation and the Creative Process," from a
lecture delivered in 1983, in *The Jazz Cadence of American Culture*, ed.
Robert G. O'Meally (New York, 1998), p. 113. Early jazz compositions
referencing train noises include (Texan) Scott Joplin's "The Great Crush
Collision March" (1896), Duke Ellington's "Choo-Choo" (1926), and
one of the most popular tunes of the war years, Louis Jordan's 1945

recording of "Choo Choo Ch' Boogie" (1946, by Vaughn Horton, Denver Darling, and Milt Gabler), with its onomatopoeic refrain.

14 Conversation with Marjorie Crenshaw in her Southside Fort Worth home, October 10, 2016. A graduate of Fisk University (Nashville) and the University of North Texas, Marjorie Juanita Hollins Crenshaw taught music to elementary school students for 32 years and was a founding member and president of the Fort Worth Jazz Society. Her husband Willie, a friend of Ornette's, played trumpet.

15 Rosa's birthdate is given as December 25, 1903, in the 1930 U.S. Federal Census. In the 1940 census it was 1904. Likewise, there were discrepancies in Randolph's birthday between the 1920 and 1930 censuses, given as 1893 and 1897 respectively, with the former date the more likely. According to the "Application for Headstone" submitted by Rosa in June of 1939, Randolph died on February 21, 1938. Truvenza was born in Rio Vista, Texas, July 16, 1920. Ornette's full name was Randolph Denard Ornette Coleman.

16 Conversation with Brenda Sanders-Wise (1949–), director of the Lenora Rollins Heritage Center, Southside Fort Worth, October 19, 2016.

17 Telephone conversation with Bobby Bradford, November 4, 2016. Trumpeter, cornetist, bandleader, composer, and educator (currently at Pomona College, California) Bobby Lee Bradford was born in Cleveland, Mississippi, and moved to Dallas in 1946. He worked most extensively with John Carter, but met Ornette in 1952, played with him in New York in the early 1960s, recorded with him in 1971, and remained a lifelong friend.

18 Conversation with Jack Carter, October 17, 2016.

19 Video interview of Marjorie Crenshaw conducted by journalist and musician Michael H. Price entitled "Jazz Perspectives," recorded for the Fort Worth Public Library archives, September 2007.

20 Bob Ray Sanders, *Calvin Littlejohn: Portrait of a Community in Black and White* (Fort Worth, TX, 2009), p. 127.

21 LeRoi Jones, *The Blues People* (New York, 1963), p. 48. Jones (1934–2014) changed his name to Amiri Baraka in 1967.

22 Clive Bell, "Plus de Jazz," *New Republic*, September 21, 1921, p. 93.

23 Jazz at the Philharmonic was named after the Los Angeles Philharmonic Auditorium, where the series (1944–83) began. Tad Hershorn, *Norman Granz: The Man who Used Jazz for Justice*, (Berkeley, CA, 2011), pp. 53–5. Hershorn provides a comprehensive

account of Granz's lifelong efforts to redress the effects of racism in
the music industry and his leading role in promoting jazz as a fine art.

24 Litweiler, *Ornette Coleman*, pp. 22–3.

25 A. B. Spellman, *Four Lives in the Bebop Business* (New York, 1966),
p. 95.

26 I am indebted to Gayle Hanson, librarian at the Prince Hall
Mosque, Fort Worth's first African American Masonic lodge, who
searched the lodge archives to determine whether the Colemans
were Masons like many of their contemporaries. African American
women also participated in the Masons, as members of the Order of
the Eastern Star or the Herons of Jericho.

27 The certificate issued by the Texas Bureau of Vital Statistics noted
Vera's cause of death on January 21, 1941 as a "fractured skull"
following an automobile accident, leaving it unclear whether she
was a passenger or pedestrian. Allen was born on July 26, 1916, and
is not listed as residing in Rosa's home in the 1940 census, which
notes Rosa's job and that she had received a third-grade elementary
school education. Allen died on April 5, 1943. I was unable to procure
documents indicating the cause of death.

28 Whitney Balliett, *American Musicians: Fifty-six Portraits in Jazz*
(Oxford, 1986), p. 403.

29 Ornette mentions being part of a church band (see N. Hentoff,
"Biggest Noise in Jazz," *Esquire* (March 1961), p. 84). If Ms.
Crenshaw's memory is correct, he would have played in Fowler's band
when he was thirteen or fourteen, perhaps overlapping with the time
he played in the I. M. Terrell High School band. Fowler instructed
other I. M. Terrell band members, including alto sax, clarinet,
and flute player Prince Lasha. Keala Griffin, "Cowtown Legacy
Competing with Fort Worth's Jazzman," *Fort Worth Star-telegram*,
November 12, 1994.

30 Charles Moffett interviewed by George Coppens, *Coda Magazine*,
191 (August 1, 1983), p. 12.

31 Pianist and composer Thelonious Monk, born in North Carolina,
toured with a Pentecostal preacher at age seventeen; Ornette's
friend the pianist, composer, and theorist George Russell grew up
in Cincinnati listening in on Holy Roller services that "rocked the
earth"; see Francis Davis, *In the Moment: Jazz in the 1980s* (New
York, 1986), p. 167. Bassist and composer Charles Mingus attended

services in Los Angeles, "the blues was in the Holiness churches—moaning and riffs . . . "; see David H. Rosenthal, *Hard Bop: Jazz and Black Music, 1955–1965* (New York, 1992), p. 138.

32 Conversation with Jack Carter, October 17, 2016. Mr. Carter recalled a Pentecostal church on Baptist Hill in Fort Worth.

33 Marjorie Crenshaw, "Jazz Perspectives" interview, September 2007. The Southside's Love Chapel Church of God in Christ was built in the 1930s on White Street, later renamed Rosedale Street. It is uncertain how many Pentecostal and Evangelical churches were located in Fort Worth, but their congregations were the likely target for an ad in an African American community paper, the *Fort Worth Mind* (November 1946): "AULT MUSIC Company, TAMBOURINES . . . 4.25$ and up."

34 Jones, *The Blues People*, p. 41.

35 Litweiler, *Ornette Coleman*, p. 152.

36 Mark Warren, "Ornette Coleman: What I've Learned," *Esquire Magazine*, www.esquire.com, December 24, 2009.

37 From the documentary *Dewey Time* (dir. Daniel Berman, 2001). Dewey lived on the corner of Leuda and Tennessee Streets.

38 Conversation with Bobby Bradford, October 28, 2016. Jukeboxes were both designed and manufactured by the Chicago-based J. P. Seeburg Piano Company.

39 "The Automatic Age, Millions in Pennies," *Popular Mechanics* (October 1932), www.jitterbuzz.com, accessed January 8, 2017.

40 David Breskin and Rafi Zabor, "Ronald Shannon Jackson: The Future of Jazz Drumming," *Musician* (June 1981), http://davidbreskin.com, accessed January 8, 2017. I am grateful to Shannon's son Clifford Jackson, to Kevin Coffey for additional information regarding Bill Jackson, and to Shannon's mother, Ella Mae Shannon (b. 1917). Bill Jackson's record store operated at least until the early 1970s.

41 Conversation with Brenda Sanders-Wise, October 19, 2016.

42 Radio aficionado Mike Shannon has compiled a wealth of information, lacking in local library archives, regarding the history of radio stations established in the Dallas/Fort Worth (DFW) area: www.dfwretroplex.com. See also Richard Schroeder, *Texas Signs On: The Early Days of Radio and Television* (College Station, TX, 1998).

43 Joseph Abel, "African Americans, Labor Unions, and the Struggle for Fair Employment in the Aircraft Manufacturing Industry of Texas, 1941–1945," *Journal of Southern History*, LXXVII/3 (August 2011), pp. 595–638. Carter was later responsible for bringing Bell Helicopter to the Fort Worth area.

44 Carter is quoted in the Amon Carter Museum's website. Selcer, *A History of Fort Worth*, p. 295.

45 Bradley Shreve, "Trent, Alphonso E.," Texas State Historical Association, *Handbook of Texas Online*, www.tshaonline.org, accessed January 25, 2017. The weekly broadcast continued throughout the band's eighteen-month engagement. Texan jazz greats who played with Trent's band include Charlie Christian, Herschel Evans, Buddy Tate, and Budd Johnson.

46 Correspondence with Kevin Coffey, January 12, 2017. Coffey has been documenting the history of American roots music for several decades, particularly western swing and other jazz-inflected country music styles.

47 Brown's band expanded to include jazz pianist Fred "Papa" Calhoun (in 1933), electric steel guitarist Bob Dunn (1934), and saxophonist Iris Harper (1935). The Light Crust Doughboys were so named for their role in a radio program promoting Light Crust Flour, a product of the Burrus Mill Company. Dave Oliphant, *Jazz Mavericks of the Lone Star State* (Austin, TX, 2007), pp. 150–51.

48 Mike Shannon's radio history site, www.dfwretroplex.com, accessed January 14, 2017. Lombardo was a Canadian of Italian descent. Performing animated if tame arrangements of popular tunes suitable for ballroom dancing, his orchestra became famous for its New Year's Eve concerts broadcast live, first via radio from New York's Roosevelt Hotel (1929–55), and then via TV across America from the Waldorf Astoria (1956–76).

49 James Head, "Durst, Albert Lavada [Dr. Hepcat]," Texas State Historical Association, *Handbook of Texas Online*, www.tshaonline.org, accessed January 14, 2017.

50 Govenar, *Texas Blues*, pp. 502–3. On the origin of "Hattie Green" see Dave Oliphant, *Texan Jazz* (Austin, TX, 1996), p. 75.

51 Selcer, *A History of Fort Worth*, pp. 426–7.

52 Head, "Durst, Albert Lavada [Dr. Hepcat]."

53 Govenar, *Texas Blues*, p. 502. In his 1984 interview, Durst recited lyrics from "Let's Talk about Jesus": "There's a man in my soul / That keeps me free from sin. / My whole life has been changed / Since Jesus moved in."

54 Ibid.

55 Conversation with James Clemons's son James Jr., also known as Butch, Fort Worth, 2016. Clemons later (early 1950s) had an hour-long program on another Fort Worth Station, KNOK, called "High Noon Ramble," whose signature opening was "Toothpick time for me, lunchtime for you."

56 Mike Shannon's radio history site, www.dfwretroplex.com. The program probably played songs from *Billboard* magazine's "Harlem Hit Parade," the name given to the list reserved for best-selling recordings by African Americans, later changed to "Race Records" (1945) and "Rhythm and Blues Records" (1949).

57 The *Dallas Morning News* ad dated November 9, 1947 is reproduced online at DFW Radio Archive, www.dfwradioarchives.info, accessed January 11, 2017. KLIF's programming included "a comprehensive sports program . . . [and] a talking parrot at station break time."

58 The Rose Ballroom opened in 1942, reopened in 1943 as the Rose Room, and was renamed the Empire Room in 1952. Govenar, *Texas Blues*, p. 87. Red Calhoun appeared as bandleader in the film *Juke Joint* (1947) by pioneering African American director Spencer Williams.

59 Govenar, *Texas Blues*, p. 215.

60 Ibid., p. 11.

61 The Pythian Temple, like Fort Worth's Allen Chapel, was designed by William Sidney Pitman, son-in-law of Booker T. Washington. Govenar, *Texas Blues*, p. 86.

62 The noun "blues," meaning "low spirits," was first recorded in 1741 and may come from "blue devil," a seventeenth-century term for a baleful demon, or from the adjective "blue," meaning "sad," a usage first recorded in Chaucer's *Complaint of Mars* (c. 1385). See Christine Ammer, *American Heritage Dictionary of Idioms* (New York, 1997), p. 191.

63 Stanley Crouch, *Considering Genius* (New York, 2006), p. 25.

64 Ibid., p. 27.

65 Govenar, *Texas Blues*, p. 215. For a full discussion of Southwest territory bands, including the Blue Devils, Moten's, and Alfonso

Trent's, see Gunther Schuller, *Early Jazz: Its Roots and Musical Development* (Oxford, 1968), pp. 279–317.

66 "Territory Bands," in *Encyclopedia of the Great Plains*, ed. David J. Wishart, University of Nebraska-Lincoln, at http://plainshumanities. unl.edu, 2011.

67 Ross Russell, quoted in Oliphant, *Texan Jazz*, p. 113.

68 Texan guitarist, composer, and arranger Eddie Durham may have contributed to this composition, but Smith does not mention him in his 1982 interview. Govenar, *Texas Blues*, pp. 213–17.

69 Gunther Schuller, *The Swing Era: The Development of Jazz, 1930–1945* (Oxford, 1989), p. 245. Gunther Schuller produced the recording session in Fort Worth's Clifford Herring Studio that resulted in the Atlantic release *The Legendary Buster Smith* (1959). Oliphant, *Texan Jazz*, p. 187.

70 Govenar, *Texas Blues*, p. 213. According to Smith, Parker acquired his nickname "because when he'd go home at night he'd say, 'I'm goin' to get my wife to cook me one of them yard birds' . . . so they called him 'Yard Bird' then shortened it to 'Bird.'"

71 Ibid., p. 215. Hear Buster Smith's "King Alcohol" (1959) on YouTube.

72 Ted Panken, *DownBeat* contributor, posted the transcript of his 1998 interview with David "Fathead" Newman on his blog, in honor of what would have been his 81st birthday, February 24, 2014: https:// tedpanken.wordpress.com.

73 Litweiler, *Ornette Coleman*, pp. 24, 31. Ornette specifically recalled two songs from his youth, "Sentimental Journey" (1944) by clarinetist/orchestra leader Les Brown, and "Flying Home." Hampton wrote "Flying Home" (1939) while with Benny Goodman's band and nervously waiting to board his first transatlantic flight. Hear Jacquet on "Flying Home" on YouTube. The transcription of Jacquet's solo, available on several online sites, has been downloaded thousands of times.

74 *The Autobiography of Malcolm X*, as told to Alex Haley (New York, 1962), p. 74.

75 Govenar, *Texas Blues*, p. 220. Illinois Jacquet performed in the first Jazz at the Philharmonic concert, in Los Angeles, 1944.

76 Ibid., p. 238. See "Texas Tenor, the Illinois Jacquet Story" (dir. Arthur Elgort, 1992), with appearances by Buddy Tate and Arnett Cobb.

77 Oliphant, *Texan Jazz*, pp. 171–3. Johnson studied music in Dallas with Portia Pittman, daughter of Booker T. Washington.

78 Ibid., pp. 13–16; quotation from Rudi Blesh and Harriet Janis, *They All Played Ragtime* (New York, 1950). Fort Worth's Euday Bowman (1887–1949) authored the popular "12th Street Rag," recorded by Louis Armstrong (1927) and every swing band of the 1930s and '40s. Oliphant, *Texan Jazz*, p. 29.

79 Documented by Gates Thomas, brother of William Thomas, an early president of the Texas Folklore Society. Govenar, *Texas Blues*, p. 13. The cultural context from which the blues originated was extensively documented in books based on the field work and recordings of John A. Lomax (Austin, 1867–1948, appointed honorary curator of the Archive of Folk Song at the Library of Congress in 1933) and his son Alan (1915–2002), who toured Texas, Louisiana, and the Mississippi Delta in the early decades of the twentieth century.

80 Robert Palmer, "Black Snake Moan: The History of Texas Blues," *Guitar World* (September 1996), in *Blues and Chaos: The Music Writing of Robert Palmer*, ed. Anthony DeCurtis (New York, 2011), p. 59. See also John Scanlan, *On the Road in America: From Delta Blues to '70s Rock* (London, 2015), pp. 14–34.

81 The voices of Lightnin' Washington and others singing "Lord, God Almighty" while chopping wood in a prison work yard was recorded by Texan musicologist John Lomax in 1934 and is available on YouTube, accessed 26 July 2019.

82 Govenar, *Texas Blues*, p. 10. The term "breakdown" may derive from "breaking down the corn" (removing the ears from the stalks), but it also refers to how while dancing, individuals transported by the sound would take turns breaking away from the group to perform a "solo" encircled by the others, literally breaking the music down into movement. For chock houses, see Govenar, *Texas Blues*, p. 215.

83 Quince Cox, cemetery caretaker in Wortham, Texas, where Jefferson is buried, interviewed in 1999, ibid., p. 10.

84 Ibid., p. 22. Paramount advertised itself as "the Popular Race Record." Ranking with Bessie Smith and Ma Rainey as a preeminent lady blues singer was Houston-born Sippie Wallace, "the Texas nightingale" (1898–), who began recording in 1923, and in 1924 recorded with Sydney Bechet and Louis Armstrong. "Queen" Victoria Spivey, born in Houston but raised in Dallas, also recorded with Armstrong, and

was known for the "proto-feminist" blues "Any Kind of Man (Will Be Better Than You)" (1934).

85 Transcript of Eddie Durham interviewed by Stanley Dance for the Smithsonian Institute, August 1978, from the University of San Marcos (Texas) Archives, p. 71. When asked how he found snakes, Eddie replied, "Turn over rocks. You know just about where they are." p. 74.

86 Ibid., p. 9.

87 Ibid., pp. 14, 22, 42–3.

88 From a 1984 interview, Govenar, *Texas Blues*, p. 72. Durham was among the first to use the DeArmond pick-up, a device introduced in 1939 that gave guitarists a bigger sound. Born in Fulton, Mississippi, Lunceford (1902–1947) studied music with Wilberforce Whiteman, father of bandleader Paul Whiteman, and achieved a master's degree in music and sociology from Nashville's Fisk University.

89 Govenar, *Texas Blues*, p. 75.

90 Transcript of 1978 Dance interview with Durham, p. 21.

91 Interview with T-Bone Walker for *Record Changer* magazine, 1947, reproduced in Michael H. Price, *Thick Lights, Loud Smoke and Dim, Dim Music: The Honky-tonk Badlands of Texas* (CreateSpace Independent Publishing Platform, 2015), pp. 90–91.

92 Gene Fowler, "Physic Opera on the Road: Texas Musicians in Medicine Shows," *Journal of Texas Music History*, VIII/1 (2008), p. 9.

93 M. Price, *Thick Lights, Loud Smoke*, pp. 90–91.

94 Govenar, *Texas Blues*, p. 209.

95 Ibid., p. 219.

96 Hear T-Bone's JATP performance on YouTube.

97 Thanks to Kevin Coffey for information (and digital files) of the first electric guitar recordings. Bob Dunn, electric steel guitarist, recorded in Chicago in January 1935 with Milton Brown and his Musical Brownies. In September 1935, Leon McAuliffe became the first to record with an electric standard guitar, playing with Bob Wills and his Texas Playboys in Dallas. Several other western swing electric guitarists appeared on records prior to their jazz counterparts. See also Fernando Ortiz de Urbina, "Who's on First?" posted September 28, 2016, at http://jazzontherecord.blogspot.com.eg.

98 Schuller, *Swing Era*, p. 567.

99 Quoted in Oliphant, *Texan Jazz*, p. 195.

100 Litweiler, *Ornette Coleman*, p. 25.

101 Balliett, *American Musicians*, p. 403.

102 Litweiler, *Ornette Coleman*, p. 25. In Nat Hentoff, *The Jazz Life* (New York, 1961), p. 283, Ornette recalls the altercation with an unnamed church bandleader, which would have been with Fowler, but the incident may have occurred later, when Ornette joined the I. M. Terrell band, under George Baxter.

103 Nat Hentoff, "Ornette Coleman: Biggest Noise in Jazz," *Esquire* (March 1961), p. 84.

104 Selcer, *A History of Fort Worth*, pp. 62–4. Born into slavery in Grimes County, Texas, Isaiah Milligan Terrell (1859–1931) learned to read and write as a child, a criminal offense for the enslaved. He attended Straight University in New Orleans, a historically black college, founded in 1868 by the American Missionary Association. Terrell was one of the first black teachers hired when Fort Worth started a public school system in 1882, and later the first superintendent of the city's black schools. I. M. Terrell (on Chambers Hill, formerly Baptist Hill) closed in 1973, a significant loss to the black community, paradoxically as a result of desegregation. Owing to alumni efforts it was reopened in 1986 as an (integrated) elementary school. It is now a school for visual and performing arts in addition to a science technology, engineering, and math academy.

105 Charles Jackson, "Trio Contemplate their FW Jazz Roots," *Fort Worth Star-telegram*, June 17, 1984.

106 A. B. Spellman, *Four Lives in the Bebop Business* (New York, 1966), p. 86.

107 Conversation with Marjorie Crenshaw, October 10, 2016. Tom Kellam, City of Fort Worth archivist, also heard the "Star Spangled Banner" story. Crenshaw said her husband Willie, a trumpeter who practiced with Ornette, was saddened when his aunts refused to let Ornette in their house because he "looked like a thug." The porkpie hat was fashionable among musicians, including Illinois Jacquet.

108 "Terrell Class Gets Diploma," *Fort Worth Star-telegram*, June 2, 1944.

109 The *Fort Worth Press* (December 17, 1945) advertised the jitterbug contest: "with [Fort Worth's] Sonny Strain, his drums and orchestra, admission 1$." The talent shows were held at the Southside's Grand Theater on Fabons Street (see Charles Jackson, "Fort Worth's Jazz

Connection: Trio Reminisce," *Fort Worth Star-telegram*, June 17, 1984. Marjorie Crenshaw recalled seeing Ornette play there.

110 Conversation with Brenda Sanders-Wise, director of Fort Worth's Lenora Rollins Heritage Center, October 19, 2016. Also known as the New Negro Movement, the Harlem Renaissance refers to the cultural efflorescence (literature, art, theater, and jazz) that made Harlem the center of African American creative and intellectual life in the post-First World War years to the mid-1930s.

111 According to Marjorie Crenshaw, interviewed October 10, 2016, "you could not play a note without a union card, even in high school, black musicians, local #99. My husband, [trumpet player] Willie Crenshaw, Ornette and [bass player] Charles Scott, [all I. M. Terrell band members], they all had union cards, as teenagers."

112 Thanks to the Fort Worth Public Library for providing access to microfilm of *The Mind,* published by the Southwestern Negro Press, 1932–84. Other African-American-owned publications based in Fort Worth included the *Lake Como Weekly*, *The Clarion* (issued by the Price Hall Masonic Lodge), and *Sepia Magazine*, which debuted Texan author and journalist John Howard Griffin's indictment of racism "Life as a Negro: Journey Into Shame," in six monthly installments beginning in April 1960. Griffin, a white man, dyed his skin brown to pass as an African American in the Deep South. The *Sepia* installments were published in book form under the title *Black Like Me* (New York, 1962).

113 Selcer, *A History of Fort Worth*, p. 342; p. 80.

114 Conversation with Butch Clemons, Fort Worth, October 20, 2016. According to William James "Butch" Clemons (eldest of Pappy's six sons, named after William MacDonald), "[The Greenleaf] is where everybody used to hang. I would go with [my father] at night time, and it was blacks only, and we'd get bacon and egg sandwiches."

115 Selcer, *A History of Fort Worth*, p. 84. Selcer quotes the *Fort Worth Telegram*, May 7, 1909, describing the Southside's rural origins. On MacDonald, see Selcer, pp. 300–303. The *Ebony* magazine quote, notes Selcer, is dated 1949. The Rainbow Terrace was located on Presidio and Kentucky, on the east side of downtown.

116 Located near Ornette's childhood homes (405 E. 5th Street and Grove), the Jim Hotel was named after MacDonald's second wife, Jimmie Strickland. Its nightclub was probably named after the

College Inn in Chicago's historic Sherman Hotel, one of that city's first post-First World War jazz venues.

117 *Fort Worth Mind*, November 17, 1946.

118 Conversation with Sarah Walker (1935–), Lenora Rollins Heritage Center, Fort Worth, October 15, 2016. A November 1944 ad for the Paradise Inn (1230 New York Avenue) announced, "Chopped Beef sandwiches our specialty, opens 11:45am daily, closes 3am, Fish oysters, chili, fried chicken. Delicious home baked pies. Plenty of cold beer. We cater to special parties."

119 Fort Worth Blues guitarist Sumter Bruton, quoted in Govenar, *Texas Blues*, p. 188.

120 Conversation with Marjorie Crenshaw, October 10 and November 1, 2016.

121 The Chitlin' Circuit refers to the venues where African American musicians could perform throughout the Jim Crow South and Southwest. Coleman Hawkins reportedly played the Bluebird in the 1930s. Blues singer and drummer Robert Ealey ran and performed at the Bluebird from 1977 until his death, in 2001. See Price, *Thick Lights*, pp. 157–9. Frequented by blues enthusiasts and musicians (including Jimmy and Stevie Ray Vaughan), the club's wild ambiance is, thankfully, preserved in an early 1980s film clip on YouTube featuring U. P. Wilson playing his lethal one-handed guitar.

122 Telephone conversation with Bobby Bradford, November 9, 2016.

123 It is possible that Ornette's injury delayed his graduation. While original documents from I. M. Terrell are unavailable, a 2001 Alumni Association booklet regarding "All Class reunions" lists him in the class of 1949.

124 Ornette admired Lynn Hope (1926–1993), an Alabama tenor player who performed wearing a jeweled turban and later converted to Islam. He also studied the records of Jimmy Dorsey (bandleader Tommy's brother), a clarinetist and alto player whose sound, said Ornette, "was so round" (Litweiler, *Ornette Coleman*, p. 28).

125 Jones, *The Blues People*, p. 172.

126 Litweiler, *Ornette Coleman*, p. 31.

127 G. E. Lambert quoted in Oliphant, *Texan Jazz*, p. 226.

128 Jones, *The Blues People*, p. 172.

129 Litweiler, *Ornette Coleman*, p. 31. In the program for Ornette's June 20, 1966, concert in Fort Worth's Will Rogers Auditorium, produced by

his sister Trudy, Ornette said one of his favorite singers was Mississippi Delta bluesman Robert Johnson.

130 A. B. Spellman, liner notes to *Ornette on Tenor* (Atlantic, 1962), quoted in Litweiler, *Ornette Coleman*, p. 98.

131 Raleigh Dailey, doctoral dissertation, University of Kentucky School of Music, Lexington, Kentucky (2007), pp. 26–7.

132 Howard Mandel, *Miles, Ornette, Cecil: Jazz Beyond Jazz* (New York, 2008), p. 113.

133 Dewey, Hopkins, and Ealey quotes from Govenar, *Texas Blues*, p. 227, p. 42, and p. 184 respectively.

134 Warren, "Ornette Coleman: What I've Learned."

135 Price, *Thick Lights*, pp. 180–82.

136 Marjorie Crenshaw interviewed on video by Mike Price for the Fort Worth Public Library Jazz Archive, September 2007.

137 Trudy quoted in Litweiler, *Ornette Coleman*, p. 34. Former music director and conductor for the Fort Worth Symphony Orchestra John Giordano (1937–), who worked closely with Ornette for several years (mid-1980s), recalled a conversation about Trudy: "At one point Ornette said 'I think Truvenza was maybe my true mother.' That was conjecture on his part, as Trudy was too young, but in those days it happened that a mother took an unmarried daughter's child and reared her as his own." This was the case with Trudy's "son," the late Sean Leach (Trudy married General Dynamics employee Sam Leach in 1961). Sean's real mother was Trudy's daughter, Sandra. Conversation with John Giordano, October 31, 2016.

138 Bob Rusch, "Charles Moffett Interview," *Cadence* (February 1997), p. 9. Jam Jiver Prince Lasha was also from Lake Como. Trudy lived in Como for a while, possibly in the late 1940s–early 1950s, and Ornette stayed with her on occasion.

139 Raleigh Kenneth Dailey, doctoral dissertation, p. 27.

140 Liner notes of John Carter's first recording, *Seeking* (Revelation, 1969), featuring Bobby Bradford. Years later Ornette introduced John Carter to Bradford, an encounter that resulted in a long and fertile collaboration.

141 Telephone conversations with Bobby Bradford, November 4 and November 20, 2016.

142 Jean-Paul Sartre, "I Discovered Jazz in America," *Saturday Review*, November 29, 1947. Dizzy Gillespie admired Sartre, promoting

Existentialism (and "left bank intellectual" fashion, that is, beret, horn-rimmed glasses, and goatee) among musicians. Dizzy's memoir was titled *To Be or Not . . . to Bop* (1979).

143 Quote from Ross Russell's novel *The Sound*, in Rosenthal, *Hard Bop*, p. 13; ad reproduced p. 15.

144 Litweiler, *Ornette Coleman*, p. 33.

145 Timothy S. Murphy, trans., "The Other's Language: Jacques Derrida Interviews Ornette Coleman, June 23, 1997," *Genre*, XXXVII/2 (2004), pp. 319–29. Ornette said he made $3 for playing a long night, that is, approximately $100 per month (Spellman, *Four Lives*, p. 94).

146 John Carter interviewed by Mark Weber for *Coda*, August 31, 1976.

147 Charles Jackson, "Fort Worth's Jazz Connection: Trio Reminisce," *Fort Worth Star-telegram*, June 17, 1984.

148 Warren, "Ornette Coleman: What I've Learned."

149 Conversation with Marjorie Crenshaw, November 1, 2016. Regarding Red Conner's style of dress see Charles Jackson, "Trio Contemplate their FTW Jazz Roots," *Fort Worth Star-telegram*, June 17, 1983.

150 Spellman, *Four Lives*, p. 92.

151 Dewey Redman interviewed by Sarah Walker on *They Showed the Way* TV program sponsored by Fort Worth's Black Genealogical Society, broadcast September 2003 on municipal access channel 7.

152 David "Fathead" Newman interviewed by Ted Panken, for *DownBeat* magazine, 1998. Available online at https://tedpanken.wordpress.com. Conner is present, said Newman, in the sound of another of his admirers, Texas tenor Booker Ervin (Denison, TX, 1930–1970), who recorded extensively, notably with Charles Mingus and Eric Dolphy.

153 Govenar, *Texas Blues*, p. 188, mentions the recording. Thanks to Kevin Coffey for sharing his research, including Conner's death certificate, which notes that he died September 30, 1957, of a cerebral hemorrhage precipitated by malignant hypertension and that he was employed in a band called the Clouds of Joy at the time. According to John Carter (interviewed by Mark Weber for *Coda*, August 31, 1976), "[Red] just used his body up." Had he lived long enough to achieve greater notice, said Carter, "of all the fine players that you listen to, he would have been one of the finest that you would have heard in your life." Ornette said, "He died of several different things. He lived a jazzman's life," in Nat Hentoff, *The Jazz Life* (New York, 1961), p. 234.

154 Spellman, *Four Lives*, pp. 91–2; Hentoff, *Jazz Life*, p. 234; Govenar, *Texas Blues*, p. 209.

155 Telephone conversation with Bobby Bradford, November 9, 2016.

156 Spellman, *Four Lives,* p. 93.

157 Rockwell, *All American Music*, p. 186. Composed by pianist Hoagy Carmichael in 1927 and published with lyrics by Mitchell Parish in 1929, "Stardust" has been recorded in over a thousand instrumental or vocal renditions by musicians of every genre, including Louis Armstrong, Frank Sinatra, John Coltrane, Texan country music singer Willie Nelson, and former Beatle Ringo Starr.

158 Warren, "Ornette Coleman: What I've Learned."

159 Christopher Evans, "The Hot-spot," *Fort Worth Star-telegram*, June 30, 1991, and, by the same author, "A Drive Through History," *Fort Worth Star-telegram*, March 14, 1993.

160 Full page ad in the *Fort Worth Mind*, January 25, 1947. Business began to decline in the mid-1950s and the Jim Hotel was demolished in 1964, when 4th Street was replaced with a highway ramp.

161 Ad in the *Fort Worther* (December 1948), a weekly newsletter published by the Fort Worth Chamber of Commerce and the city's Hotel Association.

162 United States Department of the Interior, National Register of Historic Places, Will Rogers Memorial Center. Available online at www.nps.gov.

163 Annie O. Cleveland and M. Barett Cleveland, "Fort Worth for Entertainment: Billy Rose's Casa Mañana (1936–1939)," *Theater Design and Technology,* XLIV/1 (Winter 2008), pp. 27–39.

164 Ann Arnold, *Gamblers and Gangsters: Fort Worth's Jacksboro Highway in the 1940s and 1950s* (Austin, TX, 1998), p. 6.

165 Amon Carter Museum of American Art, Fort Worth website: www.cartermuseum.org.

166 According to an ad for the Duke Ellington concert in the *Fort Worth Press* (April 8, 1946), floor seats cost $2.50 and $2.20, and balcony seats $2. In September 1949 impresario Ocie "Marble Eye" Jones presented Lionel Hampton at the Northside Coliseum and saw to it that African Americans could enjoy the show from the main floor (*Fort Worth Mind*, October 28, 1949).

167 The December 8–9, 1946, concert was advertised in the *Fort Worth Mind*. See also Selcer, *A History of Fort Worth*, pp. 315, 424.

168 Information culled from advertisements in the *Fort Worther*, December 1948.

169 Arnold, *Gamblers and Gangsters*, pp. 3–13.

170 Ibid., p. 12.

171 Conversation with Marjorie Crenshaw, October 10, 2016.

172 Selcer, *A History of Fort Worth*, p. 424.

173 Interview with Ray Sharpe, 2004, in Govenar, *Texas Blues*, p. 192.

174 Spellman, *Four Lives*, pp. 93–4.

175 Ibid., p. 95.

176 Spellman, *Four Lives*, p. 95.

177 Mandel, *Jazz Beyond Jazz*, p. 189.

178 Litweiler, *Ornette Coleman*, pp. 29, 34.

179 Ornette interview, "Making Knowledge Out of Sound," *Stop Smiling* magazine, 34 (2008), The Jazz Issue.

180 Spellman, *Four Lives*, pp. 97–9.

181 Ibid., p. 103. In a 1968 interview with Val Wilmer, Blackwell says both he and Ornette were working in "rock 'n' roll groups" at the time of their meeting, and Ornette was playing tenor. *DownBeat*, October 3, 1968.

182 Litweiler, *Ornette Coleman*, p. 39. A theater and TV writer, Aurelius Hemphill may have been related to Fort Worth composer and saxophonist Julius Hemphill, another I. M. Terrell alumnus and founder of the World Saxophone Quartet, who later befriended Ornette.

183 Conversation with musician, author, and former *Fort Worth Star-telegram* entertainment writer Michael H. Price, Fort Worth, October 18, 2016. According to Kevin Coffey, steel guitarist C. B. White and trumpeter Chubby Crank were among the western swing musicians Ornette jammed with in Amarillo.

184 January 2017 correspondence with Kevin Coffey, who interviewed Chubby Crank (1996) and was in frequent contact with Buddy Wallis (1995–8). Stories emerged in the early 2000s that Ornette played with Bob Wills's Texas Playboys, some based on interviews with Ornette, but according to Coffey, members of the Playboys never mentioned the encounter. Although it's possible that Ornette jammed with Wills's musicians, in his later years he may have simply grouped the various western swing musicians and bands he had played with under the "Texas Playboys" heading.

185 Ibid. Sock Underwood remained in Fort Worth for the rest of his life. In the late 1960s and early 1970s he played the White Sands Supper Club on the Jacksboro Highway with Trudy Coleman, and considered both her and Ornette his lifetime friends.

186 Oliphant, *Jazz Mavericks*, pp. 47–8. With Charlie Parker, Dorham performed at the 1949 Paris Jazz Festival, the first international gathering of the jazz clans. He was a founding member of the hard bop Jazz Messengers. Hear Dorham's 1960 recording of Johnny Mercer's "I'm An Old Cowhand" (with the memorable refrain "yippee kay-yo-kay-yay') on YouTube. Sampling is the use of quotations taken to the extreme, that is, sound loops borrowed from older recordings that sometimes form the entire substance of new ones. For a list of artists sampling Coleman compositions see www.whosampled.com.

187 John Carter interviewed by Mark Weber for *Coda*, August 31, 1976. Possibly the first "battle of the bands" was held on the Champ de Mars (Paris) in 1846, in order to prove the superior volume of the newly patented saxophone (invented by Belgian Adolphe Sax) lent to military bands.

188 Christopher Evans, "The Hot-spot," *Fort Worth Star-telegram*, June 30, 1991.

189 Fort Worth keyboard player and manager of Record Town Gerard Dailey obtained a scan of the poster from the collection of Chuck Nevitt (1956–2015). Founder of the Dallas Blues Society, Nevitt produced recordings of unsung local R&B heroes, including guitarist ZuZu Bollin's sole album, *Texas Bluesman* (Dallas, TX, 1989), which featured Buster Smith, Fathead Newman, Doyle Bramhal (drums), and Gerard Dailey. Formerly the Rose Ballroom, the Empire (renamed in 1951) booked top R&B and blues groups in the early 1950s, including Bollin and Clarence "Nappy Chin" Evans, a friend of Ornette's (Govenar, *Texas Blues*, pp. 87–8). Showtime for Ornette's music battle was "9pm–Until?" Of his opponent, Stan Johnson, nothing is known.

190 Bobby Bradford, describing the first time he heard Ornette play alto, at Charles Moffett's 1953 wedding in Austin, Texas, said, "he was tampering with things in an investigative kind of way." Litweiler, *Ornette Coleman*, p. 44.

Part Two: Ignition

1 From Eno's comments at the Sydney Luminous Festival, 2009: www.synthtopia.com; see also Bruce Sterling, "Scenius, or Communal Genius," *Wired Magazine*, wired.com, June 16, 2008.

2 Conversation with Bobby Bradford, November 4, 2016. Bradford met Ornette in 1953, at an all-night jam in Austin's Victory Grill celebrating Charles Moffett's wedding; Ornette was best man.

3 Valerie Wilmer, "Ed Blackwell: Well-tempered Drummer," *DownBeat*, October 3, 1968.

4 Keith Raether, "Ornette, Bobby Bradford's portrait of an emerging giant," *Jazz Magazine*, 1/3 (Spring 1977).

5 Interview with Dr. Joanne Gabbin, executive director, Furious Flower Poetry Center, in 2006, available on YouTube.

6 Jayne Cortez and D. H. Melhem, "Jayne Cortez: Supersurrealist Vision," in *Heroism in the New Black Poetry: Introductions and Interviews* (Lexington, KY, 1990), p. 197.

7 Ibid.

8 Ted Gioia, *West Coast Jazz, Modern Jazz in California, 1945–1960,* (Berkeley, CA, 1998), p. 351.

9 Peter Watrous, "Ornette Coleman's Beautiful Difference," *Village Voice* (June 1987).

10 Wilmer, "Ed Blackwell: Well-tempered Drummer."

11 A. B. Spellman, *Four Lives in the Bebop Business* (New York, 1966), p. III.

12 Francis Davis, *In the Moment, Jazz in the 1980s* (Oxford, 1986), pp. 150–51.

13 Stanley Crouch, *Considering Genius* (New York, 2006), p. 14. On Browne and his students, see Matthew Duerston, "Samuel Rodney Browne: The Music Teacher that Broke LA's Color Barrier," March 7, 2016, available on Los Angeles educational TV station KCET's website (www.kcet.org). Browne (1908–1991) taught from the late 1930s until 1973. Jefferson band alumni include saxophonists Big Jay McNeely, Dexter Gordon (1923–1990), drummer Chico Hamilton (1921–2013), trumpeter Art Farmer (1928–1999), alto player Frank Morgan (1933–2007), and pianist Horace Tapscott (1934–1999).

14 Conversation with Stanley Crouch in his Brooklyn apartment, New York, November 22, 2016.

15 Valerie Wilmer, *As Serious As Your Life: Black Music and the Free Jazz Revolution, 1957–1977* (London, 1977), p. 63.

16 Conversation with Bobby Bradford, November 4, 2016. Bradford recalled playing all of the pieces on Ornette's first album, *Something Else!!!!*, in gigs around LA prior to his 1954 departure.

17 Conversation with Stanley Crouch, November 22, 2016. Jayne Cortez also founded the Bola Press and was cofounder of the Organization of Women Writers of Africa.

18 Nat Hentoff, "Ornette Coleman: The Biggest Noise in Jazz," *Esquire*, March 1961. Hentoff quotes Ornette as saying: "My wife would start in, 'people say you're crazy' and she sounded as if she agreed." The quote also appears in Hentoff's *Jazz Life* (New York, 1961), p. 237. Hentoff met Ornette in LA during one of his first recording sessions for the Contemporary label.

19 John Litweiler, *Ornette Coleman: A Harmolodic Life* (New York, 1992), p. 56.

20 Recorded in three sessions, February 10–March 24, with Ornette on plastic alto, Cherry on cornet, Walter Norris on piano, Don Payne on bass, and Billy Higgins on drums.

21 Art Farmer's review of *Something Else!!!!*, *Jazz Review* (July 1959), p. 18. Hsio Wen Shih was also a *Jazz Review* cofounder.

22 John Tynan, "Critics' Poll," *DownBeat*, August 21, 1958.

23 Crouch, *Considering Genius*, pp. 6–7.

24 David Lee, *The Battle of the Five Spot* (Toronto, 2006), p. 54. Hear MJQ's *Pyramid* (Atlantic, 1960) on YouTube.

25 Conversation with Bobby Bradford, November 20, 2016.

26 Bley quoted in Lee, *The Battle of the Five Spot*, p. 109. Hear *Live at the Hillcrest* on YouTube, a technically mediocre recording released in 1976 that nonetheless conveys the group's self-assuredness and cohesion.

27 Dan Morgenstern, "Charlie Haden—From Hillbilly to Avant-Garde—A Rocky Road," *DownBeat*, March 9, 1967.

28 Haden quoted from his appearance in Ken Burns's epic documentary, "Jazz" (2000), Segment 9 ("The Adventure"), part 2.

29 Fred Kaplan, *1959: The Year Everything Changed* (Hoboken, NJ, 2009), p. 88. On Davis's interactions with women, see Crouch, *Considering Genius*, p. 47.

30 Lee, *The Battle of the Five Spot*, pp. 81–2.

31 Hear Raeburn's 1946 rendition of "Somewhere over the Rainbow" on YouTube.

32 Litweiler, *Ornette Coleman*, p. 69.

33 Burt Korall, "Jimmy Giuffre: Search for Freedom," *DownBeat*, December 7, 1961, p. 17.

34 The full concert program is available online at www.jazzdiscography. com. *The Lenox School of Jazz Concert* (recorded in the Berkshire Music Barn, August 29, 1959) was released in Denmark in 1990 on the Royal Jazz label, and re-released as a CD in 2009 (FreeFactory label). Ornette performs on tracks 1, 2, and 9–11.

35 Spellman, *Four Lives*, p. 134; Keith Raether, "Ornette: Bobby Bradford's Portrait of an Emerging Giant," *Jazz Magazine*, 1/3 (Spring 1977).

36 Jean-Paul Sartre, "I Discovered Jazz in America," *Saturday Review*, November 29, 1947.

37 Lewis MacAdams, *Birth of the Cool: Beat, Bebop, and the American Avant-garde* (New York, 2001), p. 46. Established in 1938 at 210 West 118th Street, Minton's Playhouse reopened as a "jazz supper club" in 2015; see Pete Wells, "Minton's in Harlem," *New York Times*, April 28, 2015.

38 Miles Davis quoted in MacAdams, *Birth of the Cool*, p. 44.

39 David H. Rosenthal, *Hard Bop: Jazz and Black Music, 1955–1965* (New York, 1992), p. 17.

40 Langston Hughes, *The Collected Works of Langston Hughes*, vol. VII: *The Early Simple Stories*, ed. Donna Akiba Sullivan Harper (Columbia, MO, 2002), p. 228. Monk claimed that he'd named the music "bip bop" but someone misquoted him. MacAdams, *Birth of the Cool*, p. 45.

41 R. Sukenick, *Down and In: Life in the Underground* (New York, 1987), p. 53.

42 MacAdams, *Birth of the Cool*, p. 82.

43 Malina quoted in Sukenick, *Down and In*, p. 23.

44 Ibid., p. 28. For an animated account of Living Theater's early history, see MacAdams, *Birth of the Cool*, pp. 185–213.

45 Conversation with John Rockwell, Brooklyn, November 8, 2016. Malina and Beck attended Piscator's workshops at New York's New School, as did actors Mel Brooks, Tony Curtis, Ben Gazara, Shelley Winters, Marlon Brando, and Walter Matthau.

46 Kaplan, *1959*, p. 233.

47 Robert Frank, introduction by Jack Kerouac, *The Americans* (New York, 1959). A reading of Kerouac's *On the Road* prompted Frank to ask Kerouac (who coincidentally, did not drive) to write his introduction. Like Kerouac's, Ginsberg's writing was jazz-inspired. He admired poet William Carlos Williams, who wrote the introduction to *Howl* (1956) and in 1923 authored the poem "Shoot it Jimmy!" in praise of improvisation: "That sheet stuff's / a lot a cheese. / Man / gimme the key / and lemme loose—."

48 The Five Spot moved to 2 St. Marks Place on the corner of 3rd Avenue in 1963.

49 Conversation with Michael Cuscuna, Stamford, Connecticut, November 21, 2016. Jazz DJ, writer, discographer, and three-time Grammy award-winning record producer, Cuscuna worked for several labels before undertaking the Herculean task of combing the Blue Note archives for precious unissued recordings, remixing them, and releasing them in box sets on Mosaic Records, which he cofounded with Charlie Lourie in 1983.

50 Wilmer, *As Serious As Your Life*, p. 50. For an illuminating overview of Taylor's career and music, see Adam Shatz, "The World of Cecil Taylor," *New York Review of Books Daily*, posted May 16, 2018.

51 Lee, *Battle of the Five Spot*, p. 11. On YouTube, hear *Thelonious in Action* (Riverside/OJC) recorded live at the Five Spot, on August 7, 1958 (with Wilbur Ware on bass and Shadow Wilson on drums), and the Coltrane Quartet masterwork, *A Love Supreme* (Impulse!, recorded 1964), with McCoy Tyner on piano, Jimmy Garrison on bass and Elvin Jones on drums. Sonny Rollins also played the Five Spot in "the late 1950s" and tweeted a photo of the gig on May 28, 2014 (@sonnyrollins).

52 Lee, *The Battle of the Five Spot*, p. 56.

53 Ibid.

54 Ibid., p. 57. The Jazztet featured Curtis Fuller on trombone, McCoy Tyner on piano, Addison Farmer on bass, and Dave Bailey on drums.

55 George Hoefer, "Caught in the Act," *DownBeat* (December 1959), p. 40.

56 Denardo Coleman mentions the New York trip in his liner notes for the box set *Celebrate Ornette* (Song X, 2016); Jayne mentions packing the suitcase her mother gave her as a high school graduation present

to take to New York in 1959. See *Heroism in the New Black Poetry: Introductions and Interviews*, p. 201.

57 Spellman, *Four Lives*, p. 79.

58 Bley quoted in Lee, *Battle of the Five Spot*, p. 57. Pianist/composer Horace Silver (1928–2014) cofounded the Jazz Messengers with Art Blakey, pioneering "hard-bop," a gutsy, R&B-flavored bebop derivative.

59 John Craddock, "Ornette Coleman at the Five Spot," *Jazz Journal*, XIII/4 (April 1960), p. 25.

60 Sukenick, *Down and In*, p. 142.

61 George Hoefer, "Caught in the Act," *DownBeat* (December 1959), p. 40.

62 Gunther Schuller interviewed Ornette and Don Cherry, February 7, 1960, as part of *The Scope of Jazz*, a weekly one-hour jazz show Gunther and Nat Hentoff hosted from January 1958 to roughly March 1960 on WBAI. Ornette discussed Cecil Taylor, who sat in with him at the Five Spot, at length.

63 Spellman, *Four Lives*, p. 124.

64 Stanley Dance, "Lightly and Politely," *Jazz Journal*, XIII/2 (February 1960), p. 23; Craddock, "Ornette Coleman at the Five Spot," p. 25.

65 Spellman, *Four Lives*, p. 125.

66 Dance, "Lightly and Politely," p. 23.

67 N. Hentoff, "Ornette Coleman, Biggest Noise in Jazz," p. 82, and Litweiler, *Ornette Coleman*, p. 82, quoting Davis from a 1963 publication.

68 Alto saxophonist Charlie MacPherson recalled playing with Mingus; see Frank Mastropolo, "Definitely a New York Hang: Jazz Musicians Remember the Five Spot Café," posted January 3, 2014, at www.bedfordandbowery.com; Joans quoted in Sukenick, *Down and In*, p. 143.

69 Kaplan, *1959*, p. 199.

70 The quotation from Yeats's autobiography appears in Dan Piepenbring, "An Inglorious Slop-pail of a Play," *Paris Review*, September 8, 2015. The "us" Yeats referred to included poets Stéphane Mallarmé and Paul Verlaine and painter Gustave Moreau. *Ubu Roi*'s opening and closing night was December 10, 1896.

71 Lee, *Battle of the Five Spot*, p. 66.

72 Wilmer, *As Serious as Your Life*, p. 61.

73 Lee, *The Battle of the Five Spot*, p. 70.

74 Hentoff, *Jazz Life*, p. 228.

75 Francis Davis, "Ornette's Permanent Revolution," *Atlantic Monthly* (December 1972).

76 Hentoff, "The Biggest Noise in Jazz," p. 86.

77 Peter Watrous, "Ornette Coleman's Beautiful Difference," *Village Voice* (June 1987), Jazz Special: "Ornette Coleman: The Art of the Improviser," p. 5.

78 Kaplan, *1959*, p. 210; Wilmer, *As Serious as Your Life*, p. 70. Coltrane sat in with Ornette's quartet briefly on one of the nights at the Five Spot and reportedly recalled it as one of the most exciting musical interactions of his life.

79 *The Avant-garde* (Atlantic, 1968) was recorded June 28 and July 8, 1960, with Charlie Haden and Percy Heath on bass, Ed Blackwell on drums, and Don Cherry on trumpet.

80 P. Watrous, "Ornette Coleman's Beautiful Difference," *Village Voice* (June 1987), p. 5.

81 "Another View of Ornette Coleman," sidebar to an article by Julian "Cannonball" Adderly, "Cannonball Looks at Ornette Coleman," *DownBeat* (May 26, 1960), p. 21. Ornette did his own "blindfold test" with Feather, in *DownBeat* (January 7, 1960), p. 39.

82 Brian Morton, "Ornette Coleman, 1930–2015," *The Wire*, www.thewire.co.uk, June 11, 2015.

83 P. Watrous, "Ornette Coleman's Beautiful Difference," *Village Voice* (June 1987).

84 Robert Palmer, "Ornette Coleman and the Circle with a Hole in the Middle," *Atlantic Monthly* (December 1972).

85 Wilmer, *As Serious as Your Life*, p. 65.

86 Rosenthal, *Hard Bop*, p. 152.

87 See "Beyond the Cool," *Time*, June 28, 1960.

88 Correspondence with John Snyder, November 16, 2016. Thanks to John Snyder for sharing two essays, one written around 1987 the other (on Denardo's request) following Ornette's death in 2015. They describe what it was like to study, work, and live with Ornette, who in the mid- to late 1970s camped out in the offices of Artists House Records, Snyder's label (1977–2006). Former director of the Horizon Jazz Series for A&M Records and of jazz

production for Atlantic Records, Snyder is current chair of the Film and Music Industry Studies department at Loyola University, New Orleans.

89 John Szwed quoted in Lee, *Battle of the Five Spot*, p. 61, describing how critics responded to Miles Davis several years earlier.

90 Lee, *Battle of the Five Spot*, p. 74; Davis, "Ornette's Permanent Revolution."

91 Conversation with former *New York Times* music critic and arts editor John Rockwell, Brooklyn, New York, November 18, 2016.

92 Recorded February 7, 1960, part of *The Scope of Jazz* on WBAI. Available online at pianist and writer Ethan Iverson's website: https://ethaniverson.com. Ornette did not always speak with a lisp. According to Bobby Bradford (author's correspondence, September 2, 2017) "the lisp came on in NY—he certainly did not have it early on."

93 Ornette Coleman, *Change of the Century* (Atlantic, 1960). Liner notes are available online. In a 1960 interview Thelonious Monk (to whose music Ornette's was sometimes compared) expressed the same sentiment: "I say you play your own way. Don't play what the public wants—you play what you want and let the public pick up what you're doing—even if it does take them 15 or 20 years." Rosenthal, *Hard Bop*, p. 132.

94 Liner notes, Ornette Coleman, *Change of the Century* (Atlantic, 1960).

95 Mark Warren, "Ornette Coleman: What I've Learned," *Esquire*, www.esquire.com, December 24, 2009.

96 Liner notes, Ornette Coleman, *Change of the Century* (Atlantic, 1960).

97 Pollock's wife, painter Lee Krasner, said he had a large collection of 1920s and '30s 78-rpm jazz records but contrary to popular belief, Pollock did not paint while listening to music. Regarding Pollock's and other contemporary painters' interest in jazz, see "Jackson Pollock and Jazz: Inspiration or Imitation?" unpublished lecture delivered April 4, 2008, by Helen A. Harrison, Director, Pollock-Krasner House and Study Center, East Hampton, New York, at a conference, "Brilliant Corners: Jazz and Its Cultures," sponsored by the Humanities Institute at Stony Brook University, New York. Available online at academia.edu.

98 MacAdams, *Birth of the Cool*, p. 104.

99 Ornette is on the left stereo channel with Cherry, Higgins, and bassist Scott Le Faro, whom he met through Gunther Schuller.

Charlie Haden is the bassist on the right channel with Ed Blackwell and two up-and-coming reedmen: Eric Dolphy, whom Ornette knew from LA, on bass clarinet, and Freddie Hubbard on trumpet. Dolphy, a close collaborator of Charles Mingus, had just released his second album as bandleader entitled *Out There* (Prestige, 1960). Hubbard, Dolphy's roommate and a friend of Don Cherry, had just released *Open Sesame* (Blue Note, 1960), his first as bandleader.

100 Serge Guilbaut quoted in MacAdams, *Birth of the Cool*, p. 82. According to art historian Chad Mandeles, someone other than Ornette chose to illustrate *Free Jazz* with Pollock's "White Light." See Harrison, *Jackson Pollock and Jazz*, n. 97.

101 Pete Welding and John A. Tynan, "Double View of a Double Quartet," *DownBeat*, January 18, 1962.

102 Mandel, *Jazz Beyond Jazz*, p. 115.

103 Schuller quoted in Nat Hentoff, "Ornette Coleman, Biggest Noise in Jazz," p. 87.

104 Hentoff, *The Jazz Life*, p. 245.

105 Naomi Beckwith, "Only Poetry," in *The Freedom Principle: Experiments in Art and Music, 1965 to Now*, ed. Naomi Beckwith and Dieter Roelstraete, exh. cat., Museum of Contemporary Art, Chicago (2015), p. 44.

106 See www.structureandimagery.blogspot.com for a photograph of Ornette and Thompson, posted November 10, 2011. Thompson's circle of friends also included saxophonists Archie Shepp and Marion Brown, drummer Sunny Murray, and Joe Overstreet, another painter Ornette befriended.

107 Emilio Cruz quoted in Rosenthal, *Hard Bop*, p. 77.

108 Allan Kaprow, "The Legacy of Jackson Pollock" [1958], in *Essays on the Blurring of Art and Life*, ed. A. Kaprow (Irvine, CA, 1993), p. 7.

109 Ibid., p. 9.

110 Ginsberg quoted in Rosenthal, *Hard Bop*, p. 78.

111 Conversation with Bobby Bradford, November 9, 2016.

112 Litweiler, *Ornette Coleman*, p. 103.

113 Garrison appeared on *Ornette on Tenor* (Atlantic, 1962), one of Ornette's rare tenor saxophone recordings, along with *Soapsuds Soapsuds* (Artists House, 1979), a duet with Charlie Haden with Ornette on tenor and trumpet. Garrison also performed on Ornette's *The Art of the Improvisers* (Atlantic, 1961), *New York*

Is Now! (Blue Note, 1968) and *Love Call* (Blue Note, 1968)
with Elvin Jones on drums, and Dewey Redman on tenor on
the latter two.

114 *Ornette!* (Atlantic, 1962), recorded January 31, 1961, with Scott
LeFaro, Ed Blackwell, and Don Cherry; *Ornette on Tenor* (Atlantic,
1962), recorded March 22 and 27, 1961, with Cherry, Garrison, and
Blackwell; *The Art of the Improvisers* (Atlantic, 1970) and *Twins*
(Atlantic, 1971) were comprised of session material recorded 1959–
60. Ornette's manager at the time, Mildred Fields, arranged the
Cincinnati concert.

115 Hentoff, "Ornette Coleman, Biggest Noise in Jazz," p. 87.

116 Litweiler, *Ornette Coleman*, p. 103. Ornette later referred to Newport
producer George Wien as "a very economical American. If I need
money and George Wien asks me to play and it's not too painful,
I'll pull down my pants and go and play." (Richard Williams,
"Ornette and the Pipes of Joujouka," *Melody Maker*, March 17, 1973.)

117 In 1983 Ornette said he'd studied architecture and had wanted to be
an architect as a child. Soundtrack, *Ornette Made in America* (dir.
Shirley Clarke, 1985). He also gave a "lecture/demonstration" at
Cornell Architectural School on March 9, 1970. See David Wild
and Michael Cuscuna, *Ornette Coleman, 1958–1979: A Discography*
(Ann Arbor, MI, 1980), p. 65.

118 Whitney worked in Hollywood for Douglas Aircraft (illustrating
guided missile projects) and in 1966 became IBM's first "artist in
residence," charged with "exploring the aesthetic potentials of
computer graphics." See Whitney's website, siggraph.org. Whitney's
seven-minute "CATALOG (1961/1962)" is available on YouTube but
Ornette's soundtrack has been replaced by Tod Machover's "Electric
Etudes" (1983). Also in the early 1960s, Ornette recorded "Soundtrack
for Improvisations," a short subject film by Stefan Sharp, according to
Wild and Cuscuna, *Ornette Coleman: Discography*, p. 23. I was unable
to find further reference to this film.

119 Spellman, *Four Lives*, p. 139.

120 Litweiler, *Ornette Coleman*, p. 104.

121 The phrase "not a bad seat in the house" was coined in reference to
Town Hall, located in Midtown Manhattan.

122 Philip Glass, "The Classical Musician Igor Stravinsky," *Time*,
June 8, 1998. Stravinsky conducted *Les Noces*, accompanied

by Samuel Barber, Lukas Foss, Roger Sessions, and Aaron Copland, who was coincidentally an Ornette supporter.

123 Mandel, *Jazz Beyond Jazz*, p. 172. The ESP issue (1965) covers only about a third of the Town Hall concert, and is missing Ornette's trio playing "Blues Misused," joined by Nappy Allen on guitar, Chris Towns on piano, and Barney Richardson on bass. Wild and Cuscuna, *Ornette Coleman: Discography*, p. 22.

124 Correspondence with John Snyder, November 16, 2016.

125 Nicholas Dawidoff, "The Man Who Saw America," *New York Times*, May 7, 2015. Although Ornette is often credited with the soundtrack for Robert Frank's "O.K., End Here" (1963, starring Sue Mingus) his music is in fact absent from the film. Apparently Frank hoped to get Ornette to compose a soundtrack, but the project never materialized.

126 Litweiler, *Ornette Coleman*, p. 108.

127 Nat Hentoff, "The New Jazz," *Newsweek* (December 12, 1966), p. 108. For an in-depth portrait of Albert Ayler, see Wilmer, *As Serious As Your Life*, pp. 92–111.

128 Ayler's first album, on a small Swedish label, was entitled *Something Different!!!!!!* (Bird Notes, 1962). In 1968 Ornette released *Love Call* (recorded in April) and Ayler released *Love Cry* (Impulse!) recorded in August. In December 1963 Ayler recorded a session with Ornette playing trumpet and violin, but the fate of those tapes in unknown. See Wild and Cuscuna, *Ornette Coleman: Discography*, p. 22. A Fred Lyman is listed as banjoist for the session that included an unnamed bassist.

129 Michael Cuscuna, liner notes to Ayler's *Vibrations* (Arista, 1975), recorded in Copenhagen September 14, 1964, with Don Cherry on trumpet, Gary Peacock on bass, and Sunny Murray on drums. James Marcellus Arthur "Sunny" Murray (Oklahoma, 1936–December 7, 2017) recorded at least ten albums with Ayler. An early experimenter with the drums as a melodic or textural instrument, Murray also recorded with Cecil Taylor and performed with Ornette.

130 Ayler performed onstage with John Coltrane only once, in the grand finale for a concert at New York's Philharmonic Hall entitled "Titans of the Tenor" (February 19, 1966) for a set that comprised "My Favorite Things" and "Om." See recordmecca.com for a reproduction of the concert handbill.

131 Coltrane quote from www.coltranechurch.org; Ayler quoted in Nat Hentoff's cover notes for *Albert Ayler in Greenwich Village* (Impulse!, 1967).

132 Curated by Alexandra Munroe, "The Third Mind: American Artists Contemplate Asia, 1860–1989," Guggenheim Museum, New York, January 30–April 19, 2009, proposes Asia as a primary influence shaping the American avant-garde. See www.guggenheim.org and www.alexandramunroe.com for related literature.

133 Released on CD as *The Love Revolution* (Gambit, 2005), bootlegged recordings from Rome and Milan summer of 1968, "Buddha Blues" features Ornette playing *shenai*, an oboe-like Indian instrument believed to convey blessings and used in temple rituals. Ornette also played *shenai* performing his composition "Sun Suite" with the San Francisco Symphony in Berkeley, California (1969), accompanied by his son Denardo.

134 Litweiler, *Ornette Coleman*, pp. 81, 51.

135 Hentoff, *Jazz Life*, p. 246.

136 Chris DeVito, ed., *Coltrane on Coltrane: The Coltrane Interviews* (Chicago, IL, 2010), pp. 269–70.

137 See www.coltranechurch.org.

138 Ornette, Moffett, and Izenzon performed "Holiday for a Graveyard," (O. Coleman) at St. Peter's Lutheran Church (NYC) on July 21, 1967. The 5 minute 17 second performance was recorded but the tape's location is unknown. See Wild and Cuscuna, *Ornette Coleman: Discography*, p. 29.

139 Dan Morgenstern and Martin Williams, "The October Revolution, Two Views of the Avant Garde," *DownBeat*, November 19, 1964. The Cellar Café was at 91st Street and Broadway. On Sun Ra, see Part Three.

140 Conversation with Rick Fiori and Francis J. Golia Jr., New Jersey-born musicians who frequented the New York clubs and lofts in the 1960s, Doylestown, Pennsylvania, November 26, 2016.

141 Shepp quoted in Geoff Dyer, "Torrential, Gut-bucket Jazz," www.nybooks.com, June 20, 2015.

142 Crouch, *Considering Genius*, p. 5. Jazz was not the only music that served as an anthem of social change. Marvin Gaye's *What's Going On* (Motown subsidiary Tamla Records, 1971) brilliantly captured life in urban, Black America and is considered one of the best albums of all time, genre notwithstanding.

143 Philippe Carles and Jean-Louis Comolli, *Free Jazz/Black Power*, trans. Grégory Pierrot (Jackson, MI, 2015), p. 21.

144 Dr. King's speech is reproduced at www.coltranechurch.org.

145 Spellman, *Four Lives*, p. 130. Ornette was approached by members of the Communist Party in LA, but found them patronizing. See Spellman, p. 109.

146 Hentoff, "The New Jazz," p. 102.

147 Malcolm X was reportedly assassinated by agents of his former mentor, Elijah Mohammed, founder of the Nation of Islam, who resented his rapprochement to both true Islam (following a pilgrimage to Mecca) and Martin Luther King's belief that violence and the demonization of whites would not further the fight for civil rights.

148 Spellman, *Four Lives*, p. 138.

149 Litweiler, *Ornette Coleman*, p. 93.

150 Kaplan, *1959*, p. 128. Leveraging his high public profile, Louis Armstrong cancelled a 1957 trip to Moscow until President Dwight Eisenhower sent the National Guard to protect black students enrolled at a white Arkansas high school who had been refused entry. Armstrong's stance heightened media attention to the racial conflict and, ceding to various pressures, Eisenhower sent in the troops. The "jazz ambassadors" toured until the early 1980s. A sanitized version of the concept was revived in 2011 on a much smaller, less newsworthy scale through the program American Musicians Abroad. See http://amvoices.org/ama.

151 In Nazi-occupied Czechoslovakia vocal improvisation ("scatting") was forbidden, upright basses had to be bowed, not plucked, and saxophones were entirely out of the question. See Josef Skvorecky, *The Bass Saxophone* (New York, 1979).

152 Dexter Gordon, speaking in *Cool Cats* (dir. Janus Køster-Rasmussen, 2015), a documentary about Gordon's and fellow tenor saxophonist Ben Webster's influence on the 1960s Copenhagen jazz scene.

153 Benjamin Piekut, "Indeterminacy, Free Improvisation and the Mixed Avant-garde Experimental Music in London (1965–1975)," *Journal of the American Musicological Society*, LXVII/3 (Fall 2014), p. 777.

154 *New Departures* cofounder and fellow poet Pete Brown (1940–) later wrote the lyrics for major hits for Cream (Eric Clapton on guitar, Jack Bruce on bass, and Ginger Baker on drums): "I Feel Free," "White Room," and "Sunshine of Your Love." For a discussion

of *New Departures* in the context of contemporary university-based
publications see Jed Birmingham, "Reports from the Bibliographic
Bunker on William S. Burroughs Collecting," posted December 12,
2007, at www.realitystudio.org.

155 Robert Irwin, *Memoirs of a Dervish: Sufi Mystics and the Sixties*
(London, 2011), pp. 14–15.

156 Ibid.

157 "Jayne Cortez: In Her Own Words," in catalogue for the exhibition
Watts: Art and Social Change in Los Angeles, 1965–2002, Haggerty
Museum of Art (Milwaukee, WI, 2003), pp. 35–7.

158 The reading was accompanied by the Mike West Quartet. Jack Cooke,
"Ornette Coleman at Croydon," *Jazz Monthly* (October 1965), p. 22.

159 Mike Horovitz, "A Free-flying Evening in Croydon with Ornette
Coleman," *The Guardian*, www.theguardian.com, June 18, 2015.

160 Cooke, "Ornette Coleman at Croydon," p. 22.

161 Piekut, "Indeterminacy, Free Improvisation and the Mixed Avant-
garde Experimental Music in London," p. 778.

162 Ibid., pp. 773–5. Ornette later hosted a performance of Musica
Elettronica Viva at Artists House, June 3, 1974.

163 Dan Morgenstern and John Tchicai, "A Calm Member of the Avant-
Garde," *DownBeat*, February 10, 1966, p. 20 (with Tchicai's photo on
the cover).

164 I am grateful to Danish pianist and historian Ole Matthiessen, Roger
Bergner of Svenskt Visarkiv (Centre for Swedish Folk Music and
Jazz Research), and Magnus Nygren, editor of *OrkesterJournalen*, for
information about Ornette in Scandinavia.

165 Ludwig Rasmusson's *Svenska Dagbladet* article (November 24, 1965)
is reproduced in the liner notes for a 2002 CD reissue of *The Ornette
Coleman Trio at the Golden Circle Stockholm*, recorded November 22,
December 3, and December 4 (Blue Note, 1965).

166 J. Hoberman, "Who's Crazy?, an Obscure Avant-garde Film Project
is Reborn," *New York Times*, www.nytimes.com, March 23, 2016.

167 Ibid. A portion of Marianne Faithfull's rendition of Ornette's
composition "Sadness" (1962) is available on YouTube. Ornette added
lyrics for the then twenty-year-old Faithfull, which include "Is God
man? Is man God?"

168 Richard Brody, "Ornette Coleman's Inspired Soundtrack for
'Who's Crazy'," *New Yorker*, www.newyorker.com, March 13, 2017.

The soundtrack was released on a 2-LP set on the Affinity (UK) label in 1982 and re-released on CD in 1994 on the Freedom label (Japan).

169 Recorded in New York with Moffett, Izenzon, and tenor saxophonist Pharoah Sanders and an eleven-piece orchestra conducted by Joseph Tekula, Ornette's soundtrack was released as a double album entitled *Chappaqua Suite* (Columbia, 1965).

170 The Library of Congress (www.loc.gov) describes the fourteen-minute film – produced by the Canadian Film Board and recorded August 1966, according to Wild and Cuscuna, *Ornette Coleman: Discography*, p. 27 – as "an animated cartoon about international injustice."

171 Ornette speaking in *David, Moffett and Ornette: The Ornette Coleman Trio* (dir. Dick Fontaine, 1966).

172 Jean-Pierre Binchet, "Honnête Ornette," *Jazz Magazine* (Paris) (June 1965), pp. 20–23.

173 Eric Drott, "Free Jazz and the French Critic," *Journal of the American Musicological Society*, LXI/3 (2008), p. 546.

174 Jacques Réda, "Du free jazz prisonnier," *Jazz Magazine* (Paris) (March 1966). Author's translation. Reda was reviewing a February 18 concert (no venue noted), perhaps referring to Ornette's performance at the Office de Radiodiffusion-Télévision Française (ORTF), to which members of the press may have been invited. Wild and Cuscuna, *Ornette Coleman: Discography*, p. 26, notes February 12, 1966, as the date for the radio broadcast recording.

175 Michel Delorme, Daniel Berger, Guy Kopelowicz, and Phillippe Nahman, "Consécration d'Ornette," *Jazz Hot* (Marseilles) (April 1966), pp. 5–6. Author's translation.

176 "Ornette Coleman Talks to Val Wilmer," *Jazz Monthly* (May 1966), p. 15. Val Wilmer (1941–) was apparently the only woman documenting the international jazz scene of the 1960s to the 1980s.

177 *The Charles Moffett Family Vol. 1* (Charles Moffett Recording, 1975), the first of several family recordings of original compositions, featured Charles Moffett on drums and trumpet; Codaryl Moffett on percussion; Charles Moffett, Jr., on alto and tenor sax; Mondre Moffett on trumpet, flugelhorn, and baritone; Charnett Moffett (named after his father and Ornette) on upright bass and trumpet; and Patrick McCarthy, also on upright bass.

178 The last stanza reads: "when one can't find / the straight line / they must zig-zag / unless there is a circle."

179 Barry McRae, *Ornette Coleman* (London, 1988), p. 47.

180 Litweiler, *Ornette Coleman*, p. 134.

181 Ibid.

182 McCrae, *Ornette Coleman*, p. 48.

183 Ornette Coleman, "To Whom it May Concern," *DownBeat*, June 1, 1967.

184 *Ornette at Twelve* (Impulse!, 1968), recorded July 16, 1968.

185 *Ornette: Made in America* (dir. Shirley Clarke, 1985). The film's footage from the March 1968 DC protest is unclear, but there was a bassist and possibly a second horn player performing with Ornette. Denardo also appears in footage from the *Sun Suite* performance, dated 1969 in the film, but as summer 1968 in Wild and Cuscuna, *Ornette Coleman Discography*, p. 64.

186 Michel Delorme, "Ornette prophéte en son pays?," *Jazz Hot* (October 1966), p. 3.

187 Govenar, *Texas Blues*, p. 225; 2004 interview.

188 "Ever since then every trumpet player I meet I always look at his lips . . . and I've seen some with some big mouths . . . Freddy Hubbard, Don Cherry, Clifford had some beauties." Dewey continued, interviewed by Sarah Walker on *They Showed the Way* TV program sponsored by Fort Worth's Black Genealogical Society, broadcast September 2003 on municipal access channel 7. "Mr. Goodman" was the bandleader at Mt. Olive Baptist Church on Fort Worth's Southside.

189 Mandel, *Jazz Beyond Jazz*, p. 153.

190 Dewey interviewed by Sarah Walker on *They Showed the Way*. In addition to his many albums as bandleader, Dewey Redman made seven with Ornette, several others with Don Cherry and Charlie Haden, and twelve with virtuoso improvisational pianist Keith Jarrett (1945–).

191 In 1974 Ornette was awarded a second Guggenheim Fellowship. Other recipients include: Gil Evans (Canadian pianist, composer, and collaborator with Miles Davis), 1968; composer George Russell, 1969; Charles Haden, 1970; Charles Mingus, 1971; pianist and composer Carla Bley (Paul's ex-wife), 1972; Keith Jarrett, 1972; Sonny Rollins, 1972; Cecil Taylor, 1973; Thelonious Monk, 1976; and Dewey Redman, 2002.

192 In February 1967, Ornette played at the Massachusetts Institute of Technology's Kresge Hall with Moffett and Izenzon. Haden joined

as second bassist for the May 14 performance of some of the music Ornette composed for his fellowship ("Inventions of Symphonic Poems"), conducted by his Fort Worth friend John Carter at the University of California at Los Angeles Jazz Festival. (Wild and Cuscuna, *Ornette Coleman: Discography*, p. 64.)

193 Litweiler, *Ornette Coleman*, p. 136.

194 Michael C. Heller, *Loft Jazz, Improvising New York in the 1970s* (Oakland, CA, 2017), p. 34. Among the several lofts hosting jazz gatherings was Rivbea, the home of saxophonist Sam Rivers and his wife Bea, at 24 Bond Street, New York.

195 Sukenick, *Down and In*, p. 142.

196 Ibid., p. 146.

197 For Ornette's concert with Yoko Ono at Royal Albert Hall, February, 1968, see Part Three.

198 Ornette's loft was known both as Artist House (as Denardo refers to it) and Artists House, as per John Snyder, who produced two Ornette albums and named his record label "Artists House" with Ornette's permission. Author's correspondence with John Snyder, May 8, 2017.

199 Heller, *Loft Jazz*, p. 35. In 1973 Rashied Ali later had a loft at 77 Greene Street he used as a restaurant and nightclub, Ali's Alley, where avant-garde musicians that clubs wouldn't hire played for the take at the door.

200 Denardo Coleman, "My Father Was Deep," liner notes for box set of recordings *Celebrate Ornette*, assembled by Denardo and released on his label Song X, 2016. Available at www.ornettecoleman.com.

201 Kiyoshi Koyama, editor of Japan's *Swing Journal*, met Ornette in Japan on his first tour there in 1967, and visited him on Prince Street in 1969. His article, "A Day with Ornette," with superb photos by Takahashi Arihara, was translated, annotated, and presented as part of a larger essay by Brent Hayes Edwards, "Ornette at Prince Street: A Glimpse from the Archives," trans. Katherine Whatley, Point of Departure (online music journal), 53 (December 2015). Available at www.pointofdeparture.org.

202 Conversation with Martine Barrat at her home in the Chelsea Hotel, New York, November 22, 2016.

203 Conversation with Chino Garcia, "mayor of the Lower East Side," at a local pizzeria, November 17, 2016.

204 See Heller, *Loft Jazz,* pp. 41–9, for a full account of the genesis and
    fate of the counter festival. Regarding Slugs, see Charles Simic,
    "Sunday at Slugs," *New York Review of Books,* www.nybooks.com,
    July 29, 2015.

205 Conversation with Felipe Floresca at the Vinegar Factory, on 91st
    Street, November 11, 2016. The Resurrection Workshop was held
    in a storefront on Madison Avenue between 111th and 112th Street.
    Floresca first met Ornette at age thirteen, when Congressman Powell
    took him to a Harlem club where Ornette was playing. After HARYOU,
    Floresca received degrees from Brown and Harvard, and then worked
    for Ted Kennedy, New York Mayor Koch, Governor Cuomo and the
    Clinton and Obama administrations, focused on issues related to
    inner-city housing and environmental policy.

206 Ibid. In her career as educator, Jayne Cortez taught at Rutgers,
    Howard, Wesleyan, and Eastern Michigan Universities and at
    Dartmouth and Queens Colleges.

207 Lyrics by Ornette. *Friends and Neighbors* was released on Flying
    Dutchman Records in 1972.

208 Paul Lewis, "Emmanuel Ghent: 77, Composer, Innovator and
    Psychoanalyst," *New York Times,* www.nytimes.com, April 13, 2013.

209 Wild and Cuscuna, *Ornette Coleman Discography,* p. 32, notes the
    recording date of "Man on the Moon" as June 7, 1969. The "B" side
    featured "Growing Up," an Ornette composition originally entitled
    "Going Up," according to the American Federation of Musicians'
    archives. See Edwards and Whatley, "Ornette at Prince Street." Also
    in June 1969, Ornette recorded "Space Jungle" at a concert at New
    York University, later released on *Crisis* (Impulse!, 1972), with a
    burning Bill of Rights as cover art.

210 Ornette's cover notes for *The Music of Ornette Coleman: Forms and
    Sounds* (RCA Victor, 1968). "Space Flight" was performed by the
    Chamber Symphony of Philadelphia Quartet.

211 Jordan was founding secretary of the board for the creation of the
    National Jazz Service Organization, and served on the Grants Panel
    for the National Endowment for the Arts. After retiring in 2005, he
    continued to travel with Ornette and manage his tours. James Jordan
    died on December 4, 2018.

212 For a masterful account of AACM's first half-century, see George E. Lewis,
    A Power Stronger than Itself: The AACM and American Experimental

Music (Chicago, IL, 2008). The AEC's Parisian experience is covered on pp. 215–59. Ornette shared the bill with AEC and Anthony Braxton's Quartet in Paris in 1969. For the visual art generated by AACM and the related AfriCOBRA collective, see *The Freedom Principle: Experiments in Art and Music, 1965 to Now*, ed. Naomi Beckwith and Dieter Roelstraete, exh. cat., Museum of Contemporary Art, Chicago (2015).

213 Rockwell, *All American Music*, p. 171.

214 George E. Lewis, "Expressive Awesomeness," in *The Freedom Principle: Experiments in Art and Music*, ed. Beckwith and Roelstraete, exh. cat., Museum of Contemporary Art, Chicago (2015), p. 127.

215 See creativemusic.org. Cofounders of the non-profit organization were musician and composer Karl Berger, lecturer at New York's New School, and his vocalist wife, Ingrid, who had worked with Don Cherry and Eric Dolphy, among others. Throughout the 1970s, CMS hosted music sessions with Cherry, Ed Blackwell, the Art Ensemble of Chicago, Leroy Jenkins, Anthony Braxton, Jack DeJohnette, Sam Rivers, Trilok Gurtu, and Carla Bley, and poetry workshops with Allen Ginsberg and Ed Sanders.

216 Richard Williams, "Ornette and the Pipes of Joujouka," *Melody Maker*, March 17, 1973. On Ornette's trip to Africa, see Part Three.

217 Richard Williams, *Jazz: A Photographic Documentary* (London, 1994), pp. 7–8. See also Williams's blog: www.thebluemoment.com

218 Correspondence with composer, guitarist, and oud player Roman Bunka (April 24, 2017), who attended the benefit with pianist Mal Waldron and bandmate Christian Burchard of Embryo, a Munich-based group that traveled the world in the 1970s and early 1980s performing and recording with local musicians. Kirk had suffered a stroke around Thanksgiving 1975 and Bunka recalls he was still "half-paralyzed."

219 McCrae, *Ornette Coleman*, p. 56. On the demise of Artists House see also Litweiler, *Ornette Coleman*, pp. 154–5.

220 Sukenick, *Down and In*, p. 142.

Part Three: Atmospherics

1 Ornette joined Miles Davis, Chico Hamilton, Tony Bennett, and others to sing in the gospel chorus of "We Shall Overcome" on *Louis Armstrong and His Friends* (Flying Dutchman, recorded 1970).

Armstrong, who died in 1971, is the lead vocal, urging everyone "to sing like they never sang before . . . for old Satchmo." And they did. Available on YouTube.

2 From the soundtrack of *Ornette: Made in America* (dir. Shirley Clarke, 1985).

3 I am grateful to Fort Worth pianist Johnny Case for a copy of the June 20, 1966 program. With David Izenzon and Charles Moffett, Ornette performed "New York," "Atavism," "Sadness," "Curtains Up," "The Misuse Blues," "Critics Holiday," "J. L.," and "Snowflakes and Sunshine," all Coleman compositions, in addition to a David Izenzon bass solo entitled "Acapella."

4 Joseph McLellan, "A Mix of Jazz and Jambalaya on the White House Lawn," *New York Times*, June 3, 1978.

5 In 1973 Izenzon received a PhD in psychotherapy from Northwestern University. In 1975 he composed a jazz opera, "How Music Can Save the World." He died on October 8, 1979.

6 Historian Roger Lotchin quoted in Kathryn C. Pinkney, "From Stockyards to Defense Plants, the Transformation of a City: Fort Worth, Texas, and World War II," doctoral dissertation, University of North Texas (2003).

7 See the Sid Richardson Foundation website, www.sidrichardson.org.

8 All quotes from Joe Nick Patoski, and Bill Crawford, "The Long Strange Trip of Ed Bass," *Texas Monthly* (June 1989), pp. 104, 123.

9 John Allen, *Me and the Biospheres: A Memoir by the Inventor of Biosphere 2* (Santa Fe, NM, 2009), previous paragraph quotes pp. 37–9; current paragraph, p. 28. On the ship's expeditions see www.rvheraclitus.org.

10 J. Allen, T. Parrish, and M. Nelson, "The Institute of Ecotechnics," *Environmentalist*, IV/3 (1984), pp. 205–18. According to Mark Nelson, Ed Bass has said that 95 percent of his wealth was invested in traditional portfolios and the balance reserved for innovative and/or ecological investments.

11 In 1984 the Bass family added a second, near-identical 38-story tower to Fort Worth's skyline.

12 Caravan of Dreams Performing Arts Center promotional brochure, 1983.

13 In Richard Burton's translation, the last story of the *Nights* is about Maruf the Cobbler, a poor, unhappy man magically transported

from his Cairo home to a faraway land. He serendipitously encounters another Cairene, a successful merchant who suggests Maruf pretend he too is a wealthy trader awaiting his caravan of goods. "In the land where no one knows you, there do what likes you," he tells Maruf and generously fronts him funds to gain confidence in the local market. Maruf runs through them swiftly, and then borrows widely on the basis of his lavish spending, assuring everyone, including the king, that a great caravan he's placed in motion will arrive any day. Convinced of his own fiction, Maruf finds a *djinn* who makes the dreamt-of caravan a reality. *Caravan of Dreams* (1988) is the title of a book by Sufi scholar Idries Shah: "May your caravan of dreams find its way to you too," Shah writes in the introduction. The name also references Brion Gysin's 1950s Tangier nightclub, the 1001 Nights.

14 Allen, *Me and the Biospheres*, p. 99.

15 Allen, Parrish, and Nelson, "The Institute of Ecotechnics," p. 215.

16 Conversation with Kathelin Gray, Santa Fe, New Mexico, September 25, 2016.

17 Ornette speaking in *Ornette: Made in America*.

18 Clarke's film was re-released in 2012 to critical acclaim and is still shown in art house theaters.

19 John Rockwell, *All American Music* (New York, 1983), pp. 189–90. *Skies of America* (Columbia, 1972), recorded April 17–20, 1972, James Jordan executive producer.

20 Rockwell, *All American Music*, p. 190.

21 Aaron Copland speaking in the 1985 documentary *Aaron Copland: A Self-portrait* (dir. Alan Miller).

22 Howard Pollack, *Aaron Copland: The Life and Work of an Uncommon Man* (Champaign, IL, 1999), p. 118.

23 Portions of the 1983 *Skies of America* performance appear in Shirley Clarke's *Ornette: Made in America*.

24 Leon Thomas conducted the American Symphony Orchestra and the Coleman quartet included Dewey Redman, Ed Blackwell, and Charlie Haden. Don Heckman, "Coleman's 'Skies of America' in Debut," *New York Times*, July 5, 1972; Phyllis Garland, "Sounds," *Ebony* (November 1972).

25 Conversation with John Giordano, October 31, 2016. See pianist, composer, and music scholar Ethan Iverson's essay on Ornette's

musical notation abilities or possible lack thereof, "Ornette: Forms and Sounds," available at ethaniverson.com.

26 Howard Mandel also attended the opening, see Howard Mandel, "Ornette Coleman is Focus of Fort Worth Celebration," *Billboard*, October 29, 1984.

27 John Rockwell, "Jazz: Ornette Coleman Goes Home," *New York Times*, October 3, 1983. Caravan's price tag mentioned in the program for the opening month festivities, 1983.

28 Mike Ritchey, "Caravan: Oasis of Art or Mirage?" *Fort Worth Star-telegram*, September 30, 1983; Michael H. Price, "Coleman's Music a Flight of Artistry," *Fort Worth Star-telegram*, October 2, 1983.

29 Liner notes of cassette box, William S. Burroughs, "Uncommon Quotes" (Caravan of Dreams Productions, 1988). The label's spoken word series included recordings of readings by Timothy Leary and John Allen (also known as Johnny Dolphin). William Burroughs later visited Biosphere 2 and, according to Gray, frequently expressed concern about Earth's destiny. "All my work is directed against those who are bent, through stupidity or design, on blowing up the planet or rendering it inhabitable," he wrote. Catalogue for retrospective of Burroughs's paintings "All Out of Time and Into Space," October Gallery (London), December 6, 2012– February 16, 2013. See also K. Gray, "William Burroughs and the Biosphere 1974–1997," *Los Angeles Review of Books*, https://lareviewofbooks.org, May 20, 2018.

30 Bands who borrowed names from Burroughs in the 1960s and '70s include Soft Machine, Steely Dan, Dead Fingers Talk, the Insect Trust, Nova Express, and Thin White Rope.

31 See http://schtinter.org for a series of Gysin-inspired films and publications by Stanley Schtinter.

32 José Férez Kuri, ed., *Brion Gysin: Tuning in to the Multimedia Age* (London, 2003), pp. 210–15.

33 Barry Miles, "The Inventive Mind of Brion Gysin," in *Brion Gysin: Tuning in to the Multimedia Age*, ed. Kuri, p. 137. On *Songs* (hat ART, 1981) featuring soprano saxophonist Steve Lacy, Gysin's long-time friend and an American expat in Paris, Gysin raps and scats phrases he'd written, systematically rearranging the words.

34 Michael H. Price, "And the Beat Goes On for Fans of Burroughs," *Fort Worth Star-telegram*, October 8, 1983.

35 Portions of the performance appear in *Ornette: Made in America*.

36 Francis Davis, *In the Moment* (Oxford, 1986), p. 149. Cherry was more comfortable living abroad than Ornette, though their lifestyles were not dissimilar. In 1970, with his Swedish wife, Moki, Cherry acquired an old schoolhouse in Tågarp (near Malmo) that doubled as a performance space, like Artists House.

37 Michael Brenson, interview with Melvin Edwards, *BOMB*, www.bombmagazine.org, *Magazine*, November 24, 2014. Denardo accompanied Jayne and Melvin on subsequent trips to West Africa during which they formed lasting ties with local artists.

38 Richard Williams, "Ornette and the Pipes of Joujouka," *Melody Maker*, March 17, 1973.

39 Robert Palmer, "Ornette Coleman and the Circle with a Hole in the Middle," *Atlantic Monthly* (December 1972). Often referred to as "Z. K." or "Zeke," Oloruntoba (1934–2014) provided the cover art for Ornette's *Body Meta* (Artists House, 1978) and exhibited at the Institute of Ecotechnics-affiliated October Gallery, London.

40 Gerard A. Houghton, "Chief Z. O. Oloruntoba—The World Is My Village," apropos an October Gallery exhibition, June 28–July 29, 2000, available at www.octobergallery.co.uk.

41 Palmer played clarinet, alto sax, and possibly flute and recorder on *The Insect Trust* (Phoenix Records, 1968) and *Hoboken Saturday Night* (Collectors' Choice, Music, 1970). Conversation with John Rockwell, Brooklyn, New York, November 18, 2016. When Rockwell decided to step down as the *New York Times'* chief popular music critic, Palmer took over, from 1981 to 1988.

42 Robert Palmer, *Blues and Chaos* (New York, 2009), p. 337. The musicians of Joujouka split into two factions following the 1982 death of elder Hadj Abdeslam Attar. The second configuration, led by Bashir Attar, "the master musicians of Jajouka," maintained ties with Ornette, performing with him on later occasions. I have chosen to refer to the group as "Joujouka" throughout, since Ornette's essential connection was with the place and its music.

43 Jason Weiss, ed., *Back in No Time: The Brion Gysin Reader* (Middletown, CT, 2002), p. 122.

44 Sidi Ahmad's name offers no indication of his origin, nor is he locatable in Moroccan hagiography, but his feast, like that

of Sayyida Aisha (daughter of an eighth-century Shi'a imam, celebrated in Cairo), involved men dressing as women and enacting traditional scenes: in the case of Sayyida Aisha, a mock birth.

45 Ibid., pp. 337–42.

46 Anthony DeCurtis, ed., *Blues and Chaos: The Music Writing of Robert Palmer* (New York, 2009), p. 342. Gysin associated Aisha with Astarte (Greek for the Mesopotamian-Semitic Ishtar), goddess of fertility, sexuality, and war, whom the Greeks accepted as Aphrodite.

47 On the origins and evolution of Joujouka as a world music phenomenon, see Philip Schuyler, "Moroccan Music and Euro-American Imagination," in *Mass Mediations: New Approaches to Popular Culture in the Middle-East and Beyond*, ed. Walter Armbrust (Berkeley, CA, 2000), pp. 146–60. Available online: http://ark.cdlib.org.

48 Palmer, *Blues and Chaos*, p. 343. Recorded in July 1968 in Morocco, *Brian Jones Presents the Pipes of Pan at Joujouka* (Rolling Stone Records, 1971), "a mélange of funky hill music and sophisticated studio techniques," was hailed as the first "world-music" album.

49 Schuyler, "Moroccan Music," n. 47; William S. Burroughs, "Face to Face with the Goat-god," *Oui* (Chicago), 11/8 (August 1972), p. 92.

50 Burroughs, "Face to Face with the Goat-god," pp. 91–2.

51 Ibid. Burroughs was presumably pleased when Ornette contributed to Howard Shore's score for the soundtrack of the film version of his novel *Naked Lunch* (dir. David Cronenberg, 1991).

52 Drew Franklin, "Playing in the Register of Light," *Village Voice* Jazz Special, "The Art of the Improviser, Ornette Coleman" (June 1987).

53 Ibid.

54 J. B. Figi, "Ornette Coleman, a Surviving Elder in the Universal Brotherhood of Those Who Make Music," *Chicago Reader*, 11/37 (June 22, 1973), p. 6.

55 Richard Williams, "Ornette and the Pipes of Joujouka," *Melody Maker*, March 17, 1973.

56 Figi, "Ornette Coleman, a Surviving Elder," p. 6.

57 Mark Warren, "Ornette Coleman: What I've Learned," *Esquire*, www.esquire.com, December 24, 2009; "Music is just something that I do, but I'd like to be doing lots of other things . . . I like to cure all kinds of illness," Ornette told Michael Jarrett, who interviewed him in 1987: *Cadence Magazine* (October 1995). Available online: https://york.psu.edu.

58 Drew Franklin, "Playing in the Register of Light," *Village Voice* (June 1987) Jazz Special: "The Art of the Improviser, Ornette Coleman."

59 Personnel on *Science Fiction* and *Broken Shadows*: Dewey Redman on tenor; Don Cherry on pocket trumpet; Bobby Bradford on trumpet; Charlie Haden on bass; Billy Higgins on drums; Ed Blackwell on drums; Asha Puthli on vocals; Ornette on alto, trumpet, and violin.

60 Webster D. Armstrong III (1922–2015) worked with Buster Smith until Dizzy Gillespie heard him on a dance night at Fort Worth's Prince Hall Mosque and hired him for gigs in New York, Chicago, and Detroit. According to Armstrong, in addition to the recording session with Ornette, they performed together at Carnegie Hall in 1973. An elegant, worldly-wise but modest man, Armstrong was a music educator at I. M. Terrell High School.

61 Ornette Coleman, "Prime Time for Harmolodics," *DownBeat* (July 1983), pp. 54–5.

62 Bertolt Brecht, ed., *Brecht on Theater*, trans. John Willett (New York, 1964), p. 119.

63 On space-related themes in music and music-related technology, see Ken McLeod, "Space Oddities: Aliens, Futurism and Meaning in Popular Music," *Popular Music*, XXII/3 (Cambridge, 2003), pp. 337–55.

64 Sun Ra's liner notes to *Sun Song* (Transition Records, 1957).

65 Rebecca Zorach, "The Positive Aesthetics of the Black Arts Movement," in *The Freedom Principle: Experiments in Art and Music 1965 to Now*, ed. Naomi Beckwith and Dieter Roelstraete, exh. cat., Museum of Contemporary Art, Chicago (2015), p. 105.

66 Much has been written about Sun Ra, towering figure in the history of jazz and experimental music, notably *Omniverse Sun Ra* by Harmut Geerken (London, 2015) and John Szwed's *Space is the Place: The Life and Times of Sun Ra* (Boston, MA, 1998). According to Geerken, while Ornette's orbit may have intersected Sun Ra's, they did not collaborate or perform together.

67 Peter Niklas Wilson, Foreword to Pat Metheny, *Ornette Coleman: His Life and Music* (Berkeley, CA, 1999).

68 Ellerbe plays on seven Ornette albums, from *Dancing in Your Head* (1977) to *JazzBuhne Berlin '88*.

69 Shannon studied with John Carter and started out with James Clay. On his background and experiences with Albert Ayler, Cecil Taylor, and Ornette, see Rafi Zabour and David Breskin, "Ronald Shannon Jackson: The Future Jazz Drumming" (June 1981), available on author David Breskin's website, www.davidbreskin.com. Shannon appears on *Dancing in Your Head* (1973) and *Body Meta* (1975). Denardo performed and recorded with a later edition of Prime Time on *In All Languages* (1985); *Tone Dialing* (1995); *Sound Museum* (1996); and *Sound Grammar* (2006).

70 Cliff Tinder, "Jamaaladeen Tacuma, Electric Bass in the Harmolodic Pocket," *DownBeat* (April 1982), pp. 20–21. Al MacDowell did not play on *Dancing in Your Head*, but he performed for Prime Time's 1977 Newport in New York concert, and appeared on subsequent recordings including *Opening the Caravan of Dreams*, *In All Languages*, *Virgin Beauty* (1988), and *Tone Dialing* (1995).

71 Howard Mandel, *Miles, Ornette, Cecil: Jazz Beyond Jazz* (New York, 2008), p. 180. On Ornette's theory of harmolodics, see Part Four.

72 Back cover notes, *Dancing in Your Head*, dated March 15, 1977 (Horizon, 1977).

73 Correspondence with Dave Bryant, August 10, 2018. Prime Time first line-up: Ornette on alto, trumpet, and violin; Bern Nix and Charles Ellerbe on guitar; Albert MacDowell and Jamaaladeen Tacuma on bass; and Denardo Coleman and Sabir Kamal on drums. Prime Time's later configuration: Ornette on alto, trumpet, and violin; Chris Rosenberg and Ken Wessel on guitar; Dave Bryant on keyboards; Chris Walker, Al MacDowell, and Brad Jones on bass; Badal Roy on tabla; and Denardo and Calvin Weston on drums. Weston was not present on *Tone Dialing* (1995), the later configuration's only album. Denardo recorded on *In All Languages* (1985), *Tone Dialing* (1995), *Sound Museum* (1996), and *Sound Grammar* (2006).

74 Ibid.

75 Susan White, "The Elegant Arts of Fort Worth," *D Magazine* (Dallas) (March 1984).

76 Paul Taylor, "In 'Caravan of Dreams', Texan Envisions a Smorgasbord of Life," *Washington Post*, September 27, 1983.

77 Terry Miller, "Hoffman's Dream Has Come True," *Fort Worth Star-telegram*, September 30, 1983.

78 Taylor, "In 'Caravan of Dreams'."

79 Allen, *Me and the Biospheres*, p. 108.

80 Peter Applebone, "Caravan of Pipe Dreams," *Texas Monthly* (January 1984), p. 124.

81 A civil action suit (*Flax et al. v. Potts et al.*) ended school segregation on September 27, 1989.

82 Allen, *Me and the Biospheres*, p. 102.

83 The development was named in honor of Harry Alonzo Longabaugh, also known as the Sundance Kid, who visited that quarter of Fort Worth when it was called Hell's Half Acre.

84 Taylor, "In 'Caravan of Dreams'."

85 Joe Nick Patoski and Bill Crawford, "The Long Strange Trip of Ed Bass," *Texas Monthly* (June 1989), pp. 102–27.

86 Ibid., p. 108.

87 Peter Applebone, "Caravan of Pipe Dreams."

88 Graham Snyder, "Caravan Travels Long Road to Fame," *Fort Worth Star-telegram* (June 12, 1987).

89 Applebone, "Caravan of Pipe Dreams," p. 128.

90 Guy Debord, May 17, 1960, reprinted in *Internationale Situationniste*, 4 (June 1960), trans. Fabian Tompsett.

91 Perry Stewart and Michael H. Price, "Club Grows, Comes of Age," *Fort Worth Star-telegram*, September 22, 1985; Mandel, *Jazz Beyond Jazz*, p. 169.

92 Ibid.

93 Dan Hulbert, "Living Theater to Make Rare Appearance," *Dallas Times-herald*, March 8, 1984.

94 "Synergy, the synthesis of energies with which Caravan once sought to be everything to everyone appears to taking on a narrowed [more mainstream] focus," wrote Perry Stewart and Michael H. Price, "Club Grows, Comes of Age."

95 Wayne King, "Cowtown U.S.A. Hesitantly Gives Way to High Technology and Culture," *New York Times*, June 19, 1985.

96 Peter Niklas Wilson, Foreword to Metheny, *Ornette Coleman: His Life and Music*.

97 Ornette co-wrote "Kathelin Gray" with Pat Metheny. Other Coleman compositions presumably inspired by and dedicated to women include: "Lorraine"; "Lonely Woman" (inspired by a portrait); "Una Muy Bonita" (1959); "Elizabeth"; "Street Woman" (1971); "Macho Woman" (1976); and "Denise K." (1995).

98 Lebel says Ono did the bag piece again at a friend's home where
    Noël Burch and André S. Labarthe were filming their documentary
    Rome is Burning: Portrait of Shirley Clarke (1970). During a filmed
    conversation about Clarke, Ono "disappeared into her Black Bag . . .
    unseen, unheard yet intensely present." To Lebel, who counted Gilles
    Deleuze among his friends, this was "a remarkable philosophical
    statement akin to John Cage's "New Music = New Listening" [and]
    . . . a precise metaphor of the true artist's modus operandi." From
    Lebel's website, posted in 2014: http://fondsdedotationjjlebel.org.

99 Ono's film was screened at the Albert Hall fifty years later, see
    www.royalalberthall.com.

100 Barry McCrae, "Emotion Modulation," *Jazz Journal*, XXI/4 (April
    1968), p. 5.

101 Located at 222 West 23rd Street and opened in 1885, artists from Mark
    Twain to Andy Warhol bedded down with the muse at the Chelsea
    Hotel, some permanently, including Dylan Thomas, who died of
    pneumonia in 1953, and Nancy Spungen, Sid Vicious's girlfriend,
    stabbed to death there in 1978.

102 See Gray's essay on Clarke and the genesis of *Ornette: Made in America*
    in the press kit issued for the restored film's rerelease (Milestone
    Films, 2012), p. 32. Available online: www.projectshirley.com.

103 William McKibben, "Involved," *New Yorker*, June 18, 1984. Funded
    by a grant from the National Endowment for the Arts, the project
    involved "a General Electric GEM-LINK microwave system, some fibre
    optic cable, and interface equipment."

104 Press kit, *Ornette: Made in America*, p. 32.

105 Author's correspondence, March 9, 2018.

106 Conversation with Felipe Floresca, November 11, 2016. Floresca did
    not recall Ornette's band members. Rites and Reasons Theatre still
    operates under the Africana Studies department of Brown University,
    where archival documentation of *Zeki is Coming* may exist but has yet
    to surface.

107 Conversation with Kathelin Gray, September 25, 2016.

108 Jon Pareles, "Jazz: Caravan of Dreams in a Play," *New York Times*,
    December 24, 1984.

109 Author's correspondence with Gregg Dugan, May 18, 2017. According
    to Kathelin Gray, one of the performances was videotaped, but no
    copies survive.

110 Author's correspondence with Kathelin Gray, March 10, 2018.

111 Saxophonist Charles Lloyd's Quartet included Cecil McBee on bass, Jack DeJohnette on drums, and Keith Jarrett on piano.

112 Six distributors wholesaled 90 percent of the recordings sold in America in the 1980s; independents shared the remaining 10 percent. John Litweiler, *Ornette Coleman: A Harmolodic Life* (New York, 1992), pp. 192–3. Alongside Gray, Jil Posner and Judy Jett helped run Caravan of Dreams Productions in the 1980s.

113 Shannon Jackson's Decoding Society albums on the Caravan label include: *Live at the Caravan of Dreams* (1986); *Slang in Trance*, with Nigerian musician and artist Chief Twins Seven Seven (1986); *When Colors Play* (1987); and *Texas* (1988).

114 Prime Time personnel for *In All Languages*: Denardo and Calvin Weston on drums; Al MacDowell and Jamaaladeen Tacuma on electric bass; and Charles Ellerbe and Bern Nix on electric guitar.

115 Robert Palmer, "At Jazz Festival, Hot as Well as Cool," *New York Times*, June 19, 1987.

116 Conversation with John Allen, Santa Fe, New Mexico, September 25, 2016.

117 On Slugs' Saloon (242 E. 3rd Street), where Ornette rehearsed for recording *Science Fiction*, see Frank Mastropolo, "'It Was a Joint': Jazz Musicians Remember Slugs' in the Far East," posted September 10, 2014, www.bedfordandbowery.com

118 René Daumal, *Mount Analogue: A Novel of Symbolically Authentic Non-Euclidean Adventures in Mountain Climbing*, trans. Roger Shattuck (Boston, MA, 1992). When tuberculosis prevented Daumal (1908–1944) from pursuing his passion for climbing, he wrote *Mount Analogue*. A poet and self-taught Sanskrit scholar, Daumal met G. I. Gurdjieff through Alexandre de Salzmann (a member of Gurdjieff's work group) and fashioned fictional characters from a composite of both these unusual men. A friend of Alfred Jarry and fellow pataphysician (master of singularities), Daumal died before completing the novel. *Mount Analogue* inspired Alejandro Jodorowsky's *The Holy Mountain* (1973) and is the title of composer and multi-instrumentalist John Zorn's 2012 album on the Tzadik label.

119 The first conference, featuring William Burroughs and two other guests, was held at Synergia Ranch in 1974. Subsequent

IE conferences included those focused on deserts, held at Synergia Ranch, 1978; jungles, held in Penang Malaysia in 1979; and so on. For a list of topics and speakers (1976–2007) see http://ecotechnics.edu.

120 Cover Notes, *Prime Time/Time Design* (Caravan of Dreams Productions, 1985). Among the other speakers at the 1982 Galactic Conference (September 17–20) that Ornette may have met were evolutionary biologists Lynn Margulis and Richard Dawkins.

121 Michael Zwerin, "Breaking the Sound Barriers of Jazz," *International Herald Tribune* (Paris), November 7, 1984.

122 *Prime Design/Time Design*. Gregory Gelman and Larissa Blitz on violin and Alexander Deych on viola were Soviet immigrants, joined by American cellist Mathew Meister and Denardo Coleman.

123 Soundtrack, *Ornette: Made in America*. McNair, the first of many astronaut musicians to perform in space, played his specially adapted tenor sax on the *Challenger* space shuttle in February 1984. See Terry Dunn, "Why Music Is Important to Astronauts in Space," www.tested.com, November 25, 2015. Regarding NASA's attempts to engage (visual) artists that began in 1962, see Hannah Hotovy, "NASA and Art: A Collaboration Colored with History," www.nasa.gov, April 18, 2017.

124 Soundtrack, *Ornette: Made in America*.

125 Peter Pearce, a collaborator of Fuller, designed the soaring, space-frame architecture.

126 Tim Leary called Biosphere 2 "a unique experiment in interspecies cooperation," according to Mark Nelson, chairman of the Institute of Ecotechnics, who kindly shared information regarding IE and Biosphere 2 for this section. The crew for the first closure (September 26, 1991–September 26, 1993) included Nelson, Roy Walford, Jane Poynter, Taber MacCallum, Sally Silverstone, Abigail Alling, Mark Van Thillo, and Linda Leigh. On Fuller and the construction of Biosphere 2 see John Allen, "Buckminster Fuller's Synergetic Algorithm and Challenges of the Twenty-first Century," speech delivered for Buckminster Fuller Memorial at U.S. International University, San Diego, CA, June 4, 1996. Available at: www.biospherics.org.

127 For a full account of life inside Biosphere 2, and the work and science of maintaining it, see Mark Nelson, *Pushing Our Limits: Insights from Biosphere 2* (Tucson, AZ, 2018), p. 60. See also the documentary film about Biosphere 2, directed by Matt Wolf and produced by Radical

Media, New York (untitled at the time of writing), scheduled for release at Sundance Film Festival, January 2020.

128 Allen, *Me and the Biospheres*, p. 10.

129 Conversation with John Allen, Santa Fe, New Mexico, September 25, 2016. Ornette accompanied John Allen's reading of his poetry in a Greene Street café (NYC) with Joe Albany on piano. *The Sacred Mind of Johnny Dolphin* debuted at Weill Recital Hall (NYC) in 1987, conducted by Joseph Celli.

130 All Ornette quotes from soundtrack, *Ornette: Made in America*. "Space Church" appeared on *In All Languages*, performed by both the quartet and Prime Time. "Biosphere" was recorded with Prime Time. Ornette attended the events surrounding the first two-year closure of Biosphere 2, September 26, 1991, and was particularly impressed by its two lungs. Designed by William Dempster, founding IE director and director of systems engineering for Biosphere 2, the lungs allowed inside air pressure to fluctuate. Without them, the structure might have exploded or imploded from differences between internal and external pressure.

131 Ornette reportedly sold the former schoolhouse (currently an apartment building) at 203 Rivington Street for $3 million in 1986–7. Litweiler, *Ornette Coleman*, p. 193.

132 Stanley Crouch, *Considering Genius* (New York, 2006), p. 282.

133 David Grogan, "Ornette Coleman," *People Magazine*, www.people.com, October 13, 1986.

134 "The Country that Gave the Freedom Symbol to America," a chamber piece for seventeen musicians, premiered in Paris at the 1989 Festival d'Automne in Paris. Saxophonist Anthony Braxton and musician-composer Conlon Nancarrow participated in the performance. Nothing ever came of the LaScala prospect.

135 A shortlist of artists who performed in the Caravan nightclub includes Dewey Redman, Cecil Taylor, Pharaoh Sanders, Sonny Rollins, Elvin Jones, Billy Eckstine, Carmen McRae, Shirley Horn, Betty Carter, Diane Reeves, Regina Belle, Sam Rivers, Marchel Ivery, David "Fathead" Newman, Frank Morgan, James Clay, John McLaughlin (with Trilok Gurtu and Kai Eckhardt), Stevie Ray Vaughan, Gatemouth Brown, Muddy Waters, John Lee Hooker, Stanley Turrentine, Kirk Whalum, Wynton and Branford Marsalis, Lonnie Liston Smith, Maynard Ferguson's

Big Band, Texan balladeer Lyle Lovett's Large Ban, and Eddie Brickell and the New Bohemians (who recorded their first demo tape at Caravan).

136 Wynton's 1987 Quintet featured Marcus Roberts on piano; Bob Hurst on bass; Jeff "Tain" Watts on drums; and Don Braden on tenor sax. Impresario and producer Larry Clothier managed Wynton, Carmen McCrae, and others who played Caravan in the 1980s and early 1990s. He became Hargrove's first manager and saw to it he sat in with all the big names. Hargrove's album *Habana* (Verve, 1997), with his Afro-Cuban group Crisol (featuring "Una," a composition by Texan trumpeter Kenny Dorham), won a Grammy in 1998. Hargrove's second Grammy was for *Directions in Music: Live at Massey Hall, Celebrating Miles Davis and John Coltrane* with Herbie Hancock and saxophonist Michael Brecker (Verve, 2002). Hargrove collaborated with a variety of vocalists, from jazz pianist and *raconteuse* Shirley Horn (1934–2005), to Macy Gray and Dallas-born Erykah Badu. Hargrove, who claimed Texan tenor David "Fathead" Newman as a prime inspiration, later cofounded New York's Jazz Gallery, a not-for-profit concert venue showcasing young musicians and composers. He died of kidney disease at age 49, on November 2, 2018.

137 *Eartha Kitt—My Way—A Musical Tribute to Rev. Dr. Martin Luther King Jr.* (Caravan of Dreams Productions, recorded March 1987).

138 Graham Snyder, "Leary Sees Baby Boomers Turning On to Revolution," *Fort Worth Star-telegram*, February 2, 1987.

139 Howard Mandel, "Ornette Coleman: The Color of Music," *DownBeat* (August 1987).

140 David Fricke, "Ornette Coleman's Time," *Rolling Stone*, March 9, 1989.

141 Michael Stephans, *Experiencing Ornette Coleman: A Listener's Companion* (Lanham, MD, 2017) provides an excellent guide to Ornette's music, but *Virgin Beauty* (Portrait, 1988), which went to #2 on Billboard's jazz chart and had larger first-year sales than any of his previous recordings, is a good place for novices to start. Prime Time personnel: Dave Bryant on piano; Ken Wessel and Chris Rosenberg on guitar; Denardo on drums; Badal Roy on tablas; and Al Macdowell on bass. Garcia plays guitar on "3 Wishes," "Desert Players," and "Singing in the Shower."

142 In Cologne Ornette debuted a quartet with Denardo, bassist Charnett Moffett, and pianist Geri Allen. Program from the

June 9, 1994 concert available online: http://reinermichalke.de/ ornette-celebration.

143 Mandel, *Jazz Beyond Jazz*, p. 186.

144 Nat Hentoff, "Old Country Jewish Blues and Ornette," in *At the Jazz Band Ball* (Berkeley, CA, 2010), p. 103.

145 Conversation with Kenny Wessel, New York City, November 23, 2016.

146 For a detailed description of the San Francisco event and the text of "Tone Dialing" read by Dr. Harding, see Mandel, *Jazz Beyond Jazz*, pp. 182–5.

147 The Harmolodics label, registered to Ornette's address (1825 Park Avenue at 125th Street in East Harlem), had a marketing and distribution deal with Verve/PolyGram. The label released several Prime Time albums, in addition to reissues of Ornette's older recordings and *Taking the Blues Back Home*, an album by Jayne Cortez, performing with the Firespitters, a group comprising Denardo and several other Prime Time members.

148 Mandel, *Jazz Beyond Jazz*, p. 186. The cover art for *Tone Dialing* is a touch-tone phone with ten words instead of numbers on the buttons. Elsewhere in the sleeve notes Ornette pairs the words to form a kind of perceptual map: smell=present, taste=quality, hearing=receptivity, touch=action, sight=territory.

149 Neneh Cherry, "Neneh Cherry Remembers Ornette," *The Guardian*, www.theguardian.com, December 27, 2015.

150 Charles Moffett interviewed by Bob Rusch, *Cadence* (February 1997), p. 15.

151 Soundtrack, *Ornette: Made in America.*

152 Mandel, *Jazz Beyond Jazz*, p. 191.

Part Four: Transmission

1 Nat Hentoff, *The Jazz Life* (New York, 1961), pp. 245–6.

2 Conversation with Kenny Wessel, New York City, November 23, 2016. Wessel performed and recorded with Ornette from 1988 until 2000.

3 John Zorn, "At the Hop," *Village Voice* (June 1987).

4 Correspondence with John Snyder, November 16, 2016.

5 Telephone conversation with Bobby Bradford, November 4, 2016.

6 Michael Jarrett's 1987 interview of Ornette appeared in *Cadence Magazine* (October 1995), available online at www2.york.psu. Jarrett

authored the wittily academic *Drifting on a Read: Jazz as a Model for Writing* (Albany, NY, 1999).

7 Schnee's essay, "Zen Buddhism, Ornette Coleman, and the Harmolodic Path," October 14, 2014, is available on his website: danielpaulschnee.wordpress.com.

8 A. B. Spellman, *Four Lives in the Bebop Business* (New York, 1966), p. 119.

9 Conversation with Ken Wessel, November 23, 2016.

10 Robert Palmer, liner notes, *Beauty is a Rare Thing: The Complete Atlantic Recordings*, a compilation of tracks recorded 1959–61, released by Rhino Records, 1993, in a six-CD box set. Personnel on *Sound Museum: Three Women* and *Sound Museum: Hidden Man* (Harmolodics, 1996): Ornette on alto, trumpet, violin; Geri Allen on piano; Charnett Moffett on bass; and Denardo Coleman on drums.

11 Born in Knoxville, Tennessee, "a cross between Brer Rabbit and St. Francis of Assisi," Beauford Delaney lived (and died) in Paris, and was a close friend of James Baldwin. His work, while known in Europe, has only recently been recognized in America. See David Leeming, *Amazing Grace: A Life of Beauford Delaney* (Oxford, 1998). Briet's gallery was at 558 Broadway. "Don't You Know By Now" is the title of a compositon by Ornette recorded on *Sound Museum* (Harmolodic/Verve, 1996).

12 Conversation with Skoto Aghahowa and Alix du Serech, in the current Skoto Gallery (529 West 20th Street), November 8, 2016. Ornette's text for the "Art in Africa" (February 7–March 14, 1992) flier: "Before the word[,] Art existed as in many concepts of thoughts and categorization. Civilization was the Art and is [the] Art of mankind. There is no Best in Art, only its Creation of Self-Expression. From the many concept[s] of human classes what one finds in today[']s concept of Art is the history of the Past with those who are taking the struggle to take Art into its own present. Take a look at the Art in Africa."

13 David Velasco, "David Hammons talks about 'Six Sites in Alexandria'," *Artforum*, www.artforum.com, November 24, 2008. Hammons dedicated his 2019 exhibition at Hauser & Wirth Gallery (LA) to "Ornette Coleman, Harmolodic Thinker."

14 Correspondence with Todd Siler, July 12, 2018. Jenette Khan, then editor-in-chief of DC Comics (of Superman and Batman fame),

introduced Ornette to a video of Siler's work at a 1995
New York gathering. A video of the group Harmolodics' rehearsals
and performance of "Ode to Art" is available at toddsilerart.com.
Harmolodics personnel: Ornette on alto, Denardo on drums, Owusu
Slater on percussion, and Tevin Thomas on keyboards. On vocals,
Avenda Khadija Ali, who recorded on *Tone Dialing* with Prime Time,
D. K. Dyson, who toured with rapper Ice-T in 1992, operatic singer
N'kenge Simpson-Hoffman, and Mari Okubo, who performed
onstage with Prime Time on several occasions.

15 Mandel, *Jazz Beyond Jazz*, p. 178.

16 Ibid., p. 118.

17 Scholarly studies of Ornette's early work (1960s) include Michael Bruce
Cogswell's "Melodic Organization in Four Solos by Ornette Coleman,"
PhD dissertation, University of North Texas (1990); Michael Block's
"Pitch Class Transformations in Free Jazz" (*Music Theory Spectrum*, 181,
Fall 1990), and Lynette Westendorf's "Analyzing Free Jazz," PhD
dissertation, University of Washington (1994). Musicologist Ekkehard
Jost's *Free Jazz* (Graz, 1974) provides technical analysis of Ornette's
compositions up to 1970, alongside those of contemporaries such as
Coltrane, Sun Ra, and the Art Ensemble of Chicago. Nathan A.
Frink's *Dancing in His Head: The Evolution of Ornette Coleman's Music
and Compositional Philosophy*, PhD dissertation, University of
Pittsburgh (2016), covers Ornette's compositional practices in the
"renaissance" 1970s. Stephen Rush, *Free Jazz, Harmolodics, and Ornette
Coleman* (New York, 2016) examines the technicalities and thinking
behind harmolodics, which Rush (who interviewed Ornette
extensively) relates to the issues of civil rights, and more broadly
human equality, that were close to Ornette's heart.

18 Conrad Silvert, "Old and New Dreams," *DownBeat* (June 1980).

19 Robert Palmer, "Charlie Haden's Creed," *DownBeat*, July 20, 1972.

20 Alan Nahigian, "James 'Blood' Ulmer and Vernon Reid:
Harmolodic Blues," *Jazz Times*, www.jazztimes.com, July 1, 2006.
London-born Vernon Reid (1958–) founded the Grammy award-
winning group Living Color, probably the most commercially
successful band inspired by Ornette and Ronald Shannon Jackson's
interpretations of harmolodics. Living Color's debut album, *Vivid*
(Epic, 1988), sold 2 million copies ("double platinum" in industry
terms), and *Time's Up* (1990) went gold (selling a half-million copies).

21 A 2004 interview with Dewey Redman in Alan Govenar, *Texas Blues: The Rise of a Contemporary Sound* (College Station, TX, 2008), p. 227.

22 Ornette Coleman, "Prime Time for Harmolodics," *DownBeat* (July 1983).

23 Howard Mandel, "Ornette Coleman, the Color of Music," *DownBeat* (August 1987). Ornette also sometimes used "sound grammar," the title of his 2006 LP, as a term for harmolodics.

24 Correspondence with John Snyder, November 16, 2016.

25 Conversation with John Giordano, October 31, 2016.

26 J. Rockwell, *All American Music* (New York, 1983), p. 188.

27 David Pantalony, "Hermann von Helmholtz and the Sensations of Tone," in *Altered Sensations*, Archimedes (New Studies in the History of Science and Technology), vol. XXIV (Dordrecht, 2009), p. 29.

28 *On the Sensations of Tone* is available online at archive.org. From an appendix: the key of G major for example, "favourite key of youth; expresses sincerity of faith, quiet love, calm meditation, simple grace, pastoral life, and a certain humour and brightness;" whereas E minor expresses "grief, mournfulness, and restlessness of spirit."

29 Pantalony, "Hermann von Helmholtz and the Sensations of Tone," p. 19. Apropos music's "action on the mind," Einstein, who played violin and piano, famously claimed to have discovered the theory of relativity intuitively, as the result of "musical perception," and once commended physicist Neil Bohr's work on the structure of the atom as "the highest form of musicality in the realm of thought."

30 John Zorn, "At the Hop," *Village Voice* (June 1987).

31 From the introduction of *On the Sensations of Tone*, available online at archive.org.

32 Ornette Coleman, "Prime Time for Harmolodics," *DownBeat* (July 1983).

33 Howard Mandel, "Ornette Coleman: The Color of Music," *DownBeat* (August 1987). Ornette's intent may be discerned in *Colors: Live from Leipzig* (Harmolodic/Verve, 1996), a superb duet with German pianist Joachim Kühn (1944–), who had worked with Don Cherry and Karl Berger, cofounder of the Creative Music Studio. The album cover featured a painting by Ornette.

34 Rockwell, *All American Music*, p. 188. Rockwell cites the "idiosyncratic theories" of Richard Wagner, Arnold Schoenberg, and Milton Babbitt.

35 Conversation with Kenny Wessel, November 23, 2016.

36 Ornette Coleman, "Something to Think About," in *Free Spirits: Annals of the Insurgent Imagination*, ed. Nancy J. Peters (San Francisco, CA, 1982), p. 119.

37 Whitney Balliett, *American Musicians: Fifty-six Portraits in Jazz* (Oxford, 1986), p. 407.

38 For a concise overview of Bergson's thinking see Leonard Lawlor and Valentine Moulard-Leonard, "Henri Bergson," *The Stanford Encyclopedia of Philosophy* (Summer 2016 edn), ed. Edward N. Zalta, available online at plato.stanford.edu. For an exploration of Bergsonian concepts' intersection with jazz, see Steven Tromans, "Experiments in Time: Music-research with Jazz Standards in the Professional Context," in *Artistic Experimentation in Music*, ed. Darla Crispin and Bob Gilmore (Leuven, 2015), published on behalf of Belgium's Orpheus Research Centre in Music in Ghent.

39 Timothy S. Murphy, trans., "The Other's Language: Jacques Derrida Interviews Ornette Coleman, 23 June, 1997," *Genre*, III/2 (2004), pp. 319–32.

40 Howard Mandel, *Miles, Ornette, Cecil: Jazz Beyond Jazz* (New York, 2008), p. 118.

41 Conversation with Michael Cuscuna, Stamford, Connecticut, November 21, 2016.

42 J. B. Figi, "Ornette Coleman, a Surviving Elder in the Universal Brotherhood of Those who Make Music," *Chicago Reader*, June 2, 1973.

43 D. Schnee, "Zen Buddhism, Ornette Coleman, and the Harmolodic Path," October 14, 2014. For his PhD dissertation, Schnee wrote *Zen Buddhism and Improvisation* (York, 2013).

44 Mandel, *Jazz Beyond Jazz*, p. 141.

45 Ibid., p. 127.

46 Conversation with painter, ceramicist and performance artist Letitia Eldredge, Coupland, Texas, October 21, 2016.

47 Conversation with Stanley Crouch, Brooklyn, New York, November 22, 2016.

48 Philip Clark, "Harmolodics and Ham Sandwiches: Meeting Ornette Coleman [in 2007]," *The Guardian*, www.theguardian.com, June 11, 2015.

49 Correspondence with John Snyder, November 16, 2016.

50 David Fricke, "Ornette Coleman's Time," *Rolling Stone*, March 9, 1989.

51 Charles Moffett interviewed by jazz critic and record producer Bob Rusch, *Cadence* (February 1997), p. 12.

52 Correspondence with John Snyder, November 16, 2016.

53 Greg Tate, "Change of the Century," *Village Voice* (June 1987).

54 Michael Jarrett's 1987 interview with Ornette appeared in *Cadence* (October 1995).

55 Tate, "Change of the Century."

56 "The New Jazz," *Newsweek*, December 12, 1966.

57 Ornette's liner notes for *Body Meta* (Artists House, 1978).

58 Soundtrack, *Ornette: Made in America* (dir. Shirley Clarke, 1985).

59 Ibid.

60 Mark Warren, "Ornette Coleman: What I've Learned," *Esquire*, www.esquire.com, December 14, 2009.

61 Kathelin Gray, "The Flirtin' Lesson" (2013), transcribed conversations with Ornette.

62 Conversation with John Rockwell, Brooklyn, New York, November 8, 2016. Ornette was invited to participate in a panel assembled by Rockwell that included Argentine composer Osvaldo Golijov and Australian singer, writer, and stage director Robyn Archer.

63 "Obituary: Dewey Redman Dies," *DownBeat*, September 5, 2006. Dewey's son Joshua (1969–) carried his father's legacy of musicianship forward, winning the Thelonious Monk International Jazz Saxophone Competition (1991) in addition to several Grammy nominations and recording and performing extensively.

64 Fred Kaplan, "Take the O Train," *Slate*, www.slate.com, October 30, 2006.

65 Gary Giddins, "Ornette!!!!," *Jazz Times* (November 2006). Technically, Ornette's last recording was *New Vocabulary* (System Dialing Records, 2014). Recorded in Ornette's home with Amir Ziv, Jordan McLean, and Adam Holtzman, its release became the subject of a lawsuit filed by Denardo (Ornette's legal guardian since 2013) in which the young musicians were accused of releasing the material from "teaching sessions" without Ornette's permission. The defendants maintained that the recording was at all times a willing act of collaboration. The case was dismissed with prejudice on procedural grounds.

66 Taylor Ho Bynum, "Seeing Ornette Coleman," *New Yorker*, June 12, 2015.

67 John Rogers, "My Friend Ornette Coleman," *National Public Radio*, www.npr.org, June 15, 2015. For Rogers's tattoo, tattoo artist David Digby used a photo of Ornette (*c.* 1959) taken by photographer William Claxton (1927–2008), who was known for his portraits of 1950s–60s jazzmen.

68 Conversation with Ras Moshe at the Brooklyn Commons, November 22, 2016. Ras spoke frequently with Ornette and the two eventually met.

69 Conversation with Matt Lavelle, New York City, November 20, 2016.

70 Kathelin Gray, "The Flirtin' Lesson."

71 Haden's introduction and Ornette's acceptance speech are available at www.jazzclinic.blogspot.com. Haden died on July 11, 2014, eleven months before Ornette. Visionary Canadian pianist Paul Bley, among the first to appreciate and perform with Ornette professionally in LA, died January 3, 2016.

72 Of the 33 musicians honored by the Kennedy Center, four were women, including pianist Marian McPartland and vocalist Nancy Wilson.

73 This thoroughly Texan awards round-up included the Alvin Ailey American Dance Troupe (founded by Alvin Ailey, Rogers, Texas, 1931–1989); actress Sissy Spacek (Quitman, Texas), best known for her role as a telekinetic teen (*Carrie*, 1976); Dallas-based retail chain Neiman Marcus (as "corporate arts patron"); and Fort Worth's Sid W. Richardson Foundation (as "foundation arts patron").

74 Ornette performs on the track entitled "Guilty." Don Cherry appeared on Lou Reed's album *The Bells* (Arista, 1979).

75 The Bonnaroo interview, mistakenly dated 2008, is available on YouTube.

76 Lawrence Van Gelder, "Ornette Coleman Collapses," *New York Times*, www.nytimes.com, June 19, 2007.

77 Telephone conversation with Bobby Bradford, November 4, 2016. For the Jazz Standard gig (October 3, 2009), Bobby played with David Murray on sax; Marty Ehrlich on sax, clarinet, and flute; Mark Dresser on acoustic bass; and Andrew Cyrille on drums. On October 4, the band was joined by Baikida Carroll

on trumpet, James Weidman on piano, and Mark Helias on bass. It was one of the last performances of trombonist Benny Powell (1930–2010), who recorded extensively with Count Basie and worked frequently with Fort Worther John Carter, Bobby Bradford's longtime collaborator.

78 John Morthland, "Unsentimental Journey," *Texas Monthly* (June 2001).

79 Michael Jarrett's 1987 interview with Ornette, *Cadence* (October 1995).

80 Mari Okubo performed with Prime Time in New York and Japan. Tracks from *Cosmic Life* are available at mariokubo.com.

81 Ornette made this remark at a luncheon after receiving an honorary degree from City University of New York in 2008. A young woman musician pointed out that she didn't have a penis, but Ornette reportedly stood by his remark. Conversation with Gary Giddins, New York City, November 23, 2016.

82 Conversation with Matt Lavelle, Brooklyn, New York, November 20, 2016. Lavelle's group 12 Houses, a "large free jazz groove harmolodic ensemble" comprised of six men and six women, released *Solidarity* (Unseen Rain Records) in 2016.

83 Michael Jarrett's 1987 interview with Ornette, *Cadence* (October 1995).

84 Gary Giddins, "Something Else, Ornette Coleman at Town Hall," *New Yorker*, www.newyorker.com, April 14, 2008.

85 Dewey quote in Mandel, *Jazz Beyond Jazz*, p. 153; *DownBeat* October 1997 article, quoted in the preface of Peter Nicklas Wilson, *Ornette Coleman: His Life and Music* (Berkeley, CA, 1999).

86 Pat Metheny's Foreword to Wilson, *Ornette Coleman: His Life and Music*.

87 "Call me trim tab" is written on Fuller's gravestone.

88 Mandel, *Jazz Beyond Jazz*, p. 112.

89 Schnee, "Zen Buddhism, Ornette Coleman, and the Harmolodic Path."

90 Roseman, Stacken, and Carney quotes from Matthew Kassel, "Jazz Musicians Tell their Ornette Coleman Stories," www.observer. com, June 11, 2015.

91 Greg Tate, "Change of the Century," *Village Voice* (June 1987).

92 Conversation with Letitia Eldredge in her Coupland, Texas home, October 21, 2016. A Fort Worth native, Eldredge met Ornette often

in the 1980s in Fort Worth and New York in the early 1990s, when Ornette was living in Harlem post-Rivington Street. Ornette's flat (125th Street on Manhattan's East Side) became Harmolodic Recording Studio, a world-class facility designed by Chris Agovino and used by hip-hop and other artists well into the 2000s.

93 Conversation with Michael Cuscuna, Stamford, Connecticut, November 21, 2016.

94 Alec Wilkinson, "Time is a Ghost, Vijay Iyer's jazz Vision," *New Yorker*, www.newyorker.com, February 1, 2016.

95 Vijay Iyer, "New York Stories: The Jazz Pianist Tackles the Question, 'Are Cities Music?'," Red Bull Music Academy, http://daily. redbullmusicacademy.com, May 15, 2013.

96 Wilkinson, "Time is a Ghost."

97 Ibid. Iyer adopted the term "creative music' following AACM musician and composer Wadada Leo Smith's distinction between creative and classical music. The former applies "to improvised music brought alive by the creative improviser, either through reference to a score provided for his or her exploitation or through absolute improvisation," whereas the latter is "brought alive by the performer through interpretation of a score." See V. Iyer, "Steve Coleman, M. Base, and Musical Collectivism" (1996), available on Iyer's website: www.vijay-iyer.com.

98 Patrick Jarenwattananon, "Why We Love Ornette Coleman," National Public Radio, www.npr.org, posted September 24, 2010. Sorey and Moran are also MacArthur grant winners (2017 and 2010 respectively).

99 Claire O'Neal, *Ornette Coleman* (Hallandale, FL, 2012) is part of a Mitchell Lane Publishers' series, "American Jazz," illustrated bios for young readers of Scott Joplin, Louis Armstrong, Charlie Parker, Billie Holiday, and others.

100 Mandel, *Jazz Beyond Jazz*, p. 141.

101 Martyn Griffin, Michael Humphreys, and Mark Learmonth, "Doing Free Jazz and Free Organizations: 'A Certain Experience of the Impossible.' Ornette Coleman Encounters Jacques Derrida," *Journal of Management Inquiry*, XXIV/1 (January 2015), p. 25.

102 Michael Selekman, *Pathways to Change: Brief Therapy with Difficult Adolescents* (New York, 2005), p. 48.

103 Ariel Weissberger, "Ornette Coleman and Music Therapy," Berko Music Therapy Center, http://musictherapynyc.com, June 15, 2015.

104 Ornette was interested in Alexander's work with vortices ("tube-like regions of trapped energy that are very common across nature"). He drew one for Ornette, who said they resemble his music. "Not only was [Ornette] improvising notes," wrote Alexander, "but also forming geometric patterns, like vortices." Stephon Alexander, *The Jazz of Physics* (New York, 2016), p. 98. Alexander's composition, "Ornette's Vortex," appears on a tribute to Ornette and Brian Eno by electronic musician Rioux, *Here Comes Now* (Human Pitch, 2014).

105 Carl Wilson, "This is his Music: Tracing Ornette Coleman's Influence on Punk, Rock, Hip-hop, and, Well, Pretty Much Everything Else," *Slate*, www.slate.com, June 17, 2015.

106 David Keenan, "Disco Mystic: Ornette Coleman, Asha Puthli and Science Fiction," Red Bull Music Academy, www.redbullmusicacademy.com, January 9, 2015.

107 David Fricke, "Vernon Reid on Ornette Coleman: 'He Set a Lot of People Free'," *Rolling Stone*, www.rollingstone.com, June 12, 2015.

108 "Neneh Cherry Remembers Ornette," *The Guardian* (UK), December 27, 2015. In homage to Ornette, Cherry covered "What Reason Could I Give" from *Science Fiction* on *The Cherry Thing* (Smalltown Supersound, 2012).

109 Patti Smith is one of several musicians whose tributes to Ornette are quoted on www.ornettecoleman.com, a website maintained by Denardo.

110 Francis Davis, "'Zorn' for 'Anger'," *Atlantic Monthly*, January 1991. *Spy vs. Spy* personnel: John Zorn and Tim Berne on alto saxophone; Mark Dresser on bass; and Joey Baron and Michael Vatcher on drums. Naked City personnel: John Zorn on alto saxophone; Bill Frisell on guitar; Fred Frith on bass; and Joey Baron on drums; Wayne Horvitz on keyboards; and Yamatsuka Eye on vocals.

111 Blue Wall Studio website, www.bluewallstudio.com.

112 Quoted in a press blurb for the Trafó House of Contemporary Arts in Budapest, where Bad Plus performed *Science Fiction* in April 2015. Additional trumpet players on the 1972 *Science Fiction* recording included Carmine Fornarotto (tracks 1 and 6) and Gerard Schwarz (tracks 1 and 6).

113 Molley Woodcraft, "Imagine all the people . . .," *The Guardian*, www.theguardian.com, June 21, 2009. Previous Meltdown curators include Nick Cave (1999), David Bowie (2002), Morrissey (2004), Patti Smith (2005), and Massive Attack (2008).

114 Jason Crane, "Review: Sonny Rollins 80th Birthday Concert," www.thejazzsession.com, posted September 10, 2010. Sonny's *The Bridge* (RCA Victor, 1962) and Ornette's *The Shape of Jazz to Come* (Contemporary, 1959) were inducted into the Grammy Hall of Fame in 2014, shortly before Ornette's death.

115 Jazz portrait photographer and audio engineer Jimmy Katz and his wife Dena produced the tribute, recording the performances so that the musicians could own their own masters. The line-up included Mark Turner, Joe Lovano, Nasheet Waits, Johnathan Blake, Kevin Hays, Joel Frahm, Matt Wilson, Seamus Blake, Marcus Gilmore, Stanley Cowell, Avishai Cohen, Joey Baron, and the Vijay Iyer trio with Matana Roberts and Gerald Cleaver. For their remarks about Ornette, see Jarenwattananon, "Why We Love Ornette Coleman."

116 Denardo Coleman, "My Father was Deep," liner notes from *Celebrate Ornette* (Song X, 2016) a box set of 24 performances on two DVDs, three CDs, and four Vinyl LPs, produced by Denardo.

117 Howard Mandel, "Happy Birthday 83—and 82—Ornette Coleman," www.artsjournal.com, March 9, 2013.

118 T. E. Martin, "The Plastic Muse, Pt. 1," *Jazz Monthly*, x/3 (May 1964), pp. 13–15. Vibe personnel: Denardo on drums, Charles Ellerbe on guitar, Al McDowell on electric piccolo bass, Tony Falanga on acoustic bass, and Antoine Roney on sax.

119 Howard Mandel, "Ornette Coleman Returned Music to Freedom and Basics," www.artsjournal.com, June 11, 2015. For clips of the Brooklyn tribute see Carey Dunne "Remembering Ornette Coleman's Final Performance," www.bkmag.com, posted June 11, 2015.

120 Rafi Zabor and David Breskin, "Ronald Shannon Jackson and the Future of Jazz Drumming," June 1981, posted on the "magazine" page of author and producer David Breskin's website: www.davidbreskin.com. Cecil Taylor died April 5, 2018, aged 89.

121 Timothy S. Murphy, trans., "The Other's Language: Jacques Derrida Interviews Ornette Coleman, 23 June, 1997," *Genre*, III/2 (2004),

pp. 319–32. Truvenza Coleman had a son, so "niece" was probably an affectionate term for a young cousin or child of a close friend. I was unable to find "Blind Date" in Ornette's discography, so he may have written but never recorded it.

122 Conversation with Michaela Deiss, New York City, November 22, 2016.

123 Ornette's 2007 acceptance speech is available at www.jazzclinic.blogspot.com.

124 Geoff Dyer, "Torrential, Gut-bucket Jazz," *New York Review of Books Daily*, www.nybooks.com, June 20, 2015.

125 Stanley Crouch, *Considering Genius: Writings on Jazz* (New York, 2006), p. 312; Brian Morton, "Ornette Coleman 1930–2015," *Wire* (June 2015). See also Adam Shatz, "Diary: Dancing in Your Head," *London Review of Books*, www.lrb.co.uk, July 16, 2015, and Taylor Ho Bynum, "Seeing Ornette Coleman," *New Yorker*, www.newyorker. com, June 12, 2015.

126 Fred Kaplan, "Serendipitous Convergence Hooks Up Sax and Splatter," www.observer.com, June 19, 2006.

127 Conversation with Denardo Coleman at his father's loft on 36th Street, New York City, November 10, 2016.

128 Produced and restored by Michael Cuscuna and T. S. Monk, *At Carnegie Hall* was released on Blue Note Records in 2005.

129 Conversation with Gary Giddins, New York City, November 23, 2016.

130 Berry Courter, "National Museum of African American Music on Track for 2019 Opening in Nashville," *Times Free Press* (Tennessee), July 16, 2018.

131 See Smithsonian website: https://music.si.edu.

132 Steven Lewis, "Musical Crossroads, Roots in Africa," see Smithsonian website: https://music.si.edu.

133 On how Heller met Juma and their work to catalogue the contents of his large trove of documents, photos, tapes, and film reels (funded in part by a National Endowment for the Arts grant) see Jarek Irvin, "Interview Series: Michael Heller, Loft Jazz," posted May 1, 2017, on the website of IASPM-US, http://iaspm-us.net.

134 Val Wilmer notes Ornette's taping of the Coltrane sessions in *As Serious as Your Life* (London, 1977), p. 70. The Ayler tapes are noted in D. Wild and M. Cuscuna, *Ornette Coleman, 1958–1979, A Discography* (Ann Arbor, MI, 1980), p. 22. Michael Cuscuna

related to this author how he'd stumbled upon the Town Hall concert
masters in 1976 while rummaging through the Blue Note Records
vault and returned them to Ornette with the idea, never realized,
of releasing them. The video is mentioned on ornettecoleman.com
as part of a description of *Celebrate Ornette* (Song X, 2016) in the
"artist profiles" menu.
135 Information regarding Burns's film is available at www.pbs.org.
See also the companion volume, Geoffrey C. Ward, *Jazz: A History
of America's Music* (New York, 2002).
136 Mandel, *Jazz Beyond Jazz*, p. 145.

Epilogue: Last Night

1 "Theatre and Science" [1943–8], in *Antonin Artaud: Anthology*, ed.
Jack Hirschman (San Francisco, CA, 1965), p. 171. Emphasis added.

Bibliography

Carles, Phillippe, and Jean Louis Comolli, *Free Jazz/Black Power*,
  trans. Grégory Pierrot (Jackson, MI, 2015)
Crouch, Stanley, *Considering Genius* (New York, 2007)
Davis, Francis, *In the Moment: Jazz in the 1980s* (New York, 1986)
Ellison, Ralph, *Living with Music*, ed. Robert G. O'Meally
  (New York, 2001)
Govenar, Alan, *Texas Blues: The Rise of a Contemporary Sound*
  (College Station, TX, 2008)
Heller, Michael C., *Loft Jazz: Improvising New York in the 1970s*
  (Oakland, CA, 2017)
Hentoff, Nat, *The Jazz Life* (New York, 1961)
Jones, LeRoi, *The Blues People* (New York, 1963)
Kaplan, Fred, *1959: The Year Everything Changed* (Hoboken, NJ, 2009)
Kuri, José Férez, ed., *Brion Gysin: Tuning in to the Multimedia Age*
  (London, 2003)
Lee, David, *The Battle of the Five Spot: Ornette Coleman and the New York
  Jazz Field* (Toronto, 2006)
Lewis, George E., *A Power Stronger than Itself: The AACM and American
  Experimental Music* (Chicago, IL, 2008)
Litweiler, John, *Ornette Coleman: A Harmolodic Life* (New York, 1993)
MacAdams, Lewis, *Birth of the Cool: Beat, Bebop, and the American
  Avant-garde* (New York, 2001)
MacCrae, Barry, *Ornette Coleman* (London, 1988)
Mandel, Howard, *Miles, Ornette, Cecil: Jazz Beyond Jazz*
  (New York, 2008)
Oliphant, Dave, *Texas Jazz* (Austin, TX, 1996)

O'Meally, Robert G., ed., *The Jazz Cadence of American Culture*
(New York, 1998)

Palmer, Robert, ed. Anthony DeCurtis, *Blues and Chaos: The Music
Writing of Robert Palmer* (New York, 2011)

Rockwell, John, *All American Music: Composition in the Later Twentieth
Century* (New York, 1997)

Rosenthal, David H., *Hard Bop: Jazz and Black Music, 1955–1965*
(New York, 1992)

Rush, Stephen, *Free Jazz, Harmolodics, and Ornette Coleman*
(New York, 2016)

Schuller, Gunther, *The Swing Era: The Development of Jazz, 1930–1945*
(New York, 1989)

Selcer, Richard E., *A History of Fort Worth in Black and White: 165 Years
of African American Life* (Denton, TX, 2015)

Spellman, A. B., *Four Lives in the Bebop Business* (New York, 1966)

Sukenick, R., *Down and In: Life in the Underground* (New York, 1987)

Wild, David, and Michael Cuscuna, *Ornette Coleman, 1958–1979:
A Discography* (Ann Arbor, MI, 1980)

Wilmer, Valerie, *As Serious As Your Life* (London, 1977)

Wilson, Peter Niklas, *Ornette Coleman: His Life and Music*
(Berkeley, CA, 1999)

Additional Resources

Of the online discographies, this one by John Eyles, while describing
only a selection of Ornette's recordings, is instructive:
www.allaboutjazz.com/ornette-coleman-ornette-coleman-by-john-eyles.php

A more thorough list of Ornette's recordings (through 2011), albeit
without commentary, can be found at the following website:
www.jazzdisco.org/ornette-coleman/discography

For a comprehensive listener's guide to Ornette's music, see Michael
Stephans's *Experiencing Ornette Coleman: A Listener's Companion*
(Lanham, MD, 2017)

See also the posts by musician and educator Ethan Iverson, including music and interviews:
https://ethaniverson.com/rhythm-and-blues/ornette-1-forms-and-sounds
https://ethaniverson.com/rhythm-and-blues/this-is-our-mystic

A site maintained by Denardo Coleman hosts news of recent, posthumous recording releases, in addition to Denardo's biography of Ornette and a moving essay entitled "My Father Was Deep": www.ornettecoleman.com

Acknowledgments

Writing about someone of Ornette's stature is "a tall hill to climb," as they say in Texas, and I would have been unable to attempt it without a lot of help. I owe a special debt of thanks to Bobby Bradford for his conversation and the rich recollections of his years with Ornette, and to the late Marjorie Crenshaw, who consulted her encyclopedic memory to conjure the youth she and Ornette shared. Howard Mandel lent his insightful support throughout this project. John Rockwell generously offered time and the bracing advice to beware of what I don't know. I am grateful to Michael Cuscuna for his "tales out of school" and for graciously providing a selection of photographer Francis Wolff's classic portraits for Blue Note Records.

Thanks to David Oliphant, Alan Govenar, and Raleigh Dailey for their invaluable research of twentieth-century Texan musicians and to John Snyder, for his vivid essays about living and working with Ornette in New York. Tad Hershorn and Joe Peterson of the Rutgers University Institute of Jazz Studies have my warm thanks, as do my New York interlocutors: Gary Giddins, Stanley Crouch, Kenny Wessell, Chino Garcia, Felipe Floresca, Skoto Aghahowa, Alix DuSerech, Matt Lavelle, Eugene Holley, Martine Barrat, Michaela Deiss, Darryl Pitt, and Jimmy Katz, who provided some of the images gracing these pages, as did David Schleifer of the Ira Cohen Estate, Megan Brown of the Frederick Brown Estate, Dan Munn of the Michael Rosenfeld Gallery, and Andy Fisher of Rhino Records. I could not have managed New York without the hospitality of my friends Sherief Alkatcha, Ilka Scobie, and Luigi Cazzaniga.

In Fort Worth, I benefitted from the assistance of Gayle Hanson, archivist for the Prince Hall Mosque; Sarah Walker and Brenda Sanders-Wise at the Lenora Rollins Heritage Center, and Linda Barrett and Jubari Jones at the Fort Worth Public Library. My thanks to Sara Pezzoni, University of Texas at Arlington's Special Collections Library and Katie Salzman, Wittliff Collections Archives at Texas State University (San Marcos). For their time and knowledge I thank Tom Kellam, Richard Selcer, Michael H. Price, Bob Ray Sanders, John Giordano, Jack Carter, Butch Clemmons, Clifford Jackson, Gerard Dailey, Duane Durrett, Johnny and Kitty Case, Duane Durrett, and Fort Worther Kevin Coffey, who corresponded extensively from his home in the Orkney Islands about the Texan evolution of western swing.

It was a joy trading stories with former Caravan of Dreams colleagues and friends: Laney Yarber, Brian Sharp, Letitia Eldredge, Rachella Parks-Washington, Scotti and John David Bartlett, Karen Minzer, David Morrissey, Chad Cox, John Reoch, Marie Antoinette Holiday, Alice Adair, Rene and Eric Brown, Kendall Cook, Kelli Brace, Kelly Jordan, Gary Leatherwood, Judy Jett, and Cydney Roach. I must take this opportunity to acknowledge Mike Dunagan and all the staff that made Caravan such an outstanding venue in those days, and to remember several co-workers who have since passed on: Tony Anderson (1966–1994); Sharon Frampton Griffin (1968–2003), Conan Reynolds (1957–2013), Cheri Throop (1945–2015), and Jo Anne Eckelman (1932–2018).

Thanks to Ulrich Hillebrand, Roger Bergner, Magnus Nygren, Ole Matthiessen, Salah Hassan, Todd Siler, Dave Bryant, Roman Bunka, and Robert Irwin, who helpfully corresponded about different aspects of Ornette's career. I'm grateful to Cairo's only jazz dentist, Sameh Barsoum, and his wife Mona, to Jean Colombain, Bernard Guillot, Cecil and Gigi Czerkinsky, Jean-Paul Lantieri, and Michael and Vlasta March for seeing me through this project. Special thanks to William Lyster, for his sharp eye, sharper wit and endless patience in reviewing my work and to Elizabeth Bolman for her constant encouragement.

I am, as ever, grateful to my friends of the Institute of Ecotechnics: Chili Hawes of London's October Gallery; Deborah Parish Snyder of Santa Fe's Synergetic Press; former Biospherian Mark Nelson; Caravan of Dreams architect Margaret Augustine; Marie Harding of Synergia Ranch; Corinna MacNeice, who helped paint Caravan's jazz mural; Gregg Dugan, former Caravan general manager; and Caravan founders Kathelin Gray and John Allen, whose invitation that I participate in their Texan adventure planted the seeds of this book and much else.

This work is dedicated to my eldest brother, drummer, educator, and composer Francis J. Golia Jr. (August 10, 1945–February 2, 2019), to whom the voices of Ornette and his contemporaries were like family. Finally, I thank my brother, cinematographer David J. Golia, for the inspiration and care that have enriched my every endeavor.

Photo Acknowledgments

The author and publishers wish to express their thanks to the below sources of illustrative material and/or permission to reproduce it. Some locations are also given in the captions for the sake of brevity.

Courtesy of Skoto Aghahowa and Alix DuSerech: p. 239; photos Marie Allen, courtesy of the Institute of Ecotechnics: pp. 222, 223; photo courtesy Archives of American Art, Smithsonian Institution, Washington, DC: p. 238; courtesy of the author: pp. 175, 178–9, 207, 227, 281; collection of the Birmingham Museum of Art, Alabama (museum purchase with funds provided by the Junior Patrons of the Birmingham Museum of Art): p. 129 (photo Sean Pathasema); photos Brian Blauser: pp. 184, 189, 205, 234; courtesy of Bobby Bradford: p. 99; courtesy of Sumter Bruton and Gerard Daily: pp. 67, 72; courtesy Caravan of Dreams Productions: pp. 8, 14, 172, 181, 184, 185, 186, 189, 190, 205, 209, 213, 216; photo Basil Clemons: pp. 43, 281; reproduced courtesy of James 'Butch' Clemons Jr.: p. 38; photos Ira Cohen: pp. 190, 194; photo Ira Cohen for Caravan of Dreams Productions: p. 237; reproduced courtesy the Ira Cohen Archives, LLC: pp. 194, 237; photo Denardo Coleman: p. 193; reproduced courtesy of the artist (Letitia Eldredge): p. 23; photo Walker Evans, J. Paul Getty Museum, Los Angeles (Open Access) p. 84; photo Fort Worth Public Library archive: p. 58; photo Hugo Van Gelderen/Anefo/National Archives, Netherlands: p. 104; photo Juan Gonzales: p. 207; photos William P. Gottlieb: pp. 45, 47, 63, 65, 70, 78, 108; photo Philippe Gras/Alamy Stock Photo: p. 202; photo Kathelin Gray: p. 254; courtesy Kathelin Gray: pp. 193, 254; courtesy of the Institute of Ecotechnics: pp. 177, 221, 225, 234; photo Scott Irvine: p. 266; photos Jimmy Katz, reproduced by kind permission: pp. 109, 200, 248, 269, 271, 289;

Library of Congress, Washington, DC (Prints and Photographs Division): pp. 50, 111, 141; Library of Congress, Washington, DC (William P. Gottlieb Collection): pp. 45, 47, 63, 65, 70, 78, 108; Library of Congress, Washington, DC (*New York World Telegram & The Sun* Newspaper Photograph Collection): p. 139; photo John A. Lomax: p. 50; photos Brian McMillen, reproduced by kind permission: pp. 101, 262; MARKA/Alamy Stock Photo: p. 144; courtesy NASA: p. 90; National Portrait Gallery, Smithsonian Institution, Washington, DC (gift of Joel and Sherry Mallin and Sebastienne and Bentley Brown © 1992—courtesy of Megan E. Bowman-Brown, Frederick J. Brown Trust): p. 252; courtesy of October Gallery, London: p. 197; photo Pictorial Press Ltd/Alamy Stock Photo: p. 53; photo Harry Pot/National Aarchief, Netherlands: p. 104; Rhino Entertainment Company, a Warner Music Group Company: pp. 8, 123, 156; © Estate of Bob Thompson—courtesy of Michael Rosenfeld Gallery LLC, New York City: p. 129; photo Marion S. Trikosko: p. 141; courtesy University of Texas at Arlington Libraries, Arlington Special Collections: pp. 43 (Basil Clemons Photograph Collection) and 20, 76–7, 80, 86, 203 (*Fort Worth Star-Telegram* Collection) and 17, 57 (Jack White Photograph Collection) and 83 (W. D. Smith Commercial Photography Collection); photo Mark Weber: p. 99; photos Francis Wolff © Mosaic Images LLC: pp. 93, 96, 98, 112, 135, 151, 158, 161, 165; photo Stanley Wolfson: p. 139; photo courtesy John Zorn, reproduced by kind permission: p. 266.

material in any medium or format, or to adapt—to remix, transform, and build upon the material, for any purpose, even commercially, under the following conditions—you must give appropriate credit, provide a link to the license, and indicate if changes were made—you may do so in any reasonable manner, but not in any way that suggests the licensor endorses you or your use; and you may not apply legal terms or technological measures that legally restrict others from doing anything the license permits.

Index

Page numbers in *italics* indicate illustrations.